Journey through a Haunted Land

BY AMOS ELON

Translated by Michael Roloff

HOLT, RINEHART AND WINSTON

New York   Chicago   San Francisco

Journey
through a
Haunted Land
The New
Germany

I would like to thank the following for their co-operation and permission to cite their work:
Bertolt Brecht, *Die Neuen Zeitalter,* from *Band 6 der Gedichte* © Suhrkamp Verlag, Frankfurt am Main, 1964
Hans Magnus Enzensberger, *Landessprache* © Suhrkamp Verlag, Frankfurt am Main, 1960
Günter Eich, *Inventur* © Suhrkamp Verlag, Frankfurt am Main, 1960
Stephen Hermlin, *Die Toten Städte,* from *Dichtungen,* Aufbau Verlag, East Berlin, 1956
Lach und Schiessgesellschaft, Munich, for "Go Quick with Flick"
Random House, Inc., for *The Andersonville Trial,* by Saul Levitt, © copyright 1960 by Saul Levitt.
Der Spiegel, Hamburg, for reference material
Stachelschweine, Berlin, for "We Have Scraped Through Again"
Thomas C. Wallace, for patience and forebearing
Die Welt, Hamburg for poem by Hans Leuschner

Designer: Ernst Reichl
82342-0117
Printed in the United States of America

For Beth

Eshet Khayil mi yimtza

Contents

Journey through a Haunted Land

Last Year at Auschwitz

At Crematorium Number 3 people are speaking German again. *"Vorsicht, Herr Kollege, the mud is slippery. Give me your hand a second." "Danke schön!" "Bitte schön!"*

How odd it sounds in this icy, bleak landscape! Under a thin cover of snow it stretches flatly into the distance, like a dirty shroud. Its limits are obscured by the haze of the horizon. The sky is lightly overcast. Barbed-wire fences run for miles, embracing bizarre silhouettes of blown-up walls; watchtowers and leafless birches stand exposed to the wet cold wind. Remnants of chimneys jut like gravestones out of the rubble field. In the distance the hollow rattling of a train leaving the freight yard of Uswiencim breaks an eerie silence.

It is a small town in Poland, a tiny speck on the map unknown to the outside world before World War II and even today missing from most atlases. Uswiencim—Auschwitz, also called Birkenau, also "Ass-hole of the World." Only thirty-five miles away, in Cracow, the delicately carved angels of the medieval German woodcarver, Veit Stoss, whom the Poles have nationalized into Vit Stvorz, gaze into the dark nave of the *Marienkirche.*

"Herr Lanz, bitte messen Sie die Entfernung zur Rampe."

"Herr Lanz, please measure the distance to the platform."

Court Officer Lanz, from Frankfurt am Main, has been in Poland for twenty-four hours on official duty. The slim, young man pulls tape measure and notebook from his coat pocket. He unrolls the narrow strip of plastic with black numbers on it. Now he pulls it through the mud. One length is not enough; he must measure twice. Then it becomes official: It is 125 yards from the wash barracks of the Women's Camp to the railroad platform, and 220 yards further from the platform along the wet dirt road to the gas chambers and crematoria. This was once the end of the world, millions of people rose as brown smoke, as cloying stench to the clouds. Two million? Three million? Three point five? One doesn't know.

One *does* know: "Death was a *meister* from Germany." These men too are from Germany: one judge, three prosecuting attorneys, three co-plaintiffs, twelve defense attorneys, two court officers, a court stenographer and one defendant. He is a gynecologist from northern Germany—former concentration camp doctor and SS *Obersturmführer* Franz Bernhard Lucas. He and nineteen other SS men are on trial in Frankfurt. Lucas is accused of the murder or abetting the murder of "an undeterminable multitude" of people here in Auschwitz in 1944. He is the only accused who has agreed to come back.

What are they doing here in this gigantic slaughterhouse, maintained by the Poles as a memorial? They have come to check the veracity of expert opinions and testimony of witnesses. The Frankfurt Court has sent them here to measure an outrage with a yard-stick. They have brought their tape-measures and cameras, like policemen to a traffic accident. More than twenty years after the liberation of Auschwitz, Germans are passing judgment on one another. Twenty defendants stand before the Frankfurt jury, today all of them solid citizens, physicians, businessmen, employees and craftsmen. They are charged with having kept the death machine in operation.

Judge Walter Hotz, forty-seven years old, heads the delegation. He gives orders. A crowd of plaintiffs, co-plaintiffs and defense attorneys follows his every step, notebooks in hand. Minutes are dictated, photographs taken, visual and oral tests performed. Distances are timed by stop watch. The distance from Barracks 9 to Barracks 11, from the railroad track to the cement posts where the thick barbed-wire is strung, has been ascertained. The posts with their electric insulators still stand. One notes the signs: "High Tension!" "*Vorsicht, Lebensgefahr!*" Another: "There is one way to freedom—its milestones are called obedience, industry, cleanliness, honesty, veracity, soberness and love of the fatherland." The crowd reads the inscription, then walks on in silence. Maps are unfolded. How many yards is it from headquarters to the old crematoria? Was it possible to see a man flogged to death at point A from a hole in the wall at B as witness X maintains he did? Back in Frankfurt the defendants disagreed. Here the camera must decide. There are other things to clear up. Judge Hotz reads into the record:

> The Court and the trial participants thereupon went into the former headquarters building. On the first floor of the part of the building which faces south, the Commandant's office lies to one's left. Opposite the hallway, facing the camp, is the Adjutant's office. . . .

In this office two of the Frankfurt defendants once worked, both adjutants of Camp Commandant Höss, who was executed in 1947. Former Adjutant Robert Mulka, today a distinguished-looking Hamburg businessman, claims not to have heard, nor to have seen, anything; he insists he gave no important orders. "The Adjutant's room," Judge Hotz continues, "has two windows facing the camp and a third window on the other side. It is estimated that the distance separating Mulka's room from the prison barracks opposite is between twelve and fourteen yards."

The Court moves along. Here is a cellar, Penal Barracks 11. A

3

great deal has been heard about it in the Frankfurt courtroom. Witnesses testifying with tear-choked voices have fainted from the violence of their recollections, have come to again and continued to testify. It is dark and damp in the cellar. The crowd peers into a dungeon, barely three by three yards wide, with a tiny air hatch. Here, forty people were stuffed together without food. They struggled for air, screamed, starved to death or suffocated. Another four cells, standing room only, one yard on each side. Men were made to crawl into these cells, through an opening as narrow as an oven door, always four at one time. They died standing up. Next morning they were scraped out through a small opening.

The Nazi administrators carefully recorded it all. Piles of black SS record folders can still be seen in the camp office. Interminable typewritten reports list precise descriptions of "crimes" and punishments, numbers, dates: Prisoner 64166 admitted on May 26, 1943; he allowed a tool to drop to the ground, the handle bent. Prisoner 64495, admitted on June 5 of the same year; he had relieved himself on the job. Prisoner 42658, admitted on March 14, 1943; he had tried to obtain a second bowl of soup.

What is written is clear; no one disputes it. Ah, but could one actually hear sounds through the cell walls? The question is important. Witness Y asserts it was possible. He says he heard the last screams, death rattles, the inarticulate sounds of men dying as they stood in the hunger cells. Conviction or acquittal, these hinge on the answer. Judge Hotz ponders it and conducts an experiment. He sends Court Officer Lanz into one of the cells. Lanz is asked to sing. He is a little hoarse. He clears his throat and begins:

Sah ein Knab' ein Röslein stehn,
Röslein auf der Heiden.
War so jung und morgenschön,
Lief er schnell es nah zu sehn,
Sah's mit vielen Freuden. . . .

It is a poem by Goethe. Judge Hotz reads into the record:
Court Officer Lanz thereupon went to standing-room cell 1. Its wooden door was closed. All entrances to cell 22 were also locked, and interested trial participants and the members of the court thereupon went into cell 23, whose door was closed from the outside. When everything was quiet, Court Officer Lanz sang the song *"Sah ein Knab' ein Röslein stehn,"* which was clearly audible in cell 23.

4

The German judge leaves the cell. He returns to the yard. His broad face remains blank, void of emotion. The evening before someone had asked him if he had ever been a member of the Nazi Party. He couldn't remember. "You see, all that lies so far in the past. As much as I would like to, I simply can't remember." Most of the other members of the Court are younger, most less than forty. The main defense attorneys, older men, have sent their younger subordinates to Poland.

Hotz continues along the camp road. His entourage follows. Some of the jurors are wearing colorful ski clothing, stretch pants and thick pullovers, warm boots. At the main gate, below the cast-iron band with the inscription "*Arbeit Macht Frei*," small talk cuts into the general silence. The language is the same German of the guards who dragged new arrivals from the boxcars. Mothers who begged for the lives of their children cried in that same language . . . yet it is not the same. There is little time to ponder this at the moment. The Court is in a hurry. Now it stands in front of "the Black Wall." Some twenty thousand people were murdered here. Naked, running in double-time, they came out of the penal bunkers to the right. *Kapos* flung them against the wall. A single shot in the nape of the neck. The blood flowed into the gutter. The killers today are taxi drivers somewhere, or carpenters, or bank employees.

A Polish guide points to a house on the left. Behind its boarded-up windows, women once were lain on bare slabs and used as guinea pigs. An SS doctor, until recently a respected German resident in Accra, reputedly a good friend of former Ghana President Nkrumah, conducted experiments on these women. He filled their wombs with a pap-like greyish substance.

The windows of the women's barracks are still boarded up. The court stands outside, facing the Black Wall. Floral wreaths lie in front of it. Hats are removed; heads are bowed. All stand silently for one minute. In the second row, defendant Lucas—otherwise erect and at attention—also bows his head, his soft felt hat in his hands. Here he is one with his victims; in Frankfurt his solidarity is with his former comrades-in-arms. He betrays neither himself nor his co-defendants. Photographers climb on the fence to get a shot of Lucas. Lucas from the front, Lucas in profile, Lucas against the background of floral wreaths at the Black Wall. It is perfect for

5

mass-circulation magazines. A murderer returned to the scene of the crime!

Lucas specializes in female diseases. Until recently he was the director of obstetrics and gynecology in a hospital at Elmshorn, near Hamburg. He lost his post in 1963, when his activities as an SS doctor in Auschwitz became known, but not his reputation as a physician.

It is not expected that Lucas will try to run away; in Germany he is out on bail and free to move about the country. An Israeli witness, alarmed at seeing him at Franfurt International Airport shortly after facing him in the courtroom, called the police. Was Lucas trying to flee the country? No, he was merely using the shuttle service to Hamburg to see his patients on days when the trial was in recess. His practice apparently has not suffered. He is widely praised by his patients. At Hamburg he is said to be a doctor who cares, a Samaritan anxious to alleviate pain, good-natured and conscientious. At Frankfurt he is accused of having selected the doomed from the living, telling them to step aside and move towards the gas chambers, a master over life and death at the railroad platform of Auschwitz.

. . . "As the prisoners arrived," Camp Commandant Höss recorded after the war, "the SS gave orders that all baggage be left in the boxcars. All arrivals had to pass single file past an SS doctor who was free to decide whether the prisoner was to go into the camp or directly into the gas chamber . . ."

Judge Hotz is still in the lead. His shoes sink deeply into the icy slush. A single railroad track turns off to the left, across a field and up to the gate of a tumble-down barn. Behind the gate the track divides; each arm stretches alone for hundreds of yards, a wide platform between them. Grass covers the muddy rusty rails from the arched barn gate to the railhead at the entrance to the gas chambers. Here and there huge greenish yellow mushrooms sprout out of the wet earth where the starving were beaten with sticks for lingering over an empty soup kettle.

This is Auschwitz II, the giant death factory. Auschwitz I was a prison, its purpose to "re-educate" people. The sole purpose of Auschwitz II was death. In Auschwitz I everything huddles together. You turn from the penal bunker to the women's barracks;

it is only a few steps from the crematorium to camp headquarters, a few more from the Black Wall to the main gate where a prisoner orchestra was forced to make music. It played early in the morning when the inmates marched out to work, and in the evening when they returned marching double-time, their dead on their backs, for the number leaving for work had to coincide with the number returning.

Auschwitz II is different. There seems to be no end to it. Buildings are symmetrically arranged, with carefully measured intervals between rows of elongated, low barracks. Originally these barracks were designed as transportable stables, each housing fifty-two animals. As many as twelve hundred humans were packed into them before going on to the gas. The barracks have chimneys but were never heated. In winter, temperatures fell to twenty-five degrees below zero (Centigrade). Jammed together, prisoners warmed each other. Eight men crouched on one crudely built crate-bed with an area of three square yards.

It is raining. The Frankfurt jurors carefully climb onto the shattered roof of Crematorium Number 3. A Polish museum employee draws the picture for them. From here one peers right into the heart of the death machine. These cement chambers were like cylinders of a motor. In one stroke of the turbine, they sucked up between six hundred and one thousand people, in another stroke expelled them as corpses. Highly qualified mechanics—most of them must still be somewhere today—operated the switchboard. One flick let in the gas, another started the ventilation system It was the "ingenious habitation of death," as the German-Jewish poetess Nelly Sachs has written, "where Israel's body dissolved into smoke and drifted through the air."

The jurors move down a cement stairway, worn by innumerable feet. Here prisoners walked downstairs to undress. Stragglers were lashed on with whips. Then, naked, they turned to the right, and squeezed through a narrow passageway to the "shower room."

The women with their children came inside first, afterward the men, who of course were always fewer (in number). Now the door was quickly screwed down and the "disinfectors" pumped the gas through hatches in the ceiling of the gas chamber down an air shaft to the floor. Gas immediately began to develop. After twenty

7

minutes at most, no one moved. The effect of the gas lasted from five to ten minutes depending upon weather conditions—damp or dry, cold or warm. Or, on the condition of the gas, for quality was not always the same, and lastly on the composition of the particular transport—healthy people, old or sick people. One-half hour after the gas had begun to take effect the door was opened and the ventilation system was turned on. The removal of corpses was started at once . . . the "special detachments" now proceeded to pull the corpses' gold teeth and to cut off the women's hair.

(Excerpts from the notes of Camp Commandant Rudolf Höss)

An electrically operated elevator transported the corpses to the floor upstairs. Here they were put on iron lorries and carted to the stoked-up crematory ovens manufactured by a German firm called J.A. Topf & Sons, whose trademark is still visible in the debris. The ovens burned day and night. Inside them all became ash and smoke. The smoke vanished into the air. The ash was buried in a nearby pond or taken on trucks to the Vistula and shoveled into the stream, where it drifted off and dissolved.

Eventually the ovens were unable to consume the mass of corpses. They could not keep up with the gas chambers. This problem must have caused concern to the Topf & Sons firm; in 1942 it applied for a patent on a new mammoth apparatus— a "crematory oven for massive requirements, functioning without interruption." According to the application, masses of corpses would be introduced into the new oven by means of electrically operated conveyor belts. The ash would then be ejected by water jets under high pressure. As far as is known, nothing came of this project, but Topf & Sons continued to exist in Wiesbaden until 1962. Allied war tribunals did not bother with the firm, and Topf & Sons resumed efforts to protect their invention even after the war. In 1952 their patent application was renewed. This time it was called: "Apparatus for the cremation of corpses, cadavers and parts thereof." The patent was granted on January 5, 1953 (German Patent 861731).

Because Topf & Sons did not complete their mammoth apparatus in time, tens of thousands of corpses had to be burned in the open, "despite Air Defense objections against the nightly fires which could be seen from a great distance" (Höss).

8

Judge Hotz turns to the stenographer, who never leaves his side. Hotz dictates: "Thereupon the Court went to the trenches in which the corpses were burned."

One of the defense attorneys questions his wording. Shouldn't it say: ". . . in which corpses were allegedly burned?" The Judge considers the objection and corrects: "In which corpses were allegedly burned." The Court must be factual; it must have no memory and no feelings. Auschwitz is still *sub judice*.

"Just a minute, Herr Kollege," another defense attorney interjects, "Something is wrong. If corpses were burned here, how was that tree able to survive? It would have burned." Mr. Kasimir Smolen, director of the Auschwitz museum, explains that the tree is young. "Nothing grew here when the fires burned. Nothing!"

"Well, that's easy to say. But actually one should inspect the tree."

The surrealistic conversation continues as the Court moves on. In a few minutes the group has reached a pond. Kasimir Smolen scoops a handful of whitish-grey, plaster-of-Paris-like matter out of the pond. "That is the ash of the dead. Tons of it were thrown into this pond."

"Well, yes," says one defense attorney, shaking his young head, "that might be true, but it should really be examined by a chemist."

The judge from Frankfurt says nothing. He seems to scurry more. He seems like a hunted animal rushing from one place to the next, dictating notes at an ever increasing pace. "Twenty-two yards, fifty-five yards. . . . Unobstructed view. . . . Obstructed view. . . ." One defense attorney leans down. He scratches the earth with his glove and straightens up again. Little yellowish stones, easily crushed, lie in his hand. This time no one demands an expert opinion. What these yellowish stones are, is obvious. They are the remains of bones. Twenty-two or twenty-three years ago they belonged to a living person. Everyone gazes at them. Knowingly. Knowing what? Knowing that these were the bones of a human and this was the cement stairway he walked down. Knowing that this was the door frame through which he looked out at the world for the last time. Not knowing another thing, whether it was night or day, nor the persons's name, where he came from, where his friends and relatives were, what he thought, what he felt. . . .

Then the Court inspects the Women's Camp diagonally across from the train platform. Black ravens circle above the rails. The air, which once smelled for miles of burning human flesh, is damp. It is quiet. "Herr Hollen" the Judge says, "please record: "The sky is lightly overcast. The view is good. The two men on the platform can be recognized by their stature." The two men he is referring to are Defense Attorney Steinacker and State's Attorney Wiese. They have agreed to pose for an important picture. The photograph, it is hoped, will check the credibility of several witnesses who worked in the wash barracks of the Women's Camp. They say they could recognize some of the doctors making selections on the platform. Was this really possible? How can this be proved? The judge decides to photograph a uniformed man on the platform. At first he asks a Polish policeman with a uniform cap. But the Pole refuses. He does not want to pose as an SS man. What if his captain allows him to do it? "Let the captain pose himself, if he likes to," says the policeman. "I will not pose as an SS doctor on the platform."

The defendant Lucas is accused of exactly this crime—standing on this platform, giving new arrivals from Hungary a fast once-over, idly flicking his thumb left, right, left, right, left, left, left. Left to die, right to live, at least for a while. Now, twenty years later, Lucas again stands on the platform.

He denies everything. He never conducted selections and never was here, except once or twice, "out of curiosity." A woman witness from America told the Frankfurt Court a different story. Lucas was the man, she swore, who sent her to the right, into forced labor, and her parents to the left, to the gas chamber. Now Lucas stands motionless on the platform, his hands buried in the pockets of his camel's hair coat. The prosecutor asks him where the trains had stopped? Lucas doesn't know. That gate over here, was it usually open or closed? Lucas cannot remember. Well, then, where was he standing when he came as he admits, as a curious onlooker? On this side or the other? Lucas cannot remember exactly. After all, he says, more than twenty years have passed. His chin trembles slightly. What makes it tremble? Is it fear? Recollection? Is it the cold?

There is something symbolic in the fact that of all the Frankfurt defendants, Lucas should be here on the platform. Here he stands patiently and silently. Around him the distance between the right curbstone of the platform and the outermost fence of Camp B II is being measured. It amounts to thirty yards. One court officer loudly calls out the figures; another writes it down. Lucas nods. He is somewhat different from the other defendants. He is not as black as some of the others; but he is not white. He is not good, but neither is he altogether bad. In Frankfurt a few witnesses even testified that he was the "good man of Auschwitz," and "friend of prisoners." Today he deplores the crimes of twenty years ago. What was he doing then? He was forced to go along, he says, but against his own will. That is why he does not feel responsible.

Millions of Germans over forty years old say the same thing. "We knew nothing" or "We had to go along." Lucas tells of the time he went to the former Archbishop of Osnabrück, Berning, for advice. Berning told him: "One must not obey immoral orders. But nor must you endanger your own life." Another adviser—a "high-placed jurist" to whom he had turned for help—had encouraged him: "We are in the fifth year of the war and all sorts of things will happen."

Judge Hotz gives the sign for everyone to depart. The inspection is at an end. The Court returns to the base camp, Auschwitz I. Here the Polish government has converted some former prison barracks into a museum. The barracks are heated now, there are curtains strung over windows blocked by rusty bars, even doormats at the entrance. The museum has little to do with the court's official mission here. It serves only as background. And yet it is here that the sober, matter-of-fact façade of the jurors suddenly disintegrates. The Judge bursts into tears. He stands with his staff before the remains of the murdered: whole rooms filled with children's shoes, spectacles, crutches, prayer books, valises, men's suits, dresses, dentures. Thousands of toothbrushes. Mountains upon mountains of women's hair, cut prior to gassing, some still in sacks labeled for shipping to a firm in Bavaria that manufactured insulating material for submarines.

Next morning, two dozen jurists, one defendant and a mass of documents fly back to Germany.

At Warsaw Airport I sit next to a young journalist from Hamburg. He was seventeen years old when the war ended; today he is married with two young children. "Oh, that I have to be a German!" he had groaned the day before as we walked through Auschwitz together. He wants to come back to Auschwitz in a few years he says—once his children are a little older. He wants them to see it with their own eyes. He would like every German to see it. He knows that most of them do not want to. They're only human, he says.

"Travel through Germany," he told me. "Crisscross the land. It has changed." "Have the people changed?" "A little," he answered.

Heaven Was Merciful

Before one knows if Germany has changed, one sees it is new. In 1945 Germany was a pile of rubble; twenty years later—a "little America." The resurrected cities—brand new, clean, sober, infinitely monotonous—stand on the former ruins. Future archeologists examining layers of civilization will easily uncover the onset of a new era that began between 1945 and 1950 almost all over West Germany.

No country in Europe appears as modern. None has as many new façades, new housing developments, coldly new and colorless market places, or as many public signs that give orders to do something or not to do it: "*Achtung*! Beautiful View to the Right!"; "No Trespassing!"; "Single File on the Left." No European country has as many ultramodern glass and concrete churches, at times almost undistinguishable from neighboring silos or electric plants. No European country has as few, as astonishingly few slums. None has as many restored Romanesque Churches, reconstructed Gothic cathedrals, regilded baroque castles. Shining and new, appointed with all modern comforts, they stand, in a forest of television antennas, surrounded by skyscrapers of glass, steel, plastic and concrete.

The cities that were almost totally bombed out during the last year of the war today radiate the coldly blinding glare of neon lights. Bright Mercedes stars (symbols of a new age?) slowly turn around invisible axes high in the air. *Original Cologne 4711, Lufthansa, Esso, Pepsi-Cola, Dortmunder Union—das gepflegte Bier für Feinschmecker!* You must seek out the ruins of World War II, except where they have been intentionally preserved, either out of piety or as admonition.

There is a building boom all over Europe. Everywhere new cities are sprouting out of the ground. Everywhere new superhighways and bridges leap across the land and seas, and underpasses burrow through the earth like moles. Yet no country seems as much as West Germany to be actually bursting at the seams. Like octopuses its ancient cities extend their tentacles into the land, swallowing meadows, forests and hills. Much of West Germany, like the East Coast of the United States, is a single, continuous megalopolis. One wide, contiguous urban conglomeration stretches along the Rhine; another runs parallel to the Elbe in the north; a third is forming around Munich.

Millions of people live in this new world of prosperity and yet the atmosphere is less than metropolitan; it is rather that of an extended provincial capital. Enormous new factories are surrounded by large parking lots. American-style shopping centers—still relatively rare elsewhere in Europe—display a practically unlimited choice of goods. Drive-in mail boxes, drive-in bank counters are common. Streets burst with traffic. Well-dressed, well-fed people crowd the sidewalks, fill the streamlined subways and spacious streetcars, create crowded bottlenecks in front of overstuffed shop windows. The homes of the rich are decorated with bearded Chagall Rabbis, on canvas or on paper. Formidable old knights' castles, where the Nazis once trained specially selected youths to be a "new elite"—"hard as Krupp steel,"—"to look at a thousand corpses without batting an eyelash" (Himmler) today flourish as whimsical hotels for romantically inclined tourists. Nearby international student centers conduct symposiums on "French-German understanding" or for "Christian-Jewish cooperation."

The Cologne cathedral, a hallmark of that city, was begun in 1248 and finally completed in 1880. In some inexplicable way it survived the war intact even though its surroundings were nearly entirely destroyed. Next to the cathedral is *Hohe Strasse*, a narrow street that runs parallel to the Rhine. Nothing remained of it in 1945. Cologne was probably the most heavily destroyed city in Germany; 80 percent of its houses were partially or totally obliterated. It is said that in 1945 not a single stone lay atop another on the *Hohe Strasse*. Today it is there again as if nothing had happened. *Hohe Strasse* is now Cologne's oldest, most modern street: a long, compactly built bazaar, Jammed full of people, closed to traffic during daytime so as not to endanger an eager crowd of buyers inspecting the long rows of sparkling shop windows.

I go to an American film playing in Cologne. The newsreel, commemorating an anniversary, is from 1937. There is a mass meeting: everyone is marching the goose step; thousands of howling, screaming people. Adolf Hitler appears, gesticulates, talks. His hoarse, barking voice fills the movie house, but the audience laughs. There's no doubt—Hitler looks funny today. And yet it is an odd, somewhat forced laughter. Are they laughing the way a man laughs at old photographs and the silly clothes he once wore?

I stand on the cathedral square and watch the people passing by. It is a beautiful broad plaza. In the background is the large main railroad station where in 1941 twelve hundred Jewish people were loaded into the East. On the right, in the direction of the Rhine, rises the magnificent façade of the old cathedral. In the foreground, just below a coffee-house terrace, people rush past. I give them a hard look. My imagination tries to invest them with brown uniforms, long leather coats and heavy boots. I attach red swastika armbands around their left arms and raise their right arms. The attempt fails. The faces look as new as the lead-grey prefabricated skyscrapers. Youth predominates the street scene. The young men in close-fitting cuffless pants and fashionable jackets could be in New York, Brussels or Lyon. The girls have open faces and long legs. They are "ungermanically" slim. "Little has changed as radically since the war as the German Woman," a friend in Bonn said proudly a few days later. But even older people look different from the men and women in photographs taken during the thirties at the Nuremberg party conference grounds or at nightly torch-light parades through the Brandenburg Gate.

Am I fooling myself? Are appearances misleading? Is it because they dress differently? Or because all the world is becoming small and homogeneous? More than twenty years have passed since the war. Sometimes one forgets a new generation has meanwhile grown up in Germany. Do human beings change or only circumstances? Or both? Every fourth West German today was born after the end of the war. The National Socialists arrived in 1933. Every West German thirty-five years old or younger—approximately 48 percent of the population—was born after Hitler's assumption of power. Adding those who were fifteen years old in 1933, you discover that approximately 64 percent of the population of the Federal Republic is neither responsible for Hitler's victories nor, in most cases, for his crimes.

"Let heaven be merciful," Hermann Göring wrote in 1939, "If we should lose this war." Heaven has been charitable toward the West Germans. Never in history have Germans been as well off as West Germans are today. In 1945 Germany was shattered (6.8 million Germans had died violently—compared with 33 million people of other nations). Nine million had no homes. What industry remained was being partially dismantled. "The snow that is drizzling over the fields and cities is shrouding the ruins and graves," wrote Hans Werner Richter, a returning soldier who later was to become a key figure in the important literary *"Gruppe 47."* "Misery and hunger increase during the long winter nights. Ovens are not heated, people are ill dressed, children malnourished. Freezing and hungry, everyone tries to survive the next few months." Up to 80 percent of the cities lay in ruin, and sickness was rampant. "The spiritual and political confusion . . . deepens the impression of hopelessness."

A journey through the flourishing cities and villages of West

Germany gives an idea of the immense energies that went into reconstruction. How tenacious, patient and irresistible must have been the people, who, exchanging conquest for production and glory for consumerism, now mass-produce cars or hi-fi sets as once they mass-produced death? How were these people revitalized after 1945? Different Germans offer different explanations. There are economists who say that the nearly total rebuilding and retooling of industry gave Germany a valuable advantage over neighboring countries saddled with prewar industries. The resumption of German production coincided with the Korean boom. Then, of course there was generous United States aid.

Some sociologists emphasise the bourgeois revolution that erupted under Allied occupation of Germany, giving control over the land—for the first time in history—to the middle classes. Psychologists see a psychic reaction to the catastrophe of the past in the widespread desire for an apolitical, Philistine existence. Ideology has given way to consumption.

Practically everyone refers to the German's proverbial zeal. "It's all the same to them if they manage the deportation of Jews from Hungary, a defamation campaign against nuns or the sale of canned chicken. They handle everything beautifully," says a character in *Halbzeit*, a mammoth novel by the West German author Martin Walser.

Today, West Germany is the third largest industrial producer in the world, the second largest international trader. The gross national product exceeds DM 400 billion; average per capita income is more than DM 6000 ($1500) yearly. The new riches are not equally distributed. Here as everywhere in Europe the entrepreneur is better off than most. Workers often must work overtime to afford modest extras, such as a used car or holiday trip. The inequity occasionally triggers protests—on paper. Rolf Hochhuth, the young playwright who put the hierarchy of the Catholic Church on trial in his world-famous drama *The Deputy*, followed it with an attack on social inequalities in West Germany. Citing West Germany's growing social inequality and increasing concentration of capital in fewer hands, he warned that West Germany's young democracy was in danger.

Despite such intellectual reservations, West Germany is marked by tranquility of a kind that is rare in the rest of Europe. Strikes are infrequent. Does this mean the Germans are satisfied? Everyone seems to have his own theory and often has the chance to record it. Few people are asked as many questions as often as the Germans. A half dozen polling institutes continually check the pulse of public opinion. Every day Germans are polled on their political views and economic condition, their view of history and even on their weight. The results are unequivocal. Most West Germans are better off than ever before. And, what is even more important, they know it.

At the end of 1964, the Bielefelden Emnid Institute (one of the polling organizations) asked the following questions: Are you better or worse off than before the war? Fifty-six percent answered in the affirmative. Twenty-six percent believed they were just as well off, 9 percent felt they were worse off. Nine percent had no opinion whatsoever. The institute for Demoskopie in Allensbach asked at the same time: "Are you better off today than you were five years ago?" The result: Almost 60 percent answered "better," only 9 percent "worse."

These figures appeared in the German press on the day that I returned from Auschwitz to the Federal Republic. It was shortly before Christmas. "Celebrate without regrets," cries the fat headline of the illustrated ten-penny newspaper *Bild*, read daily by ten million people. It goes on to rejoice: "Citizens of the Federal Republic admit: We are doing great! We are better off than ever before. We Germans are proud of our economic success. We work. We work hard and so we can celebrate without regrets."

The Hamburg newsmagazine *Der Spiegel* a few days later refers to the same subject, "The Citizens of the Federal Republic have practically attained what Wilhelm II and Adolf Hitler once promised them: Marvelous times." Even the staid financial periodical *Der Volkswirt* reviews the economic state and lyrically announces: "Heaven on earth!" Nothing is beyond the reach of the German citizen. In 1964 one out of every three West Germans took a holiday trip. Millions owned their own car, one and a half million more than in the previous year. Eleven million bottles of whiskey were consumed. For the first time more champagne flowed in West Germany than in France.

West German consumption, Veblen would say, is of the conspicuous kind. Simply look at its citizens. Returning visitors have commented on the West German male's growing corpulence. Public polls corroborate this observation. In 1952, 56 percent of all German men weighed less than one hundred and fifty pounds; in 1963 only 42 percent did. In 1952, 44 percent weighed more than one hundred and fifty pounds, in 1963 it had leaped to 58 percent. Germans ironically refer to the *"Fresswelle,"* a wave of gluttony. Two widely prevalent ailments are diagnosed by doctors as "double-chin epidemic" and "pot belly," "Well-fed Teutons, are they content?" asks a Berlin satirist. "Let me have around me men who are fat and such who sleep o'er-night," exclaims Shakespeare's Julius Caesar. "Yon Cassius, he has a lean and hungry look. Such men are dangerous." Does prosperity pacify? Does it take the sting out of extremists? Does it make people more tolerant?

We do not yet know. Everything has happened so much more rapidly than expected. The writer Hans Werner Richter reports that in 1947 many people believed it would be at least fifty years before Germany's cities were rebuilt. At that time economic experts warned that unless the old Reich borders in the East were restored, "only death or the exodus of twenty million inhabitants" would relieve food shortages in the new over-populated Germany. People were far more optimistic in 1947 about the revival of German "Geist" in a framework of true democracy. Some looked forward to Utopia within a matter of years. Even now it is a stirring experience to read the faded journals and the political pamphlets of that time, badly printed on poor paper and already collectors' items. In them, some of the young writers of 1947 poured out their hearts. They demanded a state that had never existed in history; without duress, without an army, without rulers and underlings, without exploiters and exploited. These young intellectuals envisioned a kind of picture-book democracy. Some were former members of the Hitler Youth, calling themselves "Children Who Were Burnt Once." Eagerly, they submitted to "re-education" by Allied officers. Others were returning from prisoner-of-war camps. Hans Werner Richter was one of these former POW's. He says people expected to live in ruins for at least a generation, but looked forward to "a spiritual rejuvenation" within a period of less than ten years. Today Germany is rebuilt. The spiritual rejuvenation envisioned at that time has not taken place.

• The older generation which helped put Hitler into power, cheered him on, waged his wars, watched while the synagogues were burning and their Jewish neighbors were led away—this generation still holds on. In cultural life it has little influence; press, radio and television are mostly in the hands of the young. But economically and politically this older generation still controls the new West German Republic. Adolf Hitler's generals, officials and industrialists are respected citizens today. They are found among the mighty in Bonn: in leading positions as members of parliament, as secretaries of state, lawyers and commanders of an army wholly integrated into NATO. Some two-thirds of all West German judges practiced "justice" during the Third Reich. Sixty-four percent of all army officers once belonged to the Nazi *Wehrmacht*. Half of all federal officials served the Nazi administration. When one considers that more than twenty years have passed since the end of the war, these are astonishingly high figures. The age group of senior executives (those between forty and sixty today) was severely decimated by the war. One would consequently expect to find younger men advancing more quickly. Rather than former Nazi judges handing down the law, or former Nazi generals planning Germany's defenses against Russia, one would expect to see younger judges, generals or ambassadors. But in Germany forty or forty-five is still considered too young for such a job.

• The first president of West Germany, Professor Theodor Heuss, tried hard to ban the wearing of World War II decorations and service medals. Eventually he had to give up. Cabinet members and deputies, professors and judges, generals and managers of the new economy adorn themselves with Hitler's decorations —from which the swastika has been carefully removed. Few miss an opportunity to prove on white, starched dress shirts how hard they worked to help Hitler to victory. When queried, they say "objectively" it was a bad war, but "personally" they were fighting for "good": loyal service being always honorable. West Germany—though a democracy—is marked by moral schizophrenia. At official receptions in Bonn, proud memories of war clink and shine on the breasts of the prominent. What clinks inside? The same decorations sat on the chests of men who stood guard in Auschwitz (awards that were won there because their recipients were good at throwing cyanide gas into sealed chambers packed with screaming naked human beings).

• President Heuss also fought to replace the old megalomaniac national hymn:

> Deutschland, Deutschland über alles
> Über alles in der Welt
> Wenn es stets zu Schutz und Trutze
> Brüdlelich zusammen hält.
> Von der Maas bis an die Memel
> Von der Etsch bis an die Belt
> Deutschland, Deutschland über alles
> Über alles in der Welt.

Four rivers are mentioned. None of them is German. The Maas flows through Holland, the Etsch through the Italian part of Southern Tyrol. The Memel lies in what is now the Soviet Union; the Belt is a narrows in Denmark.

Heuss wanted a new hymn for a new state. Again he had to give in. When August Heinrich Hoffmann, romantic poet and professor of German in Breslau, wrote this poem in 1841, as a flaming protest against German disunity, perhaps he only wanted to strike up a song full of naïve hope and love for his country. But words lead a life of their own. Hoffmann's anthem has acquired a heavy patina by now. To many non-German, and even German ears, it now sounds like a macabre echo from the grave. At first, the leading stanza was avoided; a third, rather harmless stanza was sung. This custom is still kept up, though mainly at official occasions. According to an official announcement made by the President's office in Bonn in the spring of 1965, the first stanza is as much part of the national anthem as ever.

• Toward the end of 1964 the semi-official *Wehrkunde* (Defense News) published without comment a longish essay by retired General Friedrich von Boetticher. Boetticher wrote: "A well-conducted war is like a great symphony . . . when educating staff officers the task is to light a holy fire in their breasts; thus they

will be fit for war, the greatest enhancement of human life [sic!] and will overcome the weakness of their time." Does the general want the new German soldiers to anticipate war as they would a concert? In 1945 Goebbels compared war with a church service.
• Excessive preoccupation with the past is to be avoided, says even an editor on such a respected liberal paper as the *Frankfurter Allgemeine Zeitung*, Erich Dombrowski. In his view history is nothing but the foam on top of the "waves of eternity." And besides, he notes, France is responsible for the wars of 1870 and 1914.

Others go still a step further, and actually rationalize Nazi crimes. This is nothing new. One reads about it before coming to Germany. Hearing it with your own ears and, of all things, from the mouth of a twenty-five-year-old, has a shattering effect. A young man sat next to me in a railroad compartment: "Oh, it can't have been as bad as all that," he said idly stretching his legs. That stuff about the six million murdered Jews is enormously exaggerated. I heard it from an absolutely trustworthy source. And besides it's the British who invented the concentration camp . . . in South Africa during the Boer War."
• Today even those who admit that millions of Jews were murdered often pretend that Germans murdered only Jews. The Soviet Union, not counting ten million dead soldiers, lost thirteen million people in occupied territories, including four million prisoners of war shot, gassed, worked or starved to death. The Soviet Union, says Alexander Werth in *Russia at War*, did not have just one Lidice, not only one Oradour, but hundreds. Lesczynski estimates the number of dead Polish civilians at two and a half million people. At least one million Poles died in extermination camps.
• It has become common to compare—even equate—the extermination camps of Auschwitz and Treblinka with the destruction of Dresden by Allied bombers a few weeks before the end of the war, or with the expulsion of the German population from East Prussia, Silesia or Czechoslovakia in 1945. Some people demand trials against "Allied War Criminals." Prominent politicians, led by former Minister of Defense Franz Josef Strauss, render lip service to this demand. It is politically useful.

It is new, this Germany; but often so obtuse you could despair. In November, 1952, President Heuss visited a former extermination camp at Bergen-Belsen to help consecrate a memorial. In his speech Heuss said bitterly: "We knew about these things." Thirteen years later, in April, 1965, the successor to the late Dr. Heuss, President Heinrich Lübke, stood at the same spot. In his speech he said: "What happened did *not* happen with the mandate, with the knowledge of the German people, but in its name."

Not with knowledge of the German people? A little Jewish girl, locked up in an Amsterdam attic, did know. On October 9, 1942, only a few months after the gas chambers of Auschwitz started working, Anna Frank wrote in her diary:

> I've only got dismal and depressing news for you today. Our many Jewish friends are being taken away by the dozen. These people are treated by the Gestapo without a shred of decency, being loaded into cattle trucks and sent to Westerbork, the big Jewish camp. Westerbork sounds terrible: only one washing cubicle for a hundred people and not nearly enough lavatories. There's no separate accommodation. Men, women and children all sleep together. One hears of frightful immoralities because of this and a lot of women, and even young girls, who stay there any length of time are expecting babies.
>
> It is impossible to escape; most of the people in the camp are branded as inmates by their shaven heads and many also by their Jewish appearance. If it is as bad as this in Holland what will it be like in the distant and barbarous regions they are sent to? We assume that most of them are murdered. The English radio speaks of their being gassed.

Few West German politicians are as courageous as Social-Democratic Deputy Dr. Adolf Arndt, who told Parliament in 1965:

> "Once in Herrenalb I had to speak to a Protestant youth club. A minister had spoken before me and had said: 'We did not know anything about that!' Following him on the rostrum I felt compelled to tell these youngsters: "If your own mother is lying on her deathbed and she swears on the Bible, invoking God the Almighty and All Knowing, that she did not know, I tell you she just cannot bring

herself to tell the truth, it simply refuses to pass her lips, because it is too horrible to have known, or to have been able to know but not to have wanted to know it. . . ."

Even Dr. Arndt, a leading figure in his party, was obliged to add: "This is my conviction. I am not speaking for the Social-Democratic Party in this case." Dr. Arndt's views are those of a tiny minority. He can not speak for a majority, neither in the nation nor in his own party. The majority speaks a different language.

Language can be a revealing, treacherous medium. It often reveals vital insights into moral conditions of society as a whole. In everyday conversation or in the press many Germans today speak of the "catastrophe of 1945." Why catastrophe? On the other hand, events leading to Hitler's rise to power in 1933 are usually not referred to as the catastrophe they were but simply as "the Nazi seizure of power." What "seizure" of power? One does not seize power when freely elected.

The phrase "worst of all times," as commonly used today, usually refers to the immediate postwar period before the panacea of currency reform and massive United States aid began to create the basis for later prosperity. It means the time when Germany's cities were in ruin and ashes and there was too little food to go around. It is not the time when smoke-stacks belched at Auschwitz or Maidanek, when trains traveled slowly through the land, stopping at sidings for hours, crammed full with half-choked people screaming with hunger and thirst, visible and audible to all who cared to look and listen.

The night in 1938 when synagogues everywhere in Germany were burned is called *Reichskristallnacht* (Night of the Crystals), a thoughtless diminution of a bloody program. Who set fire to the synagogues? Who conducted the huge extermination? Who led the war? Who fought for victory? In today's language it was not the Germans. Everything happened merely "in the name of the German people" as if perpetrated by foreign mercenaries.

In the use and misuse of language for political purposes, the Nazis were masters. In 1939, words marched into war like soldiers. An army of new words covered unspeakably hideous acts. Previously innocent words now meant something entirely different. *lösen*—originally "to solve" became *endlösen*—or "final solution"

—the extermination by industrial means of millions of people; *behandeln*—originally "to deal with" or even "to treat medically" —now meant to commit murder; *selektionieren*, "to select"—to decide whether a man is sent to death or forced labor by slightly moving a thumb. The Gestapo "attended to" its prisoners; extermination detachments went under the special name of "action groups."

These are just a few examples. The West German novelist Heinrich Böll undoubtedly had them in mind when he recently warned his countrymen of the dangers even in innocent everyday use of language. "Words," Böll wrote, "as soon as they are uttered or written down transform themselves and impose a responsibility on the speaker or writer." He who "writes down a word should know its ancestry and of what transformation it is capable." Reading German newspapers or books, or in conversation with West Germans young or old, it is easy to see how serious Böll's warning should be taken. For instance: What is a KZ? (short for concentration camp). Hans Kroner, author of a standard postwar work on semantics *Handbuch der Seismologie* overlooks its ancestry (Heidelberg 1952). KZ = *Kuhns Zeitschrift* (that is, journal) for comparative linguistics.

Another standard work, leading in its field and published in an extremely large edition, is Küppers *Lexikon der Umgangssprache* 1963 (Dictionary of Everyday Usage 1963), which reflects a similar insensitivity to the ancestry of words. It contains the following entries:

Vergasen, i.e., to gas (verb): 1. to pollute the air with noxious odors (escaping intestinal wind: Cheese, etc.). 2. *Bis Zum Vergasen:* doing something up to the point of disgust.

Nazi (noun):

1. Ridiculous, dumb man; boob, word of abuse abbreviated from the masculine first name Ignatz, Ignatius.
2. Austrian soldier; Austrian.
3. National Socialist.
4. "That's enough to make the biggest Nazi leave the party": an expression of ill humor, of despair.

In 1965, President Heinrich Lübke of West Germany addressed the Hamburg Chamber of Commerce. Speaking to some three thousand guests assembled in the gaily decorated city hall, the seventy-three-year-old man announced: "It is the mission of the hour to ask very soberly whether the present generation is a match for its fathers [sic]." Not a voice was raised in protest against this monumental tactlessness. "Anyone who succeeds to an inheritance," Lübke lectured, "should not only admire the achievements of his fathers but is obligated to preserve them and then produce something of his own."

Such moralizing is probably innocent in intent and hopefully harmless in effect. In any other country one simply accepts it as speech-making. But Germany is not just any other country. The German-American historian Hannah Arendt said in 1963:

> Everybody became accustomed to deceiving themselves, since this had become a kind of moral prerequisite for survival. The habit has persisted in such a way that even today, eighteen years after the collapse of the Nazi regime, it is sometimes difficult not to believe that mendacity and "living a lie" are an integral part of the German national character.

These are hard words, and not completely fair. We cannot disregard the intellectuals and so many of the postwar youth who continue to grapple with the past. Few governments in Europe are today as subjected to such jarring criticism as is that of West Germany. Nowhere else can one find as many young people who do not know the meaning of patriotism or who reject nationalism, completely.

Young Germans, not malicious foreigners, or professional German-haters—are the first to call attention to unsympathetic aspects of their country. A few months after my arrival some students from West Berlin, whose fathers were Nazis, took me to the West Berlin Cabaret *Stachelschweine* (Porcupines). It is a well known and successful little theater. Once a year its program can be seen live on TV. Millions watch it. As recently as the summer of 1965 the "Porcupines" presented a macabre sketch echoing the past and reflecting a present intellectual climate. The curtain rises on Hitler's bunker underneath his Chancellory in Berlin. Four high-ranking Nazi officers sit at a table drinking champagne. It is April, 1945, and the game is almost up; the Russians are at the outskirts of Berlin. The four officers are: SS-*Obergruppenführer* Lodigkeit from the State Security Office; *Standartenführer* Eichheim, "Martin Bormann's right hand"; Undersecretary Kreissler from Goebbel's propaganda Ministry; and Luftwaffe Colonel Kretschmann. They are discussing the future, now that everything seems to be lost. They sing:

The game is over—what counts now is to be a good loser,/a kingdom for a five-year's refuge!/Indeed, how foolish to commit oneself so fervently!/Where is the spirit that motivated us—gone!

Of course, my conscience is spotless./I have never used it. It has never surrendered./And it will simply be your fate/to live obediently with us and Kaduk.*

What we did will fade quite soon,/since people are so forgetful./ We will be understood and no one will hate us/for justice luckily is blind.

Who will want to hear about Dachau in twenty years?/Then Auschwitz too will be just another word like Langemarck!

We shall wear the old decorations again./Our limbs will tremble when the band strikes up./Nor will we like the Jews,/and to blame will only be the others.

The next scene opens again on the four officers. They meet again in 1965. Again they are drinking champagne. Twenty years have passed. Lodigkeit directs a successful Catholic publishing house; Eichheim is a film producer; Undersecretary Kreissler has been promoted to State Secretary in the Ministry of All-German Affairs. Colonel Kretschmann is a German army four-star General at NATO Headquarters. They sing:

* An allusion to a well-known remark by the former Minister of Justice, Ewald Bucher, who resigned in April, 1965 as a protest against the extension of the statute of limitations for Nazi-murderers. Bucher declared in an interview that it was the fate of the Germans "to have to live with the Kaduks." Kaduk was a defendant at the Auschwitz trial.

We've scraped through once again.
We were spared the twenty years.
Our past was not held against us;
on the contrary—we've taken from left and right.
In our case the past was worth it.

Only if your stakes are high can you really win
and begin the past from the beginning.
If your stakes are low, you'll remain stupid forever,
and even your future will be held against you.

We are all democrats now,
for, to be a democrat is "up to date."
We're almost more democratic than in the States.
We would never betray our own Negroes.
The only ones we penalize are the Communists.

They have scraped through once more. They have rebuilt
Pompeii, more beautiful, wealthier than ever, on the crater of
their calamitous history. Has the lava hardened and the volcano
exhausted its violent energies? In January, 1963, the thirtieth
Anniversary of Hitler's "seizure of power" the journal *Stimme
der Jungen Generation* (Voice of the Young Generation) asked
leading public figures: "Can all this happen again in Germany?"
The answer was an almost unanimous: "No!" A few of those
questioned expressed themselves more carefully and said: "Not
quite the same way!"

3

The New Metropolis

THE huge entrance hall of the Munich railroad station is swarming with people. An almost incalculable mass, in colorful pullovers and winter parkas, armed with skiis and sticks, pushes towards the gate, squeezes past the ticket controller, fills the huge waiting room with holiday shouts and laughter. Most of the crowd is young, tall postwar children with open, unworried, sympathetic faces. Their demeanor is relaxed and easygoing. The contrast between these youngsters and the stiffness still noticeable among the old is striking. Railroad policemen try to order the growing mass into manageable groups. It is no use! They give it one more try—which appears halfhearted to anyone who has seen American or French police in action—then they give up, shaking their heads. A foreign observer, part of whose mental baggage is the stereotyped idea of German discipline, cannot help chuckling with a certain relief and happy surprise at such disorder and insubordination.

It is almost impossible to get a hotel room in Munich. I spend half an hour at the station booking counter while the young woman calls one hotel after the other. "Funny," says a man from Berlin, also waiting for a hotel room, "looking at the crowds here, I thought the whole population was fleeing." The girl behind the counter laughs. "Well, for all who leave, more come in every day." Statistics bear this statement out. In 1964 almost 1.8 million people visited Munich, of which 150,000 were Americans and 100,000 Frenchmen. "Munich has become a real metropolis."

Here, Hitler began his career. In smoke-filled, sour-smelling, heroically vaulted beer cellars, which even today resound to German march music, Hitler gave his first speeches. He is said to have loved Munich, in contrast to Berlin, where he never felt at home. "There is only one city in Germany which Hitler promised to make a great city—and which became great in spite of it," *Der Spiegel* noted a few years ago. Of all present-day German cities, Munich is the pleasantest.

Munich, like most German cities, was a huge smoking ruin during the last months of the war. Barely a house was untouched; 97.5 percent of all lodgings were damaged. Of those, 17 percent were totally destroyed, another 17.1 percent heavily, 32.7 percent less heavily and 30.7 percent slightly damaged. Some of the most valuable buildings were either destroyed or heavily damaged: the famous art museum *Alte Pinakothek*, the royal *Residenz*, the Gothic *Liebfrauenkirche*. All traces of the war, with few exceptions, have been removed. The old city is restored; baroque *Bürgerhäuser*, castles, memorials and churches, quaint wine cellars, beer cellars and old-fashioned apothecaries, fountains and towers have been rebuilt. Brand-new cobblestones adorn old narrow alleys. The classical Bavarian National Theater, with its royal box (forty years after the last king) and uncomfortable aisle seats from which only half the stage is visible—everything must look again as it was once upon a time.

An explosion of piety accompanied the rebuilding of cities all through West Germany. Germans were full of nostalgia for the day before yesterday. The rebuilders hoped to return to grandpa's cozy era across a bridge of plush carpets and grandiose stucco. The price paid was the missed opportunity of rebuilding cities fit for the age of the automobile. Almost everywhere—Hanover, taking a more modern course, is one of the few exceptions—price seems to have been no consideration. This is nowhere as apparent as in Munich. "Yes, the center of the city is being choked by traffic," says a nice old gentleman in the City Works Board, "but at least we've got our good old Munich atmosphere back."

Under the Nazis, Munich was the "Capital of the Movement," the seat of their National Directorate. The Directorate was housed in a bombastic building, which certainly would not have been restored had it been destroyed. But it somehow escaped, much like Cologne's Cathedral, and today belongs to the Bavarian State Library. Ironically, it now shelters a collection of Judaic Art— Sixteenth Century illuminated prayer books, Bible commentaries, *Pessukim* and *Mishenayot*. The "Brown House," home of the Nazis prior to 1933, stands next to it—also undamaged. Today its façade is a little jaundiced, it contains the offices of the National Lottery. At America House across the street, the Stars and Stripes flutter in the wind. Young *Münchners* sit in the reading room, leafing through *Playboy*, *Time* magazine and the New York *Times*.

Another landmark, Munich's *Feldherrnhalle* (Field Marshal's Hall), remains untouched—an exact copy of the *Loggia dei Stanzi* in Florence. Hitler attempted his 1923 coup d'etat here. Sixteen rioters were felled by police bullets that day. Perhaps world history would have taken a different course if the Munich police had also shot a seventeenth man. Or even if the Munich judges handling the case of *Bavaria* versus *Adolf Hitler* had not secretly sympathized with the defendant, sending him into comfortable confinement in a gentlemen's prison and giving him time and peace to write *Mein Kampf*.

A few hundred steps away rises a triumphal arch from the last century, restored after the war. It is a military monument. Yet its vaulted arcades are inscribed in large black letters: "Consecrated to Victory. Destroyed by War. Exhorting you to peace."

"Metropolis with a heart," the people of Munich call their city.

Whether the atmosphere is heartier here than in other German cities is arguable. Perhaps it is merely rougher, beerier and more bohemian. The city owes its postwar fortune completely to Germany's defeat and its subsequent partition that shifted population centers west and south. Munich has grown almost twice as fast as any other German city. Its 1.2 million inhabitants exceed the population of 1939 by 350,000. It is still growing. There are larger West German cities—West Berlin is twice as big and Hamburg has a half million more inhabitants—but only Munich can be compared with other West European capitals. It is the only German city not completely deserted at night. Munich makes no special effort to guard against the ennui of dull provincialism; Berlin, for instance, offers special grants to artists, writers and scientists to spend a few months each year in that cutoff province. Here, such measures are unnecessary. More foreigners and more students live in Munich than anywhere else in Germany. Twenty-one thousand study at the university and another twenty thousand at the *Technische Hochschule* and other institutes. No other German city offers as rich a variety of theaters, concerts, exhibitions, museums or Nobel Prize winners (three). Munich, while smaller in area than other cities, does not as strongly feel the constriction that came with the upheaval of 1945—causing a large country to shrink like a sock.

What is still remembered as the sinister capital of the "Nazi movement" is now sometimes called "the secret capital of West Germany." When *Der Spiegel* coined this phrase it acknowledged what is generally admitted to be a cultural reality. It admits the vacuum created by the isolation, inaccessibility and deterioration of Berlin, and the longing for a new urban ideal. Small, provincial Bonn—officially still the "provisional" capital—cannot provide it.

Munich tries to. It is the brilliant infant prodigy of defeated Germany. Today young Germans are as attracted to Munich as they once were to Berlin. Munich has become a surrogate for Berlin. Life here is "easygoing," they say, using an English word incorporated into German for lack of a synonomous expression, "It is a kind of German paradise," says Hans Sepp, a forty-two-year-old columnist on Munich's *Süddeutsche Zeitung*. It has something of the atmosphere of Breugel's "Land of Milk and Honey," again on display in Munich's *Alte Pinakothek*. The slogan here is "Live and Let Live." Munich has been called "Capital of German Leisure."

One hears that Germans are learning the art of *savoir vivre* for the first time. *Münchners* preoccupy themselves far less with the grave problems of German politics than do Germans elsewhere in the country. Partition, the Berlin Wall—one hears them less frequently discussed; people here are probably more aware than elsewhere that those problems apparently are insoluble. The West German government still believes that East Germany must be absorbed by West Germany, as Germany was absorbed by Prussia in the nineteenth century. In Bonn's view this is a "purpose" of history.

Most people one meets in Munich have a different sense of history. Munich is closer to Vienna than to Berlin, and Prussia a distant unpopular land; its disappearance causes few heartaches. Munich sociologist Hans Josef Mundt, remarks: "A new, open-minded, urban society is slowly coming into existence here. This is something completely new in Germany and its influence radiates throughout the country. We have a more Southern temperament than the Berliners of the 'golden twenties.' This new society wanders beyond its borders, toward Italy, Switzerland, Austria, France and the United States. If all of Germany will be like this— well, then we can call ourselves lucky."

Joachim Kaiser, a young drama and music critic, maintains that the people of Munich are more tolerant; the influx of outsiders accustoms them to the unusual and foreign. Munich students confirm this; there are few universities in Germany where foreign students are as firmly integrated into the community. Rarely does one see so many white and colored students together, as friends or as lovers.

The townhall of Munich is a gigantic, dark looking structure, built in neo-Gothic style. Like so many in Germany, it was built, destroyed and rebuilt from scratch, all within the past eighty years. The present Lord Mayor of Munich, Dr. Hans Joachim Vogel, was first elected in 1960 at the age of thirty-four. He has since increased his unprecedented majority from sixty-three to seventy-three percent of the vote.

The Lord Mayor is of medium height; he has a friendly roundish face. He wears a large pair of horn-rimmed glasses and combs his hair loosely to the back. He stands in the doorway, hand extended,

33

and calls out "Welcome to Munich City Hall!" This informal greeting, while common in other countries, still sounds odd in a German City Hall. It is not Vogel's only trait that strikes one as American.

Like Willy Brandt in Berlin and so many young leaders of the once-leftist German Social-Democratic Party, Vogel quotes Kennedy rather than Karl Marx. Munich is "a city open to the world," Vogel says, "with firm links across its borders. No, no, not a 'new capital.' We shouldn't concentrate all of our assets in one place; let's spread them over as many cities as possible." That is the "better way for Germany—and also for democracy," he explains. For the first time in history, says Vogel, democracy has a "fair chance" in Germany. "For the first time it can establish itself quietly, in peace, in general prosperity . . . under conditions totally different from those of the unhappy twenties. . . . The twenties were not golden. The more you hear about them the more you hate them," he adds.

I ask Vogel whether conditions of the twenties might return. "It's not absolutely impossible," Vogel says. "We could suffer an economic crisis or a Social-Democratic victory might even produce a neo-Nationalist reaction. After all, there are still people who consider all Social-Democrats as unpatriotic fellows. Even Adenauer once said that a SPD victory would be the end of Germany." Vogel dislikes and fears his fellow-Bavarian Franz Josef Strauss, a volatile Catholic politician. "Strauss," he calls "an unusually vigorous power station, who unfortunately lacks a sufficient number of circuit breakers." Such a man might, he adds, exploit any crisis. On the other hand, one must not compare the Bonn Republic with the Weimar Republic. There are new realities. "We, the younger people of this country, no longer regard Germany as the navel of the world," Vogel says. "And, after all, the future depends on us."

I ask the young mayor how he happened to enter politics. "Of course I was in the *Hitlerjugend* like my contemporaries," Vogel begins. "My father entered the party in 1932. I was six years old at the time. In 1936 he left the party again. What kept me from joining was being drafted when I came of age." Did he support the cause with any enthusiasm? "Yes, I believe I did. As almost everyone else at that time. But after a while I started having my first

34

doubts; in an Army hospital I first heard about horrible things happening in the East. At first I couldn't believe they were true. But I knew the man who told me. I could depend on him. I received a terrible shock. . . . When I returned from the war, I entered the university. I tried to think about what had really happened here. I realized that young people like myself must take an interest in politics. So I studied various party programs and after some time decided the SPD suited my convictions better than any of the others." In 1955 lawyer Vogel was called in by Bavarian Minister-President Wilhelm Högner and asked to "clean up" the state's archaic provincial law. Three years later he joined the city's legal department. By 1960 he had advanced to where the SPD nominated him as candidate for the office of Lord Mayor.

Quite a contrast to Vogel is another young *Münchner*. He is often in the news. I watch him one evening in a large beer cellar. Beer and a certain kind of politics seem to be inseparable in Germany, and beer cellars still serve as main gathering places for political meetings. The young man is thirty-two years old, his name Dr. Gerhard Frey. He pretends to be the new *führer* summoning the Germans to a new rabid nationalism. He publishes the weekly *"National und Soldatenzeitung*, which claims a circulation of more than 100,000—third largest among the political weeklies in West Germany. "Blow below the belt against Germany," "The truth about Hitler," "The sadistic Czechs and their love of human blood," "In servitude to Jewry," are typical headlines in this journal. Frey and his cronies have been called "the potential murderers of tomorrow."

"It is high time we start practicing German politics again and not English, American or Jewish politics," Frey screams into his microphone. "We are not the potential murderers of tomorrow but they, the Bonn politicians who practice nothing but renunciation are the murderers of the present, the murderers of the German nation." A crowd of roughly five hundred people howls approval: "Richtig!" (true) "More! More!"

At last, here is someone who has the guts to say it out loud: "Bravo!"

From the back of the hall a young female voice calls out: "You

35

barefaced liar! You Nazi! You belong in the nut house!" She is supported by shouts of agreement from the same direction. A group of bouncers rushes over to the girl. Her friends try to protect her. After a brief scuffle the hecklers are forcibly removed as the speaker calmly waits at his rostrum. I sit in the crowd and watch the audience. About half are older than forty. Tough-looking workers in dark suits or sporting the green Bavarian national garb; mostly coarse, heavy-limbed men squatting heavily on their stools. A few women blink nervously. The other half are young people, outwardly almost indistinguishable from their contemporaries at universities, factories, offices or Munich movie houses. All are drinking beer out of large stone tankards.

Quiet is restored in the hall. Gerhard Frey continues. He is a tall muscular man. Out of his somewhat puffy face sticks a small precise nose, his double chin sags down across his spotless white shirt and elegant silk tie. His dark blue tailor-made suit is of Italian cut. This postwar product of a German University has learned a lot from the Nazis. He is a gifted public speaker. He uses short, lucidly formulated sentences. Words spring lightly and rapidly out of his small mouth; he pauses regularly for applause. His standard phrase begins: "I say . . ." "I tell you, friends. . . . " and in a soft, intimate tone of voice he announces "outrages," incredible affronts "kept secret" by the government. Then abruptly his voice rises; hysterically—either genuine or pretended—he screeches: "I fear the wages of history . . . I tremble . . . I am troubled that our politics come not from national interests but from blackmail by International Jewry. We are a people of valorous soldiers and cowardly civilians. Perhaps," he adds, "injustice was once done in the name of the German people, but must we atone for this until the last judgment?" The audience shouts bravo. And then he brings them from their seats: "We are accused of having murdered six million Jews . . . I say that it is an outright lie. The government must clarify such numbers. I tell you, friends, ignominious accusations are unjustly heaped upon us."

There exists an international conspiracy, Frey tells his audience, a defamation campaign to diminish Germany's national interest. "What is that national interest? The reconstruction of the German Reich within its old borders." It is unclear which borders he means:

those of 1937, those of 1943 or those of 1914. In any case, he wants East Prussia back as well as Pomerania, Silesia and "the Sudetenland which was robbed from us." All these areas "were German and will be German again, even if we have to wait for two thousand years like the Jews for their Palestine . . . we would be glad if the Israelis would help us in this endeavor." (Laughter) Restitution payments must be stopped, he shouts into the applause. "It is high time that we stopped being the world's fool who always pays."

Persecution of "co-called war criminals" should cease. The German people are against such trials. "Foreign countries" do not want them either. He has proof. He has just returned from the Near East, where the Sudanese Foreign Minister had told him (he claims): "What the Germans are doing is grotesque. You've let yourselves be blackmailed for twenty years." The Foreign Minister of Kuwait also opposes war-crimes trials. "He was speaking in the name of the entire Arab world." Everybody, says Frey, is against these trials. "I am for representative democracy but I say we must put an end to the dictatorship of Parliament." (Loud applause.) At the end of the evening, when the blinding kleig lights of the TV cameras are turned off, it is as though an evil spook had been extinguished. In the *18th Brumaire of Louis Napoleon*, Karl Marx wrote: "All historical personalities reoccur: the first time in the form of tragedy, the second time as farce."

A few days later "Brotherhood Week" begins in Munich. It is celebrated throughout West Germany and serves the understanding between peoples, nations and religions. In Munich there is a solemn inaugural matinee, a speech by the Bavarian minister-president, followed by Telemann's *C Major Suite for String Orchestra*. There is also a special broadcast on the radio, an exhibition, a series of lectures on "The Future of the Three Religions."

A commemorative service is held in the small glass-covered quadrangle of Munich's Ludwig-Maximilian-Universität. Vaulted colonnades surround the quadrangle and a magnificent stairway. The rector and members of the University senate, dressed in solemn vestments, stand on a raised platform. Floral wreaths bedeck a memorial stone. The beautiful quadrangle is a historic place. Here in 1943 two youngsters, Sophie and Hans Scholl, tossed anti-Nazi pamphlets from a third-floor gallery, for which they were promptly put to death. Theirs was one of the very few truly spontaneous acts of public resistance to Hitler's reign of terror. They belonged to a resistance circle called "The White Rose." Today, the wide plaza in front of Munich University bears their names. Inside the quadrangle, a memorial was dedicated to them in 1952; every year the Scholls' heroic deed is commemorated in public ceremony. A few hundred students are waiting here this year to listen to the rector's speech.

Suddenly, white pamphlets flutter down on the solemn assembly, from the same third-floor gallery where back in 1943, Sophie and Hans Scholl had tossed theirs. The new pamphlet quotes the old and adds:

> The most important things have not been said here today. The White Rose said in its pamphlet: "There is no punishment on earth that could do justice to Hitler and his followers. Their deeds are too evil. But let them at least not succeed in changing colors at the last moment, pretending that nothing has happened." They have succeeded in even more: they are back in office; what is more—they teach and lend this celebration the luster of their unshakeable authority, as if nothing had happened.

The pamphlet lists members of the University faculty, some of them present at the ceremony:

> Professor of medicine Max Mikorey: "Theoretician" of Nazi psychiatry, wrote *Jewry in Jurisprudence* and *Jewry in Forensic Psychology*.

> Law professor Friedrich Berber: Member of the Nazi party, friend and advisor of Hitler's Foreign Minister Ribbentrop; proved the war guilt of England and the Jews. (Today also Executive Director of the Institute for International Law, Government and the Philosophy of Law at Munich University.)

> Dean of the Theological Faculty Michael Schmaus: Justified the Nazi-terror from a Catholic theological point-of-view in, among other books, *Encounter Between Catholic Christianity and National Socialist World Views*. (He is also a member of the Bavarian Academy of Sciences and the Papal Theological Academy, a recipient of the Franco-Spanish Komtur Cross and the Bavarian Meritorious Service Medal.)

Law professor Reinhardt Maurach: Nazi party member, legal advisor on questions concerning the suppression of East European peoples, head of the Nazi Institute for Eastern Jurisprudence, author of *Russian-Jewish Politics* among others (today also Executive Director of the University Institute on Criminal Law).

What a peculiar country! There are old Nazis teaching at almost every university; yet nowhere do academicians expose the national madness of the past as candidly and with as much levelheaded composure. There is a research center in Munich, the *Institut für Zeitgeschichte* (Institute for Contemporary History), that exists for no other purpose.

Political science is a new concept in Germany. Ranke, a father of modern historiography, sought to know what the past was really like (*"wie es eigentlich gewesen"*). Contemporary history is a relatively new area of study. Before the war there was only one political science institute, in Berlin. "Today," according to Dr. Vogelsang of the Munich Institute for Contemporary History, "most universities have political science faculties as well as institutes for contemporary history." Here, a self-examination on a grand scale is taking place. Archives, secret up to 1945 are open to and used by scholars. Present-day German historians sometimes act like illegitimate children. Doggedly they try to discover from whence they come; it cannot be pleasant for them to find out.

Munich's Institute for Contemporary History was founded in 1952. Located in a quiet residential street on the other side of the Isar, it is the best-known institute of its kind. Dr. Vogelsang, a member of the board of directors, works under a huge map of Europe on which Nazi concentration and extermination camps have been marked. He is middle-aged. "Institutes like these," he says, "utilize information gathered about the Nazi period for civic education programs among young people." The Institute opened shortly after the Nuremberg Trials. Its original intent was to collect and study material assembled during the trials. It was not the only intention. "Perhaps we also wanted to create a favorable climate for Germany in the world," says Dr. Vogelsang. "And prove that Germans were ready to take the lessons of their own history seriously. . . . But now a new generation has grown up. It wants to know about its fathers. Young people want to find out why they are received coldly on trips abroad. Youth brings back into public consciousness the past that an older generation wants so much to suppress. As the younger generation comes of age it intervenes anew in the process of national self-examination."

The Munich Institute also offers expert opinions at trials of Nazis. Scholars preparing for their Ph.D. degrees work on their dissertations here. Like Ranke, they want to know "what it was really like." But in contrast to Ranke, who saw world history anchored in national development, these younger historians tend to regard German history as an integral part of world history.

Heinz Rohr is a twenty-six-year-old history student from Mainz. Here in Munich he works on his thesis "Big Business Support for Hitler Prior to 1933." He is blond and of medium height. His father was, he says, "an enthusiastic Nazi." Today his father is a member of the Christian Democratic Union. As far as Rohr is concerned, Hitler was not just a quirk in German politics; nor was he the inevitable result of German history. "We could have taken a different course if people hadn't been as blind." Indeed, he says, there were many "decent" people who held the stirrups for National Socialism. Long before Hitler certain jingoistic circles attacked democracy or liberalism as "foggy humanistic daydreaming" or "decadence." Adds Rohr: "I am convinced the Germans not only endured Hitler but also helped fashion him." Of course, a combined set of circumstances resulted in Hitler: World War I, inflation, economic crisis, unemployment—that was all worldwide. "But Germany was the weakest place in the European organism; that was why dangerous viruses were able to infect it so easily. People simply aren't all bad or all good. They are both, at one and the same time. It depends on circumstance which side will predominate."

In few countries are as many books published on recent national history and in such large editions as in West Germany. Young people seem pent up with curiosity; skillful publishers rush to satisfy the demand. Low-priced paperbacks on Nazism are often astonishingly successful. In book shops, at newspaper stands and in department stores, colorful pocket books are displayed on rotating iron racks (the "New Trees of Knowledge" says West German critic and poet Hans Magnus Enzensberger). Illustrated weeklies like *Stern* provide readers, alongside lengthy stories on royal romances and scandals of movie stars, with critical pictorial reports of the Nazi era. The Hamburg magazine *Der Spiegel*, with a circulation of more than one-half million, seems to be obsessed with contemporary history. Hardly an issue appears without page long excerpts from a recent book on the recent past. Such excerpts are rarely sympathetic toward Germany and the Germans. Such illustrated documentaries are as popular in West Germany as are articles on popular medicine or psychoanalysis elsewhere. Whether this onslaught in fact produces deeper understanding is still unclear. Young Germans pluck their apple off the Tree of Knowledge. Do they eat it too and learn to master present as well as future, like Adam and Eve, with the sweat of their brows? This is a key question.

Stachus is Munich's largest and most congested plaza. Here, bulldozers and drilling machines daily create an uproar. Huge steam shovels eat their way into the grey-brown earth. Munich's population will reach 1.5 million within the next ten years. A modern subway, an absolute necessity for this city, should be ready at that time. The first tunnel is being dug here at the Stachus.

"*Attenzione!*" "*Si, por favor.*"

Is this still Germany? Foreign languages echo from the open shaft. Most of the workers are foreigners. Digging is heavy, dirty work. It is hard to find laborers in Germany. They must be imported.

Notices in Spanish or Italian can be seen in many German factories today. Germany is surprisingly less "German" than one generally assumes. At all centers of industry, one meets foreign workers. Perhaps not as frequently as in neighboring Switzerland, which must import a full quarter of its labor force. West Germany imports about a million workers from Italy, Spain, Portugal, Yugoslavia, Greece, Syria, Jordan or Turkey. Foreign workers have long become vital for prosperity. "Without them," says one Munich businessman, "there can be no more economic miracles."

Increased automation permits a mass of unskilled laborers to work here without speaking a word of German. They are known as "*Gastarbeiter*"—guest-worker. Foreign worker, though less polite, might be more appropriate, and this is the customary appellation in German-speaking parts of Switzerland. But in Germany this, again, is a word with a "past," standing for the 5.3 million slave laborers, whom the Nazis deported to Germany from all over Europe, to gradually die of exhaustion and ill treatment.

Today they come voluntarily, sometimes from the same countries —a steady stream from the slums and remote villages of Southern Europe to the fleshpots of the Federal Republic. At metropolitan railroad stations, early in the morning, as better-heeled travelers, combed and washed, emerge from the sleeping cars of the *Compagnie Internationale des Wagons-Lits*, guest-workers climb out of their narrow compartments. Unshaven, in crumpled clothes, stretching their stiff limbs, they gather in the waiting halls. From there they will be bussed to their destination. Every day trains arrive. Still, six hundred thousand jobs in Germany remain unfilled. In the evening the workers gather again to socialize at local railroad stations, as though trains were umbilical cords uniting them with their distant homes.

Union leaders and industrial managers, mayors, the churches and social welfare offices are preoccupied with the problems of the guest-worker. Industrialists maintain that without guest-workers any further growth of the gross national product is impossible. A progressive union leader in Hamburg sees the Federal Republic, a "Germanic" land, becoming "the melting pot of Europe," much like the United States of America; he wants the government to offer guest-workers German citizenship. Special radio programs are broadcast for them; there are forty-five minutes each evening in Italian, forty-five in Spanish, forty-five in Turkish, and so forth.

Public relations has found a new field of activity. Out of the Cologne train which brought him from Portugal, twenty-three-year-old Armando Sa Rodrigues stepped in December, 1964. He was met by a reception committee. A brass band blared out: "*Wem Gott will rechte Gunst erweisen*," and then the march "*Alte Kameraden.*" A gentleman in a dark suit made a little speech. The bewildered young man was given a bouquet of flowers and a motor bicycle. TV cameras recorded the picture: Armando Sa Rodrigues was the one-millionth guest-worker.

A few weeks later another spectacle: the vast Cologne cathedral turned into a mosque for a few hours. About five hundred Turks knelt down on their prayer rugs in the northern aisle of the cathedral. Those who could not afford a rug knelt instead on newspapers. All faces turned southeast toward Mecca and prayer was offered to Mohammed, Prophet of Islam. They celebrated the end of Ramadden, the Mohammedan month of fasting "at the very place at which Bernhard von Clairveaux in 1147 summoned Christians to the second Crusade," as the *Kölner Rundschau* wryly observed next day. It was "a day that made religious history." The Hamburg daily *Die Welt* noted it "was probably the first time that Moslems were permitted to pray in a Christian church."

Relations between guest-workers and Germans remain tense. They are a valuable gauge for measuring to what extent Germans have learned a lesson. Are they more tolerant now than they were in the past? Attitudes to Jews in this respect have little if any significance, as the Jewish population of West Germany is a negligible minority (0.04 percent against 0.9 percent before the war.)

Guest-workers enjoy rights equal to those of the natives. Their children receive federal aid, like any German child. In some cases it is more difficult to fire a guest-worker than a German one. Guest workers are signed to a year's contract, so they are theoretically more immune to economic ups and downs. But professional advancement remains closed—for all practical purposes—to most guest-workers; there is very little social contact with the native population. Learning German does not help. It is interesting to note how similar prejudices persist moving from race to race: they focus on sexual jealousy, body and culinary odors. Guest workers "smell," as the Jews used to; they are supposed to be dirty. This in a country that in 1963 still lacked bathrooms or showers in forty-four percent of all apartments.

They are "after our girls." A few days after the Mohammedan service in the Cologne cathedral I found myself in a pub in the same city. Next to me a tall robust, approximately fifty-year-old man furiously loosed a string of epithets against the "filthy banana eaters," these "shameless bastards" who dare "make passes at German girls." He would not allow his daughter out alone at night. "Is your daughter blonde," I asked. "Of course," he said "that's what these guys are after. Her blondness fascinates them." Hitler too used to inveigh against "dark Jewish hooligans," who "waylay blonde German girls." Inferiority complexes persist; only the objects onto which they latch change.

Guest-workers are often depicted as potential murderers—quick with a knife, responsible for the rising crime rate. The Federal Bureau of Investigation in Wiesbaden disputes this, but popular mass-circulation papers continue to stoke prejudice with new explosives. Crimes in which guest-workers are involved are angrily exaggerated. The term "Jew" is taboo today, but there are headlines such as: "Guest-worker stabs German to death," "the Greek stabbed three times, three times he penetrated Laura's heart," "Giuseppe shot in blind fury," "She loses her life through dirty trick. Italian guest-worker accused of murder."

In April, 1965, the Cologne weekly *Neue Illustrierte* screamed in large red letters on a black background: "Out with the brazen guest-workers; Germany still belongs to us." The text was no calmer: "If things go on like this for another year we won't be masters in our own house. They are crowding our cafes, wolf-whistling after our girls, ogling our wives, beating up our cops—and even want to be loved by us! Four, five, six guest-workers march belligerently abreast along Kölner Ring. Germans must step aside. Who wants to be stabbed? These thoughts occur to many but they don't speak. They remain silent because they are afraid of the stilettos of our ruthless guests. They remain silent because they are afraid the world might again accuse us of racial prejudice. The *Neue Illustrierte* is not an extremist paper like the *Soldatenzeitung*. It is normally a harmless, colorful mass-circulation weekly you find in every barber shop.

New Prussia, Old Money

MORE THAN 380,900 foreign laborers work in a single state of the West German federation: *Nordrhein-Westfalen,* most heavily industrialized, most Americanized and wealthiest of the ten West German states. Stretching along the Belgian and Dutch borders it contains the famous Ruhr as well as the cities of Bonn, Cologne and Düsseldorf.

Nordrhein-Westfalen is often described in superlatives: the most populous state (16 million inhabitants, including 3.6 million refugees from Germany's lost territories in the east—mostly Protestants, whose average standard of living is higher today than that of the more lethargic, predominantly Catholic native population); the

State with the largest number of employees and the largest gross income; the state with the biggest budget, the most extensive road network and the greatest number of large cities. Its capital is Düsseldorf, and it contains the "provisional" federal capital, Bonn. It is a new Prussia and money is its god.

The old Prussia is dead, expunged from the maps. It has been divided between Poland and the Soviet Union. Königsberg—the city of Kant—is Kalingrad today. At Allenstein Castle, once the main seat of the Knights of the German Order, who pushed Germany's borders as far east as Estonia, Polish guides nowadays explain that the time of "German colonialism is gone forever from this part of the world."

The new Prussia on the Rhine and Ruhr has fed on the ruins of the old. It is a land of snug forests, smokestacks, romantic castles, coal mines, steel factories and huge industrial concerns that have a yearly turnover exceeding the national budget of many a small country.

Politically and geographically, *Nordrhein-Westfalen* is a synthetic postwar product, its borders fixed by decree of the British Occupation forces. A British Air Force marshal pasted it together in the summer of 1946 out of bits and pieces of what was then the British Zone of Occupation. Those in Düsseldorf who were listening to the morning news broadcast on the BBC on July 18, 1946 (only a negligible minority were), learned that parts of the former Prussian provinces of Rheinland, Lippe-Detmold and Westfalen were now melded as a new state to be called *Nordrhein-Westfalen*. Even the name was new, and foreign to the German tongue: a literal translation of the English North Rhine-Westphalia. There was no basis for it in the history of German principalities, such as supported the other states of Hesse, Bavaria or Baden-Wurttemberg. *Nordrhein-Westfalen* as a state had no past; and yet in so many ways it is typical of West Germany as a whole. The new Prussia reminds you at times of Texas.

In the Düsseldorf Palais, formerly the Prussian governor's residence, I talked with the state minister-president, Dr. Franz Meyers. He is a broad-shouldered, energetic-looking man, born in 1908 in the industrial city of Monchen-Gladbach, not far from the Dutch border. He is a member of the Christian Democratic Party. "It works out surprisingly well," says Dr. Meyers. "We are getting used to the fact there is such a thing as *Nordrhein-Westfalen.*" Meyer's cabinet has more young ministers than any other state cabinet in West Germany. Meyers says: "You can become almost anything if you work with me, except Minister-President." He has plucked some of his young cabinet members out of distant Bavaria. One is Education Minister Paul Mikat, born in 1924. Mikat hopes to start a series of new universities all over the sooty Ruhr region and is forming the first in the coal town of Bochum. A second university is planned for 1970. The two will add another superlative to the state. It will have more universitites than any other. At present, Baden-Württemberg with its famous old universities of Heidelberg, Tübingen and Freiburg, and the technical colleges of Stuttgart and Karlsruhe, ranks first.

"Federalism is good for Germany," Dr. Meyers says. In its present form, federalism is a novelty in Germany, introduced by the Allies in 1946, "First, it has accustomed Germans to democracy," says Meyers, "by abolishing the old concentration of power. Second, it has enabled the Social-Democratic opposition party— that never won a national majority—to govern at least in the states ... that's good, governing has to be learned." Are there clashes between the States and central government? Dr. Meyers says such clashes are not rare. "But they are almost never over the principle of federalism, which is generally accepted. Rather, we collide with an old-fashioned, central bureaucracy still schooled in Prussian methods and accustomed to a centrally organized German Reich. This bureaucracy," says Meyers, "is slowly dying out. Younger people, used to the pluralism of our new industrial society, are replacing it. They know you have to live with all kinds of powerfully organized interest groups as well as with legitimate lobbies."

What future has the federal state? It is declining in importance, complains Mayer, as it is in the United States. Its ultimate future, he says, hinges upon the future of Europe. In the case of European Union, national central governments may decline; states may again play a larger role in education and preserving local traditions.

Local traditions? At first one notices nothing of the sort in Düsseldorf. Skyscrapers in international style—Brazilia or Milan—

47

reflect in the dirty Rhine, the same Rhine once celebrated in song by the poet Heinrich Heine. In Düsseldorf, Heine's hometown, there is almost nothing reminding of the poet who warned the world of his compatriots' Teutonic fury: not a single memorial, nor noteworthy archive. Since the end of the war a part of one street bears Heine's name but *Düsseldorfers* call it by its old name. Düsseldorf has several theaters and symphony orchestras, flourishing jewelry shops, elegant fashion houses, bars and nightclubs—and the notorious *Industrieclub*—a strikingly modest private reservation for wealthy bankers and industrial magnates. Here Adolf Hitler gave a momentous speech on January 28, 1932, and won many wealthy followers who financed his way to power. Some of them are leaders in the economy even today. Their stakes were high and with the parodying Berlin "Porcupines" they can say: "the gamble was worth it."

"Who marched behind the first tank? It was Dr. Rasche of the Dresdener Bank." This couplet, which made the rounds in Germany in 1943, underlined the close liason between the financiers and the military. The financier whose name adorns all West German banknotes today, Carl Blessing, since 1957 President of the Federal Bank, was a member of the exclusive "circle of friends of *Reichsführer* SS Heinrich Himmler." This circle "of friends," the shady activities of which are described at length in records of the Nuremberg Trials, provided the SS with financial support. They met with the hangmen to discuss proper ways of exploiting the labor of concentration camp inmates.

Himmler's "circle of friends" had thirty-six members. Another well-known member is Düsseldorf billionaire and industrialist Dr. Friedrich Flick, a major shareholder of Daimler-Benz (Mercedes) and Auto-Union (DKW). A third prominent member was Dr. Heinrich Butefisch. His story is particularly interesting. He was a founder of the I.G. Farben branch at Auschwitz, where countless prisoners were worked to death. Today Dr. Butefisch is deputy chairman of the board of directors at Ruhrchemie-Oberhausen, a successor firm to I.G. Farben. Dr. Butefisch's career as an honorable citizen was only briefly interrupted after the war, when the Allies condemned him to six years in prison. The Nazis had given him a "Knight's Cross" in addition to a Meritorious Service Medal.

But West Germany was not less grateful for his services. On March 11, 1964 President Lübke of West Germany again rewarded him with one of the nation's highest decorations, the large Federal Meritorious Service Cross. When by sheer coincidence his name cropped up a few days later at the Frankfurt Auschwitz trial, public uproar forced President Lübke to ask Butefisch to return the medal immediately.

These are a few Düsseldorf names, picked at random. The harmless present camouflages a noxious past. Düsseldorf and other Ruhr cities are like a double-exposed negative: a pretty modern technicolor photo superimposed on the black-grey shadows of a massacre. Nowhere is this sinister hocus-pocus as striking as in Essen, the famous Ruhr and Krupp metropolis, only thirty-one kilometers from Düsseldorf. En route factories and slag heaps, refineries, mines and endless housing developments break the flat landscape. High-tension wires spread like cobwebs above the land. Huge steel pillars sprouting six, eight legs like Martians in an H.G. Wells novel stalk through the bleak landscape. The heavily traveled Autobahn crosses a black river. Sad-looking, almost tumbledown, two-story houses that Krupp built in the nineteenth century (for "my faithful miners") line the road. Miners and factory workers still live here. And now each roof has its TV antenna. At street corners there are pitiful, glum restaurants, their drabness broken only by the cigarette and beer advertisements adorning the outside. The landscape along the river Ruhr has a prehistoric feel to it. It seems like a geological deposit of the nineteenth century with steel skeletons instead of trees, and dark red brick houses with sooty curtains. A putrid haze hangs above roofs and chimneys. "The sun only rarely penetrates the smog," writes Heinrich Böll, the postwar writer from Cologne, "and this robbery has been taking place for a whole century."

In the center of Essen, new skyscrapers have gone up next to Krupp's old red brick enormities. Essen is the old armory of the Reich. Its fate is intricately enmeshed with the industrial revolution and the debacles of the German nation.

In 1945 the center of town lay for the most part in ruins; today it is completely rebuilt. Fourteen large department stores and many smaller shops make Essen the shopping center of the entire Ruhr

49

region. The large Jewish synagogue has been transformed into an industrial exhibition hall; it had become too large for the few Jews still living here. A small plaque commemorates its former function: "Synagogue of Essen, built 1912. More than 2,500 Jews lost their lives! Thou shalt love thy neighbor as thyself."

Krupp headquarters dominate the middle of the city. It is an ugly brick building dating from the nineteenth century. On November 16, 1945, a dozen shabbily suited men and one uniformed officer stood here in a gloomy conference hall. The civilians were Germans, leftover Krupp directors and section chiefs. The officer was British Colonel Douglas Fowles, a former accountant from Leeds. His job was to liquidate the firm.

Dirty, half-shattered windowpanes of the formerly proud conference hall faced the factory grounds: a forest of smoke stacks and grotesquely bent steel frames, warehouses and railroad installations, blast furnaces and towers, cranes and chains—or whatever remained of them after the heavy air attacks. Colonel Fowles pointed expressively at the remants of the cast steel factory and announced in German: "*Meine Herren*, you will never see those stacks smoking again. Grass and weeds shall grow where this steel factory now stands. The British Military Government has decided to finish Krupp off for all time. That's all, *Meine Herren*."

The master of the house, "Cannon King" Dr. Ing. Alfried Krupp von Bohlen und Halbach, was already in prison that day, waiting to be tried as a war criminal. "We Kruppians are not idealists but realists," he is said to have told his cross-examiner; people had not been unhappy under Hitler; he hadn't known anything about the extermination of the Jews, but "If you buy a good horse you have to accept a few shortcomings." At the time of his arrest (the butler in red spats and white kid gloves had said to the soldiers storming into his sumptuous palace: "Herr von Bohlen is expecting you. May I ask the gentlemen to step inside please.") a young American lieutenant is suppposed to have half-jokingly inquired about his future plans. "It goes without saying that I will rebuild my factories and start manufacturing again. As you know, I'm a businessman, not a politician." The anecdote made the newspapers; the world was amused. This boast by a man who, with his father, had oiled Hitler's war with money and cannons, who had established a factory in Auschwitz and employed ten thousands of slave laborers, this boast, which grotesquely overlooked all that had transpired, was generally shrugged off as typical Krupp vanity. At that time, the world believed Colonel Fowles. But Fowles was wrong; it turned out that Krupp was right after all.

Today at Essen, Rheinhausen and Hannover, at Bremen, Bochum and Hamburg, the vast empire of Krupp is working overtime again. It reaches from India to Brazil; the sun never sets on it. West Germany has been rebuilt and so has Krupp, who for an entire century embodied the unholy alliance between militarism and capitalism. His blast furnaces are burning again—but they are no longer casting cannons. Coal is mined; heavily laden freight trains crisscross the Ruhr, Krupp's shipyards build passenger ships and freighters. The large steel works of Essen, on whose ruins Goebbels allegedly broke into tears and swore revenge, have been reconstructed and are producing again, "but for peace only, for peace," according to Krupp's public relations men. From the same gloomy office building in which Colonel Fowles condemned the company to death, Alfried Krupp von Bohlen and Holbach runs it again. Krupp is larger and wealthier than ever.

How times change! In 1939 "Krupp" was synonymous with "cannons." In 1945 "Krupp" was equivalent to "war criminal." In 1967 "Krupp" simply means "Germany's largest industrial undertaking." Within the short span of six years the firm was condemned to death, its master sentenced to twelve years in prison and to confiscation of his entire fortune, the prisoner released and the fortune returned. Today Krupp may well be the wealthiest man in Europe, the fifth-wealthiest man in the world, following only oil magnate Paul Getty, the King of Saudi Arabia, and the Sheiks of Kuwait and Quatar.

In 1947 the judges at Nuremberg declared Alfried Krupp guilty of plundering and aiding and abetting the enslavement of men. Eighty thousand forced laborers were said to have worked in Krupp plants. It was an odd trial. The real defendant was his father, Gustav. Shortly before the end of the war, in November, 1943, Alfried, by special order of the *Führer*, had replaced his ailing father. In the twenties, together with the generals of the *Reichswehr* and prob-

51

ably behind the backs of most democratic members of government, Gustav Krupp had helped break the Versailles Treaty by illegally producing arms. Thus, in 1936 he could write: "After Adolf Hitler took over the government I had the satisfaction of being able to report to the Führer that after only a brief retooling period, Krupp was completely ready for the rearmament of the German people—the blood of the comrades of Good Saturday, 1923 has not flowed in vain." (On Good Saturday, 1923 the French Army occupied the Krupp's factory. Thirteen faithful Krupp workers were killed defending it.) It was Alfried's father, Gustav, who had helped Hitler finance the decisive election campaign of March, 1933.

Lying paralyzed on his deathbed, Gustav Krupp was alive in 1947 but could not stand trial. An American military policeman sat at the foot of his bed. Son Alfried, a shy, pale young man, a victim perhaps of paternal severity, stood in the dock as a substitute defendant. He was condemned. But he was lucky: the confiscation order was not executed. The Western powers, fearing Russian claims for a share and a foothold on the Ruhr, preferred to leave the property to Krupp.

In 1951, six years before his sentence was up, Alfried Krupp was released from prison. The confiscation order rescinded, Krupp hired a new general manager—the young, imaginative Berthold Beitz, an insurance man who knew nothing about coal and steel. But Beitz had an invaluable asset—a spotless past. He was appointed "*Generalbevollmächtiger*" (a kind of commander-in-chief). As war criminal Alfried Krupp would be unfit for good society for some time, he must stay in the background. The firm was still in a precarious situation; it had been restituted to Krupp, but under the express condition that its vertical structure be reshaped. Everything underground, such as coal and iron ore, must be sold at a "reasonable price"; reconcentration of so much economic power in one hand must be prevented.

In 1967 this condition still has not been met; it is questionable whether Krupp ever meant to fulfill it. Krupp's official explanation sounds almost like a joke: the firm has been unable to find buyers. The total value of Krupp's mines is estimated at 300 million dollars; this represents 31 percent of the firm's total turnover. The owner tactfully publicly avoids speaking on this issue; he still shuns the limelight. But Commander-in-Chief Beitz has declared that the injunction to sell is "not feasible, is unjust and nonsensical." Meantime, Krupp is buying more and more mines, and the government supports Krupp. Changing Krupp's present structure—from the coal pit to the finished screw—does not interest the government. Chancellor Erhard says: "I am firmly convinced that the injunction to sell represents an anachronism and is totally unjustified." The Western powers too, have lost interest in the matter; a little-known member of the British House of Lords and the American Jewish Congress are almost the only ones who still protest occasionally. There is an international committee headed by a Swiss banker that occasionally reminds Krupp of his obligation; it meets once a year to deliberate the issue; each time it grants Krupp a further year to sell his mines. The committee last met in 1966, confirming another year's stay of the injunction. "And if they haven't died by then. . . ." as it says in the German fairy tale, the committee's resolution in 1975 will probably still be the same.

A friendly man showed me through the reconstructed factory in Essen. Georg Volkmar Graf Zedtwitz-Arnim is in charge of Krupp's *Stababteilung* (staff unit) for information. (German industrial concerns have a preference for military terms; branches are managed along lines similar to those by which staff officers run their armies. Employees are strictly graded, and boast complicated titles borrowed from military jargon. More than a dozen such titles crowd the Krupp executive roster, from *Handelsbefugte* to *Oberhandelsbefugte* to member of the board of directors, to *Generalbevollmächtigter*.)

Count Zedtwitz is one of millions of Germans banished from Prussia after the war. He was practically a child at the time. Before coming to Krupp he did public relations for Air France and wrote an amusing book titled *Doing Good and Talking About It*. He likes to talk about "Krupp today. Krupp is doing much good, he says, "and on principle manufactures no weapons" and besides, Zedtwitz adds, Krupp's past role as cannon king is greatly exaggerated. Manufacture of arms never exceeded twenty percent of total production."

Of course it is true that "Krupp supported the Nazi machine," Zedtwitz says, "but not voluntarily . . . it was the dreadful result of a tragic entanglement of fate," not unlike the "tragic entanglement that forced the Jewish elders of Theresienstadt to collaboration with the Nazis to transport Jews to the gas chambers. . . ." As this comparison is not immediately clear to me, he adds: "Two members of the Krupp family were put into concentration camps for participating in the conspiracy of July 20, 1944. Someone who did not live under the tyrannical regime cannot understand the futility of all resistance. An individual was utterly helpless." Even such a powerful man as Krupp? "Even he," Zedtwitz says.

Krupp's workers are almost fanatically loyal to their chief. "It was to save our jobs that Krupp collaborated with the Nazis," says a foreman in Krupp's apprentice shop, a Krupp employee for thirty-five years. "Weren't you also in the Party?" I ask. "Yes, but everybody had to be in the Party," he answers. "Krupp's first concern was always for his workers." Would the workers have lost their jobs if Krupp hadn't given Hitler money or manufactured cannons? "No," the foreman says, "but we wouldn't have gotten extra allowances." As far back as 1840, Krupp workers allegedly enjoyed the best social conditions in Europe. "If all employers had been like Krupp there would be no revolutions," Zedtwitz says. The arrangement was always a strictly paternal one—workers were given cheap housing, health insurance, old age pensions, schools and kindergartens by the company. Strikes were not fought against Krupp, but for him. In 1949, when the English began to blow up the Essen factory, the workers called a sympathy strike for Krupp who, at the time, was still in prison. They also struck specifically for his release. There has been no strike since his return.

"To be a Kruppianer," as the saying goes in Essen, you don't have to be employed there. "Kruppianers" by birth, or marriage as well, belong to a feudal system that provides for Krupp employees. A typical incident occurred in 1953 when Krupp returned home from jail. While inspecting the factory he asked a foreman: "Tell me, Herr Waldeck, can we rebuild?" "Of course," was the answer, "after all, we are still "Kruppianers." A Düsseldorf union leader comments, a bit sardonically: "The workers will go through hell for Krupp. We published a caricature of Krupp once in our union paper. What happened? Large scale cancellations from Essen."

Less satisfied were some eighty thousand slave laborers who worked in Essen during World War II: approximately six thousand prisoners of concentration camps, eighteen thousand prisoners of war and fifty-five thousand "foreign workers" from the East. The luckless came to Krupp as part of the Nazi "extermination through work" operation. Jewish workers who survived have been paid indemnifications by Krupp. A 1959 West German Court decision finally acknowledged such claims in principle; only then Krupp began paying some ten million marks to the Jewish Claims Conference. No others have received indemnifications. Giants like Krupp or Flick, who enriched themselves at the expense of slave labor, are occasionally reminded of their past activities. The Munich cabaret "*Lach und Schiessgesellschaft*" a few years ago offered the following refrain:

> Flick and consorts
> never took a loss.
> They were boss
> when they got their workers from Poland,
> workers who had no choice—
> that's why they were so cheap,
> and when they sat in the cattle cars
> Flick & Compagnon would chant:
> Be smart
> Go Flick
> and you won't ever get back!

We walked slowly through the Essen factory. Upon its return to its owner in 1953, Zedtwitz reports, most of the plant was either destroyed or dismantled. Much equipment had been sent as scrap metal to England or as war indemnities to Yugoslavia and Russia, "where it rusted under the open sky without being put to any use." Nonetheless, the destroyed plants employed more than 70,000 people even in 1951; 78,000 in 1953. Today Krupp employs 115,000 workers. The turnover in 1952 was 1931 million marks; in 1964 it was 5175 million.

Krupp is no mere ironmonger anymore. His chief business since 1953 has been manufacturing, construction and trade. Krupp builds bridges across the Nile, supplies steel stages for theaters, dentures, railroad cars, ships, diesel motors, screws and razors. Art reproductions? Krupp prints them. Superhighways? Krupp builds them.

Prefabricated skyscrapers, electric elevators, coal, lubrication oil—Krupp has them for sale. Krupp offers Russian caviar, Polish ducks and Hungarian Tokay, thanks to three-way deals with the Communist countries. Krupp, Europe's largest orchid grower, builds shipping plants in American ports, steel factories in India and Brazil. "But for God's sake, no weapons!" When Alfried Krupp was released from prison in 1953 he told the assembled press: "I hope I will never again be forced (!) to manufacture arms." So far he has not been forced to. In 1960, former Minister of Defense Strauss allegedly requested Krupp to build battleships for the new German Navy. Krupp apparently refused.

Alfried Krupp still comes to the office every day, but he does not grant interviews. He is the first member of his dynasty who does not manage the firm himself. His *Generalbevollmächtiger* Berthold Beitz does it for him, and also speaks in his behalf. "Why don't you want to build any battleships?" I asked Beitz. "We are greatly oppressed by our past," Beitz replied. "We must overcome it. And besides," he adds, laughing, "peace is far better business."

Berthold Beitz, the man who people say has "complete authority over 5,000 million marks" is in many ways the exact opposite of his chief. Whereas Krupp venerates Wagner and Bach and seems buried in a world of Teutonic melancholy, Beitz is an extrovert who prefers jazz, bars and boxing. He has been known to play the drums when he goes to a nightclub. Beitz carefully cultivates an American "image." He is in his early fifties. He is said to have brought Krupp "into the twentieth century." Yet at Krupp, where directors were always conservative representatives of a feudal overlord, Beitz is still an outsider. People say he has broken time-honored principles. Unlike old Krupps (and their directors who imitated them), he does not show up in the workshops at the head of a solemn procession. He is more likely to take off his jacket, roll up his sleeves and lend a hand, like an American department head who wants to be liked by his workers . . . and must be, too. He scolds workers who address him as *Herr Direktor*. "You can call me Berthold as long as I am satisfied with your work."

These are superficial matters. But in the Ruhr region they cause unrest, which merely goes to prove how necessary a little unrest is for the Ruhr region. Beitz is no industrialist, no steel man. He is a businessman who at age thirty-nine left a successful insurance company and came to Essen. Magic concepts such as "steel," "production," "nation" or "continuity" are less decisive for him than for the Krupps. Unlike Krupp he was no Nazi. During the war he worked as a representative of Shell Oil Company in Poland. There his humane behavior toward Poles and Jews was noticed. It must have been a rare thing. He was able to help people; he saved some by providing forged papers. One of those he saved is a well-known Jewish economics expert, Professor Ehrlich, who today plays an important role in Polish economic planning. Ehrlich helped to pave the way for Krupp's first far-flung business deals with a number of East European Communist states.

Before Beitz's time everything at Krupp was tightly and centrally controlled. Under Beitz, Krupp has been decentralized. Older directors who objected had to resign. Krupp is no longer primarily an iron and steel producer, or maker of relatively uncomplicated railtracks, steel structures or cannons. Since the war, manufacture has risen to 37 percent of yearly turnover as against a diminishing 31 percent for producing raw materials. Pure trade constitutes 26 percent of annual turnover. Even if the Allies had not wanted to separate Krupp from his mines, the company would have had to turn to manufacture and trade, or face stagnation.

Today steel is manufactured almost everywhere, in India as well as in Brazil; Stalin, apparently for doctrinaire reasons, forced most Communist countries into the steel business. But the expertise necessary for turning ore into complicated machinery is still primarily available only in highly developed industrial countries of the West such as Germany. Beitz realized this and unlocked new, seemingly unlimited markets in Asia and Africa, in South America and Eastern Europe. Business has increased rapidly. Among German concerns, Krupp had the fourth-largest turnover in 1965 and was the second-largest employer.

Like his successful American prototype, Beitz excels as a master of the new art of public relations. "This," he says, "was one of the most difficult jobs. Dreadful associations are evoked by Krupp." The name itself practically sounds like a shot. In Germany it is not merely the name of a flourishing industrial undertaking; for an older generation it is still a political and military concept. "To be as hard as Krupp steel," is an old German aphorism, a counter to "humanitarian hogwash" or un-German "seditious liberalism." Some older people still use this aphorism today.

In 1953 Beitz established a "staff unit for information." Today it has more than a hundred employees. Their job is to dispel the "cannon myth" and disseminate the new Krupp slogans: "No more cannons" and "All for peaceful development." On one of his many trips to the United States, Beitz launched his "point 4½ program," its avowed purpose to enlarge on President Truman's famous "point 4 program" by offering private industry's aid to under-developed countries. The idea was well received. Beitz sent Krupp teams to India, Pakistan, Egypt and Latin America, financing development projects in their wake that helped transform Krupp's "cannon king" image into that of "development king."

Beitz travels a lot. In Communist countries he is more ceremoniously received than West German government officials. In Moscow he became friendly with Mikoyan, showed him a photograph of his daughter and said: "Children instead of cannons." His attitude towards Germany's neighbors in the East is softer than many Bonn politicians would like. West Germany still refuses diplomatic relations with Czechoslovakia or Poland because they recognize the East German regime. Beitz considers this policy an anachronism and seeks to "normalize" relationships especially with Poland. He wants to "establish contact with East Germany" and is probably even willing to recognize it. He calls Bonn's official claim to the Reich borders of 1937 "sheer nonsense . . . one should finally look at reality as it is . . . we simply have to put up with the Oder-Neisse border."

He is just as critical of West Germany's "Gaullists" who want to conduct "independent German politics" in the East. Beitz supports the opposing pro-American wing which looks to a United Europe in close cooperation with the United States. He is worlds apart from the nationalist Weimar politician Hugenberg, who was also a Krupp director (1915) and achieved cabinet rank in Hitler's government.

What draws Beitz to the East and into the so-called Liberal camp? Personal feelings that developed in Poland during difficult times? A modern sense of life, uncrowded by past myths and prejudices? The political ruthlessness of a man interested above all in profitable business dealings? Political ambitions? It is probably a combination of some or all of these factors. "Beitz is no longer an exception in the Ruhr," says a local observer. Up to a point he typifies the new West-German manager. Old-fashioned manager-generals who walked about in black frock coats, squinting through monocles, clenching cigars between their teeth, full of disdain for labor unions and subservient admiration for the army, have been replaced in most large companies. Coupled with the name of Beitz, one often hears of Wilhelm Zangen (Mannesmann), Gunther Soll (Thyssen) and Friedrich von Schulenburg (Wolf). Do general managers found dynasties too? Perhaps it is no accident that both the Ford and Rockefeller foundations—today devoted primarily to cultural activities—are being considered as models for transformation of at least part of Krupp into a public institution upon the death of its sole owner.

5

Raise Your Voice and Fear Not

Jn Hamburg the air is cool and damp. Fresh breezes blow across the river Alster that lingers like a shimmering lagoon in the heart of the city. The lagoon freezes over in winter; in summer it is filled with sailboats and flag-bedecked floating cafes. Along its spacious quays it is framed by luxury hotels and banks, warehouses and headquarters of shipping companies. Wedged between the Alster and the Elbe is the old city of Hamburg. Behind it in the huge port, large ships and small float in and out in a never-ending procession.

In the older part of the city, streets bear the names of old dams that were levelled during the nineteenth century: *Wall, Neuer*

Wall, Steintorwall, Holsteinwall. Many are as narrow as alleys. Hamburg, with a population of 1.8 million, is a special kind of German City. There was no feudal lord to build magnificent wide streets for parades in this old Hanseatic merchant town. "The town of Hamburg is a good town," Heinrich Heine wrote in the *Memoirs of Herr Schnabelowopski,* "nothing but solid houses. Not vile Macbeth, but Banquo rules here. Banquo's spirit rules everywhere." This city, built and ruled by businessmen, was constructed to show a profit; the merchants wasted as little space as possible. They lived in narrow gabled houses like their partners in Bergen or Amsterdam, preferring, if possible, to have their storage rooms under the same roof. Only a few restored examples from the eighteenth century are left today. They stand in narrow alleys and along dank canals called "fleets." The few large plazas and thoroughfares for modern traffic were built later. They were made possible not by design but by disasters.

A large part of the heart of Hamburg burned down in 1842; of the remaining part not much was left after phosphorous bombs rained down during World War II. "My old Hamburg . . . the places of my youth . . . are a smoking heap of rubble," Heine cried after the 1842 fire. In that innocent age, disasters were still considered blind blows of fate. Erich Lüth, a chronicler of recent Hamburg history, contemplating another harrowing disaster one hundred years later, wrote: "The inheritance of the Nazi regime in Hamburg expresses itself in the form of 40 million cubic meters of rubble."

Lüth, after the war headed Hamburg's official press bureau. He was not content with words alone. In 1951 he started a "Peace with Israel" movement. Two years after the establishment of West Germany as an independent democracy, the government had not yet formally ended the war Hitler had declared on the Jews; the thought of beginning restitution for material damages had not occurred to it. Early in the summer of 1951 the Western powers were ready to end the state of war with Germany (even without a formal peace treaty); the Israeli government protested, demanding concrete proof of a true change of attitude. Erich Lüth and his friends published an appeal: "We ask Israel for peace." It met with a strong response both within and outside Germany, culminating a few months later in Chancellor Adenauer's offer of September 27, 1951 to enter into diplomatic negotiations with Israel and the Jewish organizations.

Today, Erich Lüth lives in retirement in Hamburg. He was active in many good causes after 1951 and finally was forced to vacate his position with the city government. "He left himself too wide open . . . after all he was an official," says his successor at City Hall. "But he's typical Hamburger: a citizen, not a servant—headstrong, open-minded, skeptical of those that govern."

Twenty bronze reliefs of German emperors adorn the façade of Hamburg City Hall, a sandstone building built in the late nineteenth century. Statues of "four bourgeois virtues" hover above the main entrance. A splendid staircase leads to the mayor's office. It is a staircase of some fame. The proud Lord Mayors of Hamburg rarely meet official guests at the foot of the stairs, as is the custom in other cities. Even royal guests must first walk up to meet the mayor's outstretched welcoming hand—a tradition the city has been able to preserve from the time it was a member of the medieval Hanseatic League. This custom was broken only for Adolf Hitler and, recently, for the Queen of England (in the case of the latter "only because she is a lady").

Lord Mayor of Hamburg Dr. Nevermann, a self-made lawyer, son of a poor worker (a Social-Democrat since 1919), is a lean, somewhat stiff, white-haired man. During World War II he was a defense attorney at the Nazi "People's Court," trying to defend those accused of treason. As Lord Mayor he is also head of the Federal City-State of Hamburg.

He is less satisfied with West German federalism than is his colleague in *Rheinland-Westfalen*. The central government, he feels, is still too much in a position to do as it pleases. States are too weak to oppose it. Dr. Nevermann uses the English expression "checks and balances." People in Hamburg employ a noticeable number of English words and expressions; they are said to be incorrigible Anglophiles, harboring a sentiment not even the bombs of World War II were able to expunge. "Hamburg was an oasis," Dr. Nevermann says, speaking of the war. "But, of course, you find oases only in deserts."

Erich Lüth's "forty million cubic meters of rubble" have disappeared. The old gabled houses are rebuilt and so is the huge port. It is no longer the third-largest port of the world. Still, its turnover during 1964 was 35.6 million tons of freight as against 22.1 million in 1936. Hamburg is proud of its port. Judging by the Hamburg postwar charter, the port is meant to play a political role. To quote the city charter: "as a world port this city has been assigned, by history and law, a special task on behalf of the German people. Imbued with the spirit of peace, it seeks to be a mediator between all parts and peoples of the world." On tours around the port, official tourist guides proudly point out Soviet ships, one even flying the flag of hated East Germany. "Everyone is welcome in this free Hanseatic city." Czechoslovakia, with whom the Federal Republic still has no diplomatic relations because Prague recognizes East Germany, owns the so-called Czechport here. It is a duty-free storage and reloading point for the Czechoslovak fleet and its origins go back to the Treaty of Versailles.

In the narrow streets close to the harbor, elegant shop windows have been fitted into restored façades of old Burgher houses. Traffic crowds the alleys from the Alster banks to a point on the Elbe where, from a high pedestal, a mammoth Bismarck gazes stonily down on the port and its brothel district, St. Pauli.

In the west, a new university campus dominates the city's grey silhouette. Hamburg has almost five times as many students as before the war (18,500). The heart of the University is a skyscraper. It is called "Philosophers Tower"; its top floor serves the Faculty of Theology.

Before the war, Hamburg was the most important port of central Europe. But the new borders of 1945 and Germany's partition into two distinct states, have separated Hamburg from its hinterland. The Iron Curtain is a bare thirty-five miles from here; it is a well-guarded military secret on which side of the atomic trip-wire the port lies. It seems doubtful that it could be defended by conventional forces. In face of its vulnerability, the city not only rebuilt its port but also became an industrial metropolis. Hamburg produces 300 percent more than before the war. New industrial centers are clustering together in the south, along the Elbe and around the suburb Altona, which belonged to Denmark until 1864. (Jules Verne had his professor start his famous *"voyage au centre de la terre"* in Altona.)

But large-scale industrial production is not all that is new in Hamburg. A far more important innovation is the city's new role as the center of the German press.

Herr Walter Bönisch, editor-in-chief of the mass-circulation sheet *Bild*, a good-looking young man dressed in elegantly fitted suits of English cut, notes that "here in Hamburg, there occurred a revolution of the German press . . . it became thoroughly Americanized." Does this signify an improvement in any manner or form?

Bild, modeled after English and American examples, is an illustrated sheet that sells for 10 pfennig. Its columns are a mixture of philistinism and sensationalism, deliberate stimulation of primitive emotions, hatred of foreigners, sex, nationalism, astrology, politics and social gossip. When the German Near East policy hit snags, because Bonn delayed diplomatic recognition of Israel, *Bild* screamed: THE AMERICANS HAVE FORCED THIS DOWN OUR THROATS. (This echoed the famous "stab in the back" legend of 1918). When Britain imposed import restrictions to bolster its currency, *Bild*'s headline ran: GERMAN GOODS OUT OF FAVOR IN ENGLAND, as though import restrictions were aimed only at Germany. Rarely does *Bild* even mention the numerous trials of Nazi murderers, still held all over Germany to serve not only justice but also to provide training in citizenship. When two former colleagues of Adolf Eichmann (Otto Hunsche and Hermann Krumey) were given astonishingly light sentences, *Bild*'s leading article announced ambiguously:

The Frankfurt verdict is worse than no verdict at all. We understand the judges' qualms of conscience, their desire for complete proof, which the constitution obligates them to seek. But it is politically and humanly unacceptable for a German court—even if only indirectly—to punish participation in mass murder with an acquittal and a five-year sentence. Evidently our system of justice is asked to do too much. Is it possible to overcome our past with legal paragraphs? The Frankfurt trial should make us think twice before extending the statute of limitation for Nazi murders. An acquitted murderer is worse than an undiscovered one.

It has become clear once again: Judges cannot atone for the misdeeds perpetrated by madmen in the name of the German people. The German past cannot be overcome in a court of law. Not any longer.

Like most tabloids *Bild* defends itself: We are just a mirror of popular opinion. "Democracy means the people rule. And it will stay that way, no matter if 'Panorama' (a critical TV program that had attacked *Bild*) foams at the mouth, learns to live with it or disappears because of it."

Bild is printed simultaneously in eight cities. It is Germany's largest daily, the sixth largest in the world. Only Japan's *Asahi Shimbun* and *Manahi Shimbun*, Russia's *Pravda* and England's *Daily Mirror* and *Express* are larger. Roughly 4.5 million copies are sold daily and are read by some 11 million people. Many Bonn politicians take it seriously, read it as their first morning paper, clamor to be interviewed in it. Eleven million readers are a quarter of the adult population.

Bild belongs to Axel Cesar Springer, whose astonishingly rags-to-riches career began in 1945 with an Allied license to publish a radio program guide. An Allied officer, in charge of licensing would-be-publishers, had spent a long day interviewing candidates, all claiming to have been persecuted by the Nazis. His first exasperated question to Springer was: "And who persecuted you, Herr Springer?" "Nobody," he answered, "except women." He got his license almost immediately.

Today Springer is Germany's acknowledged newspaper king. His share of the West German press keeps increasing; the fear is occasionally voiced by his opponents that an opinion-making monopoly such as has not been seen in Germany since the collapse of the Nazi regime is in the making here. Axel Springer not only controls *Bild* but 89 percent of all newspapers with national circulation, 31 percent of all West German newspapers put together, 67 percent of Hamburg papers and 69 percent of all newspapers appearing in West Berlin; he controls 85 percent of the circulation of all Sunday papers, half of all radio and TV program guides, almost a third of the illustrated family and women's magazines. Not all are on the same level as *Bild*. *Die Welt* is a serious prestige organ. But all Springer papers and magazines exude an unpleasant nationalistic air. Over Springer's imposing skyscraper in Hamburg flies the German national flag—a superficiality to be sure, but still a rare ostentation in flag-shy postwar Germany.

The great majority of the more than five hundred West German dailies are dull, badly written and provincial. Their undeviating loyalty is to those in power; they do not actively partake in the vital dialogue of democracy. Many draw a distorted picture of the world; their language at times seems regulated by some central bureau. Even international press agency reports or syndicated articles by foreign journalists are frequently edited to conform them to the reigning preconceptions. The treatment of East Germany is a good example: If Reuter's—or an American history professor— writes "East Germany," referring to the other German state, it is quickly changed to "Central Germany." For "East Germany" is the area beyond the Oder-Neisse line, "stolen" by Poland and Russia, but really belonging to Germany and at present merely under temporary "Polish administration," according to current West German nomenclature. Large German newspapers keep correspondents in most important capitals of the world, but no West German newspaper has a correspondent in East Germany East Germany is always referred to as "the so-called DDR" or simply SBZ (German abbreviation for Soviet-Occupied Zone).

At one time Berlin was the newspaper capital of Germany. Six million out of a total 22 million daily newspaper copies in 1932 were printed in Berlin. Hamburg's share was then barely 900,000. Today the roles are reversed. Of 18 million newspapers rolled every day in West Germany, Hamburg prints 5.3 million and West Berlin less than one million. No single important paper is printed in Berlin. In addition to *Bild*, four of the largest and most important interregional newspapers and weekies come out of Hamburg: The daily *Die Welt* (300,000), the weekly illustrated *Stern* (1.7 million), the newsmagazine *Der Spiegel* (633,000) and the weekly *Die Zeit* (250,000). Hamburg is also the home to the German Press Agency, a news service serving the entire country. Finally, the large, wealthy North German Broadcasting Corporation, whose excellent news broadcast *Tagesschau* is carried every evening by the entire German TV network, is centered in Hamburg.

It may be mere chance that Hamburg became the postwar German press center. "A lucky accident," says Hans Gresmann, a young editor of Germany's best political weekly, *Die Zeit*. Hamburg is thought of as a "sober," "open-minded" city where one doesn't lose one's head so easily. It became a newspaper city because a few large printing plants and editorial offices were still intact in 1946 and because a few English occupation officers with grandiose plans for the re-education of the Germans happened to meet here. The English, Gresmann says, were prepared to give the occupied country a voice sooner and more emphatically than the Americans and the French, on the premise that a people that were to be tutored in democracy needed a press, the sooner the better. The English bestowed "licenses," permits to publish a newspaper; they were bits of paper that could make a man rich overnight. The licenses purported to be proof of political trustworthiness; it was no accident that their recipients were often very young and politically untainted men who, incidentally, lacked journalistic experience.

No area of public life was so thoroughly politically cleansed in 1945 as were press and radio. Big industry could remain in the same hands; the schools, the courts, the civil service and the police moved largely unchanged to a new order. Only press and radio made a completely fresh start. The best and the most courageous present-day German newspapers were licensed at that time: the *Frankfurter Rundschau*, the *Süddeutsche Zeitung* of Munich, the *Stuttgarter Zeitung*, the *Augsburger Allgemeine* and the two Hamburg weeklies *Der Spiegel* and *Die Zeit*. The courage and intellectual honesty of these publications is in no way inferior to comparable organs in Europe and America. Springer's *Bild* was launched long after Allied licenses for newspapers were abolished.

Old Nazis and nationalists frequently annoyed by *Der Spiegel*, *Die Zeit* or the *Süddeutsche*, vilify them as "license journalism." The connotation: Foreign agents are at work here, sycophants of the victorious powers, "defiling their own nest." And yet, these "license sheets," staffed mainly by enthusiastic young people, address themselves above all to a people they fear is still far too submissive to authority. They are muckrakers, zealous to expose injustice. Reading them daily for some length of time, one concludes they take their democratic duties seriously. They certainly do not believe, as a famous Prussian once put it, that a citizen's first duty is to keep quiet.

Most of the young men working on these papers would disavow the notion of collective guilt but not Germany's collective responsibility; they are full of shame and contempt for the crimes of their fathers. As a rule they are dedicated to dislodging former Nazis from public life by relentlessly exposing shoddy pasts. There are fifty former Nazis exposed in the West German press to every one attacked in foreign newspapers. Some West-German journalists are ready to go to prison for their views, as did the editors of *Spiegel* in 1962.

The "Spiegel Affair" as it is now called, dominated domestic politics for almost a year; it illustrates the difficulties these young muckrakers are facing. Good journalism is vital for any democracy; in Germany it never commanded, and still does not command, much respect. "*Er lügt wie gedruckt*" (he fibs like the printed word) is a figure of speech existing, it seems, only in German. Here reporters feel the need to upgrade themselves to "journalists," journalists to "editors," editors to "publicists," publicists to "authors" and authors, even when writing novels, to "poets." Even top literary figures such as Rolf Hochhuth (*The Deputy*) or Günter Grass (*The Tin Drum*) incur powerful government displeasure when they speak out about politics as citizens and voters. Chancellor Erhard has called them "runty dogs" and "idiots" who should keep their mouths shut and not become involved in politics.

A political leader would not dare to make such remarks elsewhere. If it should happen, as when Harry S. Truman lashed into a music critic who ridiculed his daughter's performance, it can even turn into a national joke. But in Germany, power and ideas, learning and government, at times seem to occupy different compartments of the mind. The Swiss playwright Max Frisch has described this trait thus: ". . . People who can converse intelligently and fervently about Bach, Handel, Mozart, Beethoven, Bruckner [can] just as easily be butchers. . . . Their special, always distinguishable, mark is the careful separation in their minds of culture and politics. . . . A moral cultural schizophrenia is typical of our century."

What must have been uppermost in Frisch's mind was the Nazi era, when doctors read Goethe in the evening and next morning conducted "selections" in a concentration camp. This schizophrenia seems to have survived the Third Reich, although today it is certainly less crass. While it is by no means an exclusively German trait it is very much more noticeable here than in other European countries. No Western government has slandered its writers and artists as badly during the last fifteen years as has West Germany (while using them at the same time as visible proof of a "new, changed Germany"). In Ravensburg on May 29, 1965, Chancellor Erhard resurrected, surely unconsciously, the vocabulary of Nazi Propaganda Minister Goebbels by speaking of "unappetizing signs of degeneration in modern art."

In public opinion polls rating professions, journalists occupy the lowest rungs. Professors (especially medical) rank disproportionately higher. Unlike their French, English or American colleagues, professors in Germany think it undignified to write for newspapers. "Opposition papers," Bismarck once said "are to a large extent in the hands of Jews and discontented elements who have missed their vocation." Not so long ago a whisper campaign arose against publisher Rudolf Augstein of *Spiegel*—he was a Jew, his name proved it. The same rumor was directed against Sebastian Haffner, a Berlin columnist known for his critical stands. Augstein let it pass; Haffner felt the need to publicly deny the rumor.

In France, England, or America it is an easy move from journalism to politics and vice versa. In Germany it is rare. The average American is proud of his "free press." Even the most conservative Englishman is amused when journalists flay sacred national cows. This relaxed self-assurance is somehow denied to most Germans.

Their peculiar relationship to press and free discussion is evidenced by many of the letters received by nonconformist publications. Many letter writers feel independent thinking has a "debilitating effect," is by definition contrary to national coherence. Even Acting Chairman of the governing CDU party, Hermann Dufhues, in 1962 expressed the fear that a few nettlesome literary figures endanger the "authority" of the State. Former Minister of Defense Franz Josef Strauss has suggested that intellectuals who criticize their country should emigrate. In no Western country as many "legal inquiries" are held against journalists suspected of "high treason." Accusations of this sort have a notorious precedent in Germany. In 1931, the crusading journalist Karl von Ossietzky, who later won the Nobel Prize, was found guilty of high treason. His crime: he exposed the secret and unconstitutional rearmament of the German Wehrmacht.

The same penal code is still in effect today and was applied in the 1962 "Spiegel Affair." At the time Franz Josef Strauss, then minister of defense, was continually feeling victimized by the *Spiegel*, which had accused him of corruption. Suddenly Strauss triggered the arrest of *Spiegel* publisher Rudolf Augstein and several other editors. One, Konrad Ahlers, was on holiday in Spain; the Spanish police arrested him at the request of the German military attaché in Madrid and deported him to Germany. Federal policemen occupied the magazine's editorial offices in Hamburg and Bonn. The official explanation was that *Spiegel* had committed "treason" in an article reporting recent NATO maneuvers.

What exactly was treasonable in the article was never officially explained. But it is encouraging that the subsequent public outrage forced the resignation of Defense Minister Strauss. The career of an abrasive personality who might easily have reached the Chancellor's office was at least temporarily interrupted. Two years later the Federal Supreme Court dismissed the case and the defendants were freed from further persecution due to "lack of proof."

The Bonn government reacted in a far less reassuring manner. Chancellor Adenauer did not wait for judicial inquiries. A few weeks after Augstein's arrest he declared: "Treason has been committed—it is very probable—by a man with great journalistic power. . . . We have an abyss of treason in the country. . . . In Augstein's personality you see two elements. First, he makes money [!] from treason, and I find that simply vulgar. Second, he makes money from incitement in general and against the coalition parties in particular." The dubious arrest of *Spiegel* editor Ahlers and his wife in Spain never disturbed Adenauer. "I couldn't care less whether the man was arrested in Malaga or in Hamburg." Minister of the Interior Höcherl, who admitted that Ahlers was not arrested "in a perfectly legal manner," retained his post.

Neither Adenauer nor Höcherl retracted their statements after the Supreme Court acquittal. And the decisive question—Is it permitted in Germany to publicize unconstitutional secret government actions? —was not clarified. Is a new Ossietzky case possible? The question is not purely theoretical. Two international treaties prohibit the Federal Republic from producing atomic weapons. Is it impossible that a future West German government could try to circumvent these treaties, just as the Weimer Republic violated the Versailles Treaty? Does a German journalist who reveals such activities risk being condemned for "high treason?" Most lawyers answer in the affirmative. The law, enacted by the Kaiser in the nineteenth century, is still in effect.

How much more important, then, are these men who nevertheless "raise their voices and are not afraid." Rudolph Augstein spent months in prison awaiting completion of his investigation. (A peculiarity of German law allows a defendant not only to be detained for months without proper trial but also to be left afterward neither clearly guilty nor clearly innocent. Prosecution can simply be halted due to "lack of proof." The blemish remains. This is what happened to Augstein.) He is a small, fragile-looking man. His speech is slow, almost halting, yet he is one of the most brilliant polemical writers in Germany. He looks younger than he is, almost like a college boy, though he never went to college. Augstein was ten years old when Hitler came to power and twenty-two when the war was over. He was an American prisoner of war for less than an hour. He explains: "An American soldier said 'turn left'; I went off to the right and that wasn't the way to the camp." Instead, he found the way to his hometown, Hannover, which like most German cities, was rubble and ashes. Young ex-soldiers like Augstein who stood on the ruins of their hometown in 1945 were later described as "the men of year zero," full of melancholy contempt for their father's generation, which had inflicted such dreadful misfortune on them, on Germany, and on the world.

Another man of the "year zero," the well-known West German writer Erich Kuby, writes of Augstein: "This young man with razor-sharp intelligence, a small but well-proportioned figure, is filled with sadness and pessimism. In spiritually settled times he would surely have taken another road, would have abided by the traditions of his haute-bourgeois Rhenish-Catholic family. His grandfather was an unusual man . . . who hated Kaiser Wilhelm, prohibited his son from entering his home in uniform. . . . [Augstein] is imbued with the fear he could fall prey to emotions and be taken in by the intellectual fraud perpetrated in all places where cynical opportunists are juggling the 'true,' the 'genuine' 'occidental' values because they lack the courage to draw the balance."

In 1945, instead of going to a university, Augstein joined with twenty-three-year-old John Chaloner, a British major in charge of running occupation papers, to found a news magazine called *This Week*. This eventually became *Spiegel*, an institution which, some people claim, constitutes the actual "opposition" in West Germany.

Augstein and *Der Spiegel* passionately opposed the rearmament of Germany. "Rearmament swindled us out of our new beginning," Augstein says today. "I also feared an armed country will demand the return of Breslau and Königsberg much sooner than an unarmed one. . . . If Adenauer had spoken truthfully—if he had said Königsberg is lost forever, that because there are now two German states that cannot be reunited West Germany must be protected and rearmed—well then, we could not have objected to rearmament. But Adenauer never said that. He even said the opposite. It was a dangerous swindle. If we had only waited with rearmament, until we had dispensed at least with Nazi generals, Nazi judges, and Nazi officials! But no, the old State structure was left intact, prettied up a little with a nice new petticoat. We have been swindled out of a new beginning."

I asked Augstein what kind of new beginning he had had in mind. "To put it frankly," he said, "we were thinking of a Germany that would not be the cause of World War III. The Germans happen to be people who before defeat never care about the rights of others. After defeat they can't bear the consequences and shout: 'We insist on our rights! We insist on our rights!' Give them reunification with East Germany—soon they will want to rearrange all of Eastern Europe."

Augstein thinks the danger of Germany causing a new war has been considerably diminished by two disconnected events; the Hungarian uprising and the death of Secretary of State John Foster Dulles. But, he adds, the possibility of disaster continues. This lack of stability, says Augstein, is the main reason why he and *Spiegel* inveigh against former Minister of Defense Strauss. A boyish smile crossing his face, Augstein says: "I succeeded just in time in shooting down a future chancellor." It had been imperative to do so, he continued. Not only because of Strauss's corruption, but because "he is dangerous as a person. This impetuous man who dreams of atomic weapons and combines militant Catholicism with alacrity and German thoroughness . . . in an unpredictable world, this man could have a disastrous effect."

Augstein asks the Germans to look at facts as they are. The most important fact is the existence of a second German state. It is illusory to believe that Western pressure or an inner weakness will cause the collapse of East Germany. East Germany exists not only because of Soviet dictate. It is already part of a new European system, emphasizes Augstein. West Germaany ought to make it easier for East Germany to improve the lot of its population instead of treating it as a pariah state. West Germany can help it to acquire the self-assurance of a Hungary or Poland. That is a prerequisite for liberalization. "We can live with an East German Communist state, that is gradually evacuated by Soviet troops. Perhaps not forever, certainly for a long time." These are views many West German politicians would consider treasonable, even though—albeit privately—some share Augstein's ideas. Among West German college students, Augstein is a hero. He travels a great deal, lecturing. A recent lecture sold over one million copies. Thousands wrote back and asked for extra copies.

Spiegel is produced by young men. Their average age is between thirty and forty-five. Of the hundred-odd staff members listed on the magazine's masthead, forty-nine finished high school after the war. There are some former Nazis among the older staff members; others spent the war years outside of Germany. They practice a technique of journalism developed in the twenties by *Time* magazine. *Time* has been copied in many countries, but never with such Teutonic thoroughness. Like *Time*, *Spiegel* relates events in stories," endless enumerations of facts and "inside information," that frequently lack tension and, without beginning and end, are mounted like pearls on a string. The aim is exactness. If the *Spiegel* occasionally misses the bull's-eye, most of its articles "corner" the truth like a beast about to pounce on its prey. *Spiegel*, unlike *Time*, is a crusading magazine. It is notorious for its ruthless indiscretion. No German newspaper has become enmeshed in as many lawsuits.

At the heart of the *Spiegel* operation are exceedingly comprehensive archives. When the police occupied the *Spiegel*'s offices in 1962 they immediately rushed to the archives. They found no state secrets; just, it seems, West Germany's best-arranged cross-file index. Franz Josef Strauss once said *Spiegel* was Germany's "new Gestapo." What he meant was that there is something delicate about every German politician in *Spiegel*'s archives; that fact alone gives the magazine too much power. "You see," Strauss told an interviewer, "in Germany almost everyone has something to hide. . . ." One of *Spiegel*'s specialties is its long interviews with public figures. These are published almost verbatim. Wolfgang Hammer, a Swiss pastor, has parodied a *Spiegel* "conversation with God."

SPIEGEL: ". . . we made such an effort . . . we wanted to be objective."

God: "My son has already suffered a greater humiliation than your objectivity. He has prayed for you. You should have studied his methods, not his footprints."

SPIEGEL: "What is his method?"

God: "Love and forgiveness, nothing else, solidarity even with the dumbest."

SPIEGEL: "But that's no way to run a newspaper."

God: "I had higher expectations of you than of anyone else."

Another *Spiegel* specialty is its letters column. Here, extraordinary insights can be gained into the insecurity of the average German mind. No other German publication evokes such a voluminous response. Many letters have a touch of the pathological, running a gamut from obstinate rantings of old Nazis to the young intellectual's loathing for the world.

In recent years, notably since Augstein's arrest, the magazine

74

has become less a one-man show. Its aggressive tone has become more sedate. Augstein himself, developing into a kind of Tom Paine of the new German democracy, is constantly off on lecture trips; his three chief editors—Konrad Ahlers, Johannes Engel and Klaus Jacobi—steer the magazine into calmer waters. They are less interested than Augstein in crusades, more in factual reporting. Jacobi and Engel are five years younger than Augstein, have fewer political resentments than those who were around during the stormy "rearmament" years. This does not imply that the *Spiegel* is any less candid than it used to be, or less critical where criticism is required. But the West German political climate has become more temperate since Ludwig Erhard replaced Konrad Adenauer as Chancellor.

There seems to be no letup in *Spiegel*'s efforts to confront the Germans with their past. It came out clearly in 1965 for extending the statute of limitations for Nazi murders, filling its pages with Nazi atrocity stories and pictures.

Long excerpts from books describing Nazi crimes or noting the inefficacy of possible resistance from such forces as the Catholic church crowd almost every issue. *Spiegel* published excerpts from Alexander Werth's book *Russia at War*, Guenter Lewy's *Striding Firmly into the New Reich: The Catholic Church Between Cross and Swastika* and Erich Kuby's *The Russians in Berlin*. *Spiegel*'s interest lies not only in most recent history; it has lately been as preoccupied with the origins of World War I. It excerpted Barbara Tuchman's brilliant description of the outbreak of World War I, *Guns of August*, published in Germany under the title *When the Leaves Fall* (an allusion to Kaiser Wilhelm's promise that the soldiers would be home by fall), and Fritz Fischer's controversial *Der Griff Nach Der Weltmacht*. Fischer, a young history professor in Hamburg, attributes a large share of the guilt for World War I to Prime Minister Bethmann-Hollweg's reckless war aims. As Fischer describes these aims, they seem to forecast Hitler's expansionary policies. Even if fifty years old, history does not grow stale for the *Spiegel*.

Die Zeit, another large German weekly, is infinitely more dignified than *Spiegel*. Still, it sells 250,000 copies, a remarkable figure

75

considering circulation of similar newspapers in the West, such as *Economist* and *New Statesmen* in England, *New Republic*, *New York Review of Books* in the United States or *Le Nouveau Observateur* in France.

Political editor Marion Dönhoff and literary editor Rudolf Walter Leonhardt determine the content and line of the paper. Though *Zeit* may differ in temperament and detail with *Spiegel*, its commitment is usually similar. It will not write "SBZ" (Soviet-occupied zone) or "the so-called DDR" when it means East Germany; it calls the child by its name, even compliments it on occasions. This is, of course, superficial; more than skin deep is its opposition to a militarily strong Germany. *Zeit* favors coexistence with East Germany and the East European Communist states and a lasting reconciliation with France (without, however, submitting to Gaullism). Its editors favor a united Europe, no "*Europe de patries*." *Zeit*'s untiring effort on behalf of civil rights is unmatched in the German press. Unadorned reports about anti-Semitic outbreaks, campaigns to banish former Nazis from official and academic posts, are common. Exposés in the *Zeit* forced the resignation of Hans Oberländer, a former Nazi member of Adenauer's Cabinet. As a Cabinent member, he demanded the return of the "stolen Eastern territories"; earlier he had been Hitler's *Reichsführer* of the "*Bund des Deutschen Ostens*"—an organization formed to fight "foreign national characteristics" in eastern border areas of Germany. *Zeit* also uncovered the so-called telephone affair of 1963. Through unauthorized use of special NATO equipment, West German secret police were tapping private telephone conversations of leading figures in Bonn.

Less successful was *Zeit*'s campaign against Bonn University. When this university (whose sorry honor it is to have rescinded Thomas Mann's doctorate in 1936) elected a new Rector in 1964, it was unable to find a better choice than Professor Hugo Moser. Professor Moser had once attempted to provide Nazi ideology with a "philological" foundation. For many weeks *Die Zeit* attacked Moser and the West German capital's university, which was willing to be represented by him. In the end, a German professor's inviolability was stronger than public uproar. Moser remained in office. But *Zeit* had led a persistent fight for intellectual integrity.

A magazine like *Zeit*, read by many university people, will often trace the intellectual roots of Nazism back to their pre-Hitler sources. Typical was a documentation about the late German writer Rudolf G. Binding. Binding, whose works are still taught in German schools, was not a Nazi. He was, however, a defender of Hitler. In 1933, when Romain Rolland accused the Hitler regime of inhumanity, Binding answered the French poet, sounding high praise for the National Socialist movement:

> We are struck dumb by this unification through strength. This longing for Germany. Germany, this Germany is born of furious yearning . . . the bloody birth pangs of wanting to forge Germany; at any price, at the price of complete annihilation. No accusation can stand up to such desire. We deny nothing . . . neither the incitement to violence, nor the proclamation of racism which must injure other races such as the Jews . . . nor the autos-da-fé of ideas, the immigrations and proscription. But all these things, as horrible as they might appear . . . are peripheral matters that do no harm to the actual sovereignty, the heart, the truth, of what is happening.

Zeit draws conclusions not guaranteed to be popular ones: (1) One did not have to be a Nazi to play an active role in the disaster. (2) People did know what things were leading to. (3) There is a strong connection between emotional beliefs of many Germans of that time and the criminal consequences that followed. (4) The Nazis did not, in the manner of a natural catastrophe, overwhelm a naïve and upright people—as many like to believe today. On the contrary, roots link later events to earlier ones, even though the connection is not always immediately apparent.

Marion Dönhoff, *Zeit*'s political editor is a delicately built, enthusiastic lady from East Prussia, where her family settled in 1666. Her features reveal both energy and stubbornness. Until the end of the war she had supervised her family's many estates. The defeat of Germany and her subsequent banishment from East Prussia led the fifty-seven-year-old Countess into journalism. In the middle 1950's, before *Zeit* took to its present liberal course, this strong-minded woman resigned in protest against publication of an article by the ultra-right-wing Professor Karl Schmitt, a man who had helped undermine the Weimar Republic. The Countess moved her belongings out of her *Zeit* office within an hour of her resignation. She remained away for an entire year, then returned when younger, more liberal journalists replaced some of the old editorial staff.

"The great danger in Germany" she says, "is that people today simply prefer to tread well-worn paths, every new idea is suspected of being traitorous." *Zeit* wants to be a platform for new ideas. It wants to bring politicians and alienated, embittered intellectuals closer together. The paper created a considerable stir when three of its editors—young Theo Sommer, literary editor Leonhardt and Mrs. Dönhoff—reported on a joint trip to East Germany (their report afterward became a best-selling book). It was a rare report in the German press—a cool and factual description, without blinders or resentments, on what is seen and heard in East Germany. The report's conclusion: East Germany exists as a state and is a political entity, even though people are suppressed.

Unique in the West is the position occupied by West German radio and television. Radio broadcasts, especially in the evening hours, are a stronghold of nonconformist thinking. Television exists primarily to inform, and daily political reports are painstakingly objective. They appear free of any official or party influence and stand comparison with the best models, such as the BBC.

German television regularly produces critical programs designed to expose abuses in public life. They are genuine schools of everyday democracy. Once or twice a week, sometimes more frequently, critical and mocking programs appear on TV screens in millions of living rooms to shock the German citizens' overdeveloped sense of loyalty and obedience. One rarely sees such programs on Gaullist-supervised French TV, they are rare even on English TV, and almost unheard of in the United States.

German television is never "sponsored"; it is allowed a maximum of twenty minutes of advertising spot announcements per day. As a result, programs are more cutting and daring certainly than the daily press—at times more than muckrakers like *Spiegel*. Television is not afraid of lambasting national taboos, of "touching hot irons." Of course, producers responsible for these programs can suffer unpleasant consequences. Scandals are no exception. Political pressure as well as intellectual exhaustion can halt a series. But they are usually replaced by other, equally tough shows and the game goes on. New producers are often as critical as those they have replaced. Qualified people are few; that there are not too many to replace them strengthens the position of individual producers, allows them more freedom than would a dozen hypothetical constitutional paragraphs guaranteeing the freedom of opinion.

The number of discussion programs on radio and TV is also impressive. Panelists rush into these debates with genuine ardor. Impudent interviewers will cross-examine controversial politicians; drive them into a corner to sweat unhappily under glaring kleig lights. With ruthlessly directed cameras, a victim's facial expression becomes a lie detector. It is interesting to speculate whether Nazism would have developed if a large-scale TV network had existed during the Weimar Republic. Would the masses have been misled even more quickly by television? Even more intensively? Or would National Socialism have been unmasked—as Senator Joe McCarthy was by American TV—earlier and more devastatingly?

The occupation powers can take some of the credit for the independence of German television. The victors intended that German broadcasting should be independent of government, they therefore created an almost totally decentralized network of self-sufficient broadcasting institutions. Though it is more expensive than a centrally managed system would be, it provides a better guarantee for the freedom of opinion. The system has continued despite furtive government efforts to establish government-controlled television similar to the French. The central government's effort has been frustrated by the combined resistance of press and state governments. In 1962 the Federal Constitutional Court ruled a potential government broadcasting system unconstitutional as it would violate a basic law of free reporting.

There are nine regional television centers—in Hamburg, Cologne, Bremen, Frankfurt, Stuttgart, Baden-Baden, Munich, Saarbrücken and Berlin. They are self-governing independent public bodies, supervised by a board of overseers representing parties, churches, universities, unions and business. A director appointed by the overseers is responsible for his station's program. At 8 o'clock every evening all stations broadcast jointly, but there is no central studio. One joint program will emanate from Munich,

79

another from Hamburg, and so forth. The other stations transmit the program or (very rarely) will not if, for some reason, it does not suit them. A tenth German television center in Mainz produces the "second program." This UHF channel, in contrast to the "first program," is not a local station. National, but also beyond the control of the Federal Government, it is a publicly chartered body created by special treaty among the various state governments.

The advantages of a decentralized network are evident. It protects stations against infringements by central government; it tends to strengthen the position of directors vis-à-vis their own board of overseers and powerful local factions. Most individual directors can pick and choose; they may have constant offers to switch to a new job at another station, frequently with an increase in pay. Not all superintendents stand up for their convictions with equal courage. But if there is only one out of nine who allows his associates to say the right word at the right time, the joint program sends it through all of Germany. Decentralization also affords independent writers a greater market to sell manuscripts. One director may find the subject too risky (for instance, a treatment of the "Spiegel Affair" or "Nazis in the legal system")—the writer can always try his luck with another station. Thus, it is not rare that Cologne will broadcast a program, emanating from Hamburg, based on a manuscript it has itself originally rejected.

Despite protests by offended viewers, despite shows which may sometimes fall short of the mark, German television frequently achieves what government and political parties avoid for tactical reasons: it pinpoints the consequences of the Nazi regime and the defeat of 1945. Gripping documentaries about Nazi crimes are common. Millions are thus made to see—some perhaps for the first time—the profound mark of Cain that Germans still bear in the eyes of the world. German television fills this role with great distinction.

Equally commendable are frequent television broadcasts on former German territories to the east. Hour-long telecasts describe life in "stolen" areas east of the Oder-Neisse line: Wrozlaw (Breslau) filled with Polish life . . . the rubble has been cleared away, the ruins rebuilt, a young Polish generation is growing up, and Wrozlaw is its home. An honest viewer's conclusion is bound to be: we could not possibly have it back.

Another example: It is August 13, anniversary of the erection of the Berlin Wall; most official speakers go through the worn-out anti-Communist routine and wallow in self-pity. In this atmosphere of undiluted self-righteousness, Thomas Mann's son, Professor Golo Mann, is picked to read the daily political comment following the evening television news. Professor Mann, a noted historian, tells his listeners: "The Berlin Wall is no 'Wall of Shame,' as the politicians say, but should be rather a wall of lament at which to shed tears over Germany's crimes and mistakes. Neither the East German Communists nor the men in the Kremlin are the real builders of this wall. Hitler was the mason. The Wall is a consequence of the war which Germany started, bringing Communsim into the heart of Europe and into the city of Berlin. The West German government's refusal to come to an understanding with the East German regime perpetuates the wall and prolongs the suffering of those Germans who must live in its shadow."

Press, radio and television are bitter pills. What is their effect? How influential are they in West Germany? Few agree on the answer. Walter Jens, professor of literature at the University of Tübingen, says: "Nonconformists have been treated like court jesters in Germany since 1945." Leo Bauer, an editor of *Stern*, maintains that most Germans, despite the existence of *Stern*, *Spiegel* or Springer, still get most opinions from small provincial papers. Benno Reifenberg, the venerable, old editor of the *Frankfurter Allgemeine Zeitung*, speaks of a peculiar difference between published opinion and public opinion, between what people read and how they feel.

This difference can be shown by a few crucial examples: (1) When the new German republic was established after the war, its founding fathers agreed with poet Paul Celan's famous line that "death is a master craftsman from Germany." One of their first deeds was to eliminiate the death penalty. The vast majority of West German newspapers and magazines still oppose the reintroduction of death penalties. But public opinion polls show that almost 80 percent of the population favors the death penalty. (2) A majority of German newspapers report the many trials of Nazi war criminals. According to reliable estimates, 46 percent of all readers do not wish to hear anything more about the atrocities.

(3) A large part of the German press also came out in favor of the extension of the statute of limitations for Nazi war crimes. But 63 percent of the adult population oppose extension and want the court to bury the past.

Similar discrepancies between public and published opinion certainly exist in many countries. In Germany, the role of the press is accentuated by the apparent decline in the national political debate. The stormy debate between the Social-Democrats and the Christian Democratic government party, which prevailed in the West German Parliament during its first decade, has abated considerably. In 1959, Europe's oldest Socialist party officially divorced itself from Marxism; it no longer opposes German rearmament. Opposition leaders go on pilgrimages to Rome, have become faithful churchgoers; some have lately even gone on hunts with generals and industrialists.

Political debate has naturally suffered as a consequence. Political programs and platforms of the two great parties have become nearly identical on all major issues. Both expect the East German state to vanish from the face of the earth; both publicly demand the restoration of the borders of 1937. Both woo the refugee Sudeten Germans, who demand the right of self-determination back in their old Czech homes under the 1938 Munich Agreement.

Germany's unsolved national problems are unique in that they endanger world peace. And yet key questions such as these are rarely—if ever—discussed between Government and Opposition. The debate is on an altogether different level: between a large establishment comprising all parties, on the one hand, and intellectuals disseminating their views on television and through the press, on the other. Peace and prosperity and the decline of ideology have dulled the edge of politics everywhere. But it seems that only in West Germany, the debate on key questions of national and human survival has moved away from the political arena into press and TV.

The *Pressehaus* in Hamburg is a large dark building occupying an entire block. It houses the editorial offices of the *Zeit*, the *Spiegel* and the *Stern* as well as two daily newspapers. Familiarly, the building is known as the "Hamburg hangout." The imposing brick building looks almost like a fortress (and for a time it was, when the police occupied the *Spiegel* offices in 1962). Its top floor looks out on beautifully reconstructed Hamburg. After the great fire of 1842 Heinrich Heine wrote:

> Rebuild your houses
> And drain your puddles
> Equip yourselves with better laws
> And better fire engines.

After a more recent catastrophe the Germans seem to have taken Heine's advice. They have rebuilt their houses and obtained better laws. Their newspapers have no real power; but they are fire engines. They are certainly better in this respect than those of the Weimar Republic. The best newspapers in West Germany act as watchdogs: they do this with energy, fantasy and without fear. It is the best thing to say about the press of any country.

6

Captain's Ball on a Stranded Ship

ALL OVER Germany—in shop windows, on kiosks and billboards—there are colored advertisements inviting: "Berlin is worth a trip," or "Berlin—Germany's meeting point," or "Berlin—the German capital." An added enticement is the portrait of Willy Brandt, the Mayor of West Berlin, his youthful face slightly warped by a forced smile. "Dear Countrymen," Brandt appeals to the Germans, "visit Berlin—the Wall is not our border. It can never be."

Twenty years after the war that first reduced Berlin to rubble and then condemned it to provincial isolation, the Germans have in Bonn a "provisional" capital; in Munich a "secret" capital; in Berlin a *Reichshauptstadt* that isn't one. To West Germany, Berlin is both burden and symbol, distant memory and faint hope. On the other side of the Wall that divides the city there is still a fourth German capital. There, in East Berlin, is the center of Communist rule over 18 million East Germans.

Cut-rate flights to Berlin from all airports in the Federal Republic help one to avoid the long, strenuous train or car trip through the territory of East Germany. Flight tickets are subsidized by the Berlin Senate. But despite intensive advertising and ever-present slogans—"Berlin remains our capital"—an astonishing number of educated, well-to-do and widely traveled people in West Germany have not been back to Berlin since the end of the war. Why this is so is not easily explained. "Capitals" are perhaps not as important as we think, especially one that played the role for less than seventy-five years. "Why have you never been back to Berlin?" I asked the wife of a Bonn parliamentarian, whose last visit was in 1942. "I have no urge to," the woman, born not far from Berlin in Brandenburg, answered. Many Rhinelanders and South Germans in particular have no great enthusiasm for Berlin. There is a apocryphal story about former Chancellor Adenauer. When he was a Reichstag deputy in the twenties, Adenauer traveled frequently from Cologne to Berlin. As the sleeping car crossed the Elbe into central Germany, Adenauer supposedly turned over in bed, muttering: "Ach, Asia!"

Only American, British and French planes fly the Allied air corridors into Berlin. Flights from Frankfurt, Cologne, Hannover or Hamburg take barely an hour but are as suspenseful as any in the world. Just before reaching Berlin the plane banks to the east, makes a wide turn over Potsdam and approaches the eastern (Communist) sections of the city. It flies low across empty streets, over ruins, above roofs of former Nazi ministries now serving the Communist administration, over brown minefields and high barbed-wire fences at the Wall. A few seconds later the plane lands at the West Berlin airport, Tempelhof.

Young West Berliners alight, sunburned from a holiday trip to the Mediterranean. They rush toward the main building across the paved field. On the terminal façade hangs a large portrait of President Kennedy, underneath his famous saying "I am a Berliner." Flags flutter in the wind—some international congress is

85

taking place. An American Negro in clerical habit stops to ask for information. The huge marble hall, only a few steps further, is haunted by ghosts of the past. Built by Hitler in the thirties, it mirrors the taste of his regime: enormous pillars support the red ceiling of this late-Teutonic pharaonic temple. Porters rush about the huge hall. Modern architects have sought to exorcise the spirits of the past with new colors, a lowered plastic ceiling, curtains and colorful advertisements—among them a placard of the Israeli airline El-Al. The attempt does not quite succeed. A Berlin student who arrived in the plane with me shrugs his shoulders: "Funny, isn't it? It's like dressing the giant statue of *Germania* at the Niederwald memorial on the Rhine in a bikini and hoping she'll look like Brigitte Bardot."

West Berlin is a fortified island of 481 square kilometers. It is surrounded by barbed wire, and watchtowers armed with machine guns and searchlights. The city hovers in the air somewhere between Moscow and New York like a balloon anchored on thin threads, a paradox of physics as of politics, defying all criteria. The West German constitution calls Berlin part of the Federal Republic, the eleventh state of the Federation. But the West German constitution is not valid in Berlin. The East German constitution, on the other hand, regards all of Berlin as an integral part of the "First German Worker and Farmer State." However, the East German constitution is worth as little in West Berlin as the West German one. The Western occupation powers have the simplest view of the matter: twenty two years after the war and seventeen after the creation of two German states, Berlin is still an occupied area.

The Western half of the city is controlled by the three Western powers. Reluctantly, the Western Powers allow the West German parliament sometimes to hold sessions in West Berlin. Such sessions take place in the restored west wing of the old *Reichstag* building, which stands right by the Wall—a *Reichstag* without *Reich*, surrounded by no-man's land and within range of the guns of the East German border police. "For the German people," it says inscribed in large letters above the main entrance through which Bismarck entered and Hitler, and lately tourists who take photographs. Once or twice a year TV men set up their cameras, a

86

Bonn cabinet minister places himself on the steps and solemnly intones into the microphone: "The capital city of Berlin . . . indivisible Germany . . . inalienable claim." There is something unreal about these scenes which are already part of German political ritual. Nowhere in Europe are truth and half truth, fact and fiction as inseparable as here. Close by, hidden in the bushes, linger a few British armored cars.

Not far away, a few yards behind the Wall, in East German territory, stands the Brandenburg Gate. Here too the Cold War has become a tourist attraction. From raised platforms on each side of the Wall, Eastern and Western tourists gawk at each other. One group looks from East to West, the other from the opposite direction—mirror images in a political zoo. Through the gate can be seen the ruins of East Berlin.

In West Berlin most of the ruins have been cleared away; across the city's flat expanse a large number of modern skyscrapers have been built. Although the economy is flourishing and there are more jobs than job seekers, the city still must be subsidized. West German subsidies for West Berlin have reached an estimated thirty-six billion marks, plus four billion marks from Marshall Plan funds. West Berlin businessmen enjoy special tax concessions; exporters receive premiums for goods manufactured in Berlin; West Berliners pay less income tax than people in West Germany.

West Berliners are not conscripted into military service. Young West Germans who go to Berlin to work are reimbursed for their travel expenses, receive rent allowances for living quarters that are cheaper than those in West Germany. The Berlin Senate has made every effort to turn the city into the cultural center it once was. Writers, painters, musicians and literary people from West Germany and foreign countries are offered special grants and occasional free housing to live in Berlin a few months each year. West Berlin has a large university and a technical college that together enroll twenty-three thousand students. New museums, galleries and libraries, many good theaters, concerts, lectures and a ballet, even "happenings" and Pop Art form an impressive superstructure that draws its lifeblood from a reservoir hundreds of kilometers away. It is a heartrending but somewhat contrived attempt: a captain's ball on a stranded ship.

Berlin has much in common with Vienna, another capital without torso or limbs. Vienna today has less inhabitants than before 1914. West Berlin with its 2.2 million inhabitants has fewer people than the same area in 1939; the population of the Federal Republic at the same time increased by 35 percent. A lot of active people—between thirty and forty-five—have migrated from Berlin to West Germany. Their absence is immediately conspicuous along any street: in no other European metropolis totter so many frail old men and women. Twenty percent of West Berlin is over sixty-five years old, a percentage twice as high as in West Germany. Every second West Berliner is over forty-six.

In the heart of the city, shiny glass palaces look out on elegant main streets. Colorful sidewalk cafes enliven the boulevards, expensive cars park in front of luxury hotels; the sound of jazz wafts out of bars. Still, war's traces are more visible here than in any other West German city. Submachine gun bursts still interrupt the night in this lively, outwardly happy city. From East German watchtowers, which look very much like the wooden structures that surrounded Auschwitz, light beams pierce the dark and bore into freshly plowed earth. A man throws himself into a furrow, crawls forward, reaches the West in safety or dies in a ditch, or is caught in the barbed wire and bleeds to death. Police on the Western side shoot back. Is this where World War III will start? "There must be secret troop deployment plans that include every public building, every street corner," writes a Berliner, Helmut Jaesrich. At the same hour that somone is bleeding to death in the barbed wire, someone else only a few hundred steps away celebrates a birthday or decides to quit smoking; several thousand comfortably seated music lovers are listening to a concert in the ultramodern, newly built Philharmonic Hall. Next morning they read the headline: "One was shot. Another got away."

People in Berlin are used to this; it is almost an everyday occurrence. Hitler's heritage has worked like a time bomb; the Wall went up sixteen years after his death. People in Berlin take little note of it. The city lies on a plain; the Wall is visible only when directly confronted. Most West Berliners visit it as they would a museum. Usually to show it to visitors.

The complaint that American tanks did not demolish the Wall immediately on August 13, 1962, is heard much less often in Berlin itself than other parts of West Germany. Berliners are sober, have a capacity for wit, skepticism and irony. The Wall, rather then weakening their sense of security and stability, has paradoxically strengthened it. The influx of people from West Germany has grown since the erection of the Wall. Investments are increasing, too. Conversing with Berliners, one has the impression that the Wall, while it has created many difficult human problems, has put an end to others even greater.

Every imprecisely marked section of the border between the two antagonistic super-powers is likely to increase tension, multiply chances of a clash that could have catastrophic consequences. "Before the building of the Wall," a leading member of the West Berlin senate said in an intimate conversation (he does not feel he can utter such opinions in public), "Berlin was a bridge that permitted millions of East Germans to flee, a sort of a hypodermic needle which gradually drew off East Germany's lifeblood. East Germany lost its best workers, its young people . . . the division of Germany is a sad and brutal thing. But I know that it is a reality and a part of the nuclear status quo. How can one be surprised that the Communists finally stopped this exodus?"

In the circle around Mayor Willy Brandt, there are quite a number of people who share this view. They are more interested in improving living conditions and increasing liberties of people in East Germany than in the allegedly imperative need to reunite the two parts. They privately hope the closing of the escape hatch will enable the East German regime to stabilize its economy, raise living standards and gradually permit more liberty, as in Hungary. "Then one day perhaps we will have a rapprochement within a confederation. . . ." says another Berlin senator who also will not be directly quoted. "Only police officials think of Communists automatically as criminals nowadays . . . we in Berlin know that we must live with them . . . I am no friend of the East German boss, Walter Ulbricht. I am as much for the downfall of his inhuman regime as any other person . . . but it is sheer nonsense to continue to treat a neighbor state as though it didn't exist. We have done so for fifteen years and have not accomplished anything. Ulbricht will not live forever. We must make it easier for his eventual successors to find their way back to freedom, back to us."

It is an exhilarating walk along the Kurfürstendamm, a splendid and luxurious avenue. From the heart of West Berlin the broad, divided boulevard runs westward, lined on both sides with elegant shops, cafes, movie houses and modern office buildings. It exudes a cosmopolitan air (something rare in present-day Germany) and a certain sophistication that has nothing to do with money. Carefree lovers kiss each other in the noon sun, the pavement under their feet vibrates from the subways roaring underneath. Yet turn a few dozen steps from this magnificent boulevard, around a corner, and suddenly it is another world, where streets yawn as in sleepy villages and a few old ladies are walking their dogs.

Almost everything of historical significance in Berlin is "on the other side," in the Eastern sector. Memorials and museums, remnants from the Kaiser's time, old Nazi ministries and monuments, are mostly east of the Wall. West Berlin has only a few of the old palaces: the former royal Charlottenburg, where today the Lord Mayor receives official visitors, the Bellevue in the Tiergarten, seat of the West German president when he comes to Berlin, the small classical palace in the northern suburb of Tegel in the French sector, that used to belong to the scholarly brothers Humboldt. All these palaces have arisen anew out of their ruins to their old splendor.

At one end of the Kurfürstendamm stands the ruin of the Kaiser Wilhelm Memorial Church. It is a neo-Romanesque relic dating back to the Kaisers. The plan after the war was to blow up the ruin and replace it with a new church. But Berliners, usually so sober, turned sentimental. They loved this church as it used to be and wanted to reconstruct it. A passionate controversy raged between traditionalists and modernists. The solution was a compromise: Keep the ruined main tower, both as a reminder and an admonition, and build a completely new church around it. The resulting conglomeration is at least unique. Next to the weatherbeaten tower ruin, which juts like a huge rotting tooth into the sky rises an avant-grade cement-and-glass octagon that glows enchantingly at night in shades of blue—like a huge, many-sided, polished sphere. Traffic rushes all around. The past stands next to the present, recollection next to hope, ghosts haunt the ultramodern glass enclosure. It is a combination that would seem utterly incredible anywhere but in Germany.

The area north of the broad Kurfürstendamm is mostly residential. The war destroyed a third of all housing in Berlin. Almost 250 thousand new apartments have been built since the end of the war. In the new Hansa district, a former upper-class residential area almost entirely destroyed during the war, approximately five thousand people live today in large high-rise apartment buildings. Leading architects from all over the world—Le Corbusier, Gropius, Niemeyer, Aalto and others—are represented here. Bold new churches of cement and steel abound; one such church—Maria Regina Martyrum—was only recently consecrated. Its leitmotif is a closed, gloomy vestibule: it is designed to look like a concentration camp. The church was consecrated to commemorate the faithful of all religions who were murdered by the National Socialists. A bell tower of reinforced concrete slabs, separated from the main building, purposely called to mind a watchtower. A large Star of David hangs suspended above the main entrance. The church, it says in the official guidebook, is to be a landmark of expiation and memory in the midst of a living community. It is to remind the living of the dead, the innocent of the guilty, the guilty of the innocent. The church is filled every Sunday, says the young priest. He speaks a little Hebrew; several years ago he spent a month in a kibbutz in the Negev Desert.

Toward the east, the ruins increase—desolate factory buildings lining filthy canals, old dwellings with sooty walls, plaster crumbling from them; then comes another thickly populated residential district. A long perfectly straight row of houses running north-south is called Bernauer Strasse. Here ten yards are like a thousand miles. A man living on the left side of this street has no way of visiting friends, or even parents who live across the street, no way, that is, since the erection of the Wall. The left side belongs to West Berlin, the right side to East Berlin. All windows and doors on the Eastern side have been bricked up. Moss is growing between the cobblestones of the sidewalk. No one walks here anymore. Most of the former inhabitants of these houses were forcibly resettled. A simple wooden cross, driven into the pavement on the Western side designates the spot where one of them jumped to his death while trying to escape. The number of East and West Berliners separated from relatives by the Wall is estimated to be 1.2 million.

Armed, tough-looking guardsmen are on the roofs opposite, in the East. Sometimes they shoot; usually, only loudspeakers bellow their messages into the West, praising "freedom" and "justice" in the First German Workers State and calling the Bonn Government "a gang of Nazis and revanchists." The view into the streets that lead from Bernauer Strasse into the Eastern sector is blocked by the Wall. Immediately behind it begins a forty-yard-wide blockade zone; only trusted Communist Party members are allowed to live here. Then, beyond the last barricade, begins the proper territory of the second German state of the postwar era, the "German Democratic Republic." (DDR)

7

In the Penal Colony

THERE ARE people in Germany who say that God is using the DDR to punish Germans. Partition, and the introduction of a particularly brutal kind of Communism into half of Germany, have hit some Germans directly, others only passingly, and some not at all. Approximately twenty-five or thirty million lives have been drastically affected by the creation of two Germanys. Next to the loss of East Prussia, Pomerania or Silesia to Russia and Poland, it is the most dramatically felt consequence of the lost war. A people who never in their history knew precisely where Germany started and where it ended—on the Rhine or on the Marne, in the marshes of East Prussia or in the vast plains of Russia—now stare across at one another along a new border that cuts straight through their heartland.

The new border between the Germans begins in the north, in the Bay of Lübeck. Here barbed wires run like breakwaters out into the greenish sea; armed motorboats, their sirens howling, skit through the waves. The border runs south, following for a while the course of the Elbe, passes a few kilometers east of Brunswick, and then draws a wide arc around Eisenach, the town where Luther began his translation of the Bible in 1521 and where in 1685 Johann Sebastian Bach was born. Since 1945, Eisenach serves as headquarters of a Soviet division. Then the frontier runs eastward along the northern edge of Bavaria to the Czechoslovak border.

It is the most zealously guarded border in all of Europe, one that sees a shooting almost every day. Men, women and children are lost here, victims in a German civil war which began in 1945 and whose end is still not in sight. The "front" is 880 miles long and consists of two to four rows of barbed-wire fences, some electrically charged. Between the fences lie wide, plowed death strips. Minefields and trenches, concrete bunkers and watchtowers are placed along the border. Signs warn: High Tension! Danger! Looking from a nearby hill or out of a low-flying helicopter, it all recalls a former time. There is no mistaking it; it is the architecture of Nazi concentration camps. Wires and bunkers tear the landscape apart like the scars produced by the tattooing machine that, in Franz Kafka's short story "In the Penal Colony," burns the story of his crime onto the convicted man's naked body.

To speak of the "punishment of God" sounds almost like an admonition from the Old Testament. I heard it for the first time in West Berlin, coming from a Protestant provost, Dr. Heinrich Grüber. Provost Grüber is a charming old gentleman who saved many Jewish lives. Twice he asked the Gestapo to deport him to a ghetto to share the fate of the persecuted—much like Gerstein in Hochhuth's play *The Deputy*. Speaking of East Germany, he recounts the hard lot of people on the other side. Political partition does not particularly disturb him. His concern is for the people, who for nearly four decades have not lived normal lives. Fate is blind and punishment unfair in its inequality.

In West Germany people are free, prosperous as never before.

Firm ties bind West Germany to three of its former enemies, who lavished their riches on the devastated land after 1945. What was destroyed in the war was rebuilt, better and more magnificent than before.

The other half, East Germany, the DDR—a police state suppressing any resistance in the bud—for many years was run by remote control from Moscow. After the war, the Soviet Union used the DDR as hostage for all Germany. Soldiers pillaged the land, technicians dismantled factories and transported them to the U.S.S.R.: half of the East German railroads were dismembered. The Western powers in their òwn occupation zones—not wanting to give Germany another "Versailles complex"—decided to forego such demands. In East Germany the Soviets demanded and levied huge indemnifications. Eighteen million East Germans have paid the Russians about the same in war reparations as fifty-six million West Germans have received in the form of Marshall Plan and other aid, practically as a gift. The Soviet Union's original demand for reparations from all of Germany amounted to forty billion marks. Today it is estimated that indemnifications to the extent of 55 to 65 billion marks have flowed into the Soviet Union from East Germany alone.

In West Germany new cities are flourishing everywhere. Streets can scarcely accommodate the flow of traffic, shop windows are overflowing with goods which just about everyone can afford.

In East Germany huge fields of rubble still disfigure the cities. Entire areas have been leveled and will probably not be rebuilt until the end of the next decade. Even in major cities, some main streets are nearly as deserted during the day as at night. Traffic is sparse; the shop windows display a meager assortment of low-quality commodities, most of which would be unsaleable in the West. Here they are prohibitively expensive; normal wage earners must carefully consider before sacrificing a month's pay for a radio.

Forty percent of all houses in West Germany were put up after 1950; they lend the country its characteristic modern and clean air. The parallel figure for East Germany is 15 percent. The rest are mostly old neglected buildings with crumbling plaster. Modern plumbing and elevators in working order are rare. Gloomy courtyards accentuate the scarcity of lawns and flowers.

In West Germany every eighth inhabitant owns a car; in East Germany, every forty-third. People without special connections or privileges wait several years for the car they order. A small "Wartburg" car costs sixteen thousand East German marks, more than three times the average yearly income. A similar car can be bought in West Germany for five thousand D-marks, or about one-half of an average workers yearly income.

During the first years after the war, West Germans shared the suffering. Devastated cities, unemployment, de-Nazification and millions of refugees pouring in from the East made life difficult. But then good fortune spiced with the sweet taste of freedom allowed them to recover in a relatively short time. Not in East Germany. Its society has been turned upside down since 1945, its economy radically revamped. Unbelievable mismanagement and doctrinaire misplanning, the seemingly unavoidable ailments of every young Communist regime have prevented the raising of the living standards for many years. As recently as the late fifties, the 80-kilometer distance between Lübeck (West Germany) and Rostock (East Germany), was the distance between eras. A dismaying result of their postwar plights is that—according to reliable reports—many people in the DDR nostalgically look back on the Nazi era as the "best time" of their lives: the seven euphoric years 1935 to 1942, after the slump, and before the first military reverse.

More than three million people have fled from the DDR into the "golden West," most of them young people or trained professionals, the most active and dynamic forces in the population. They left behind a bled, dismembered torso, a huge excess of women, and old people. Until about 1962, the DDR was the only country in Europe, if not in the entire world, with a constantly decreasing population. The excess of births over deaths per one thousand inhabitants in the DDR since 1950 has fluctuated down from 5.5 to 2.7 while rising in the Federal Republic from 4.2 to 7.4. Only since the Wall went up has the population of the DDR been increasing. Still, statisticians estimate that it will take at least thirty or forty years until the population returns to normal proportions.

What of those left behind in the DDR? They have been under constant police supervision, subjected to a brainwashing that places a close second to Goebbel's methods. They live cut off from West Germany and Europe, in an outcast state which most countries in the world regard as nonexistent. Even with a hard-to-get passport to leave the country, East Germans are turned away by most European states. Even Poland and Czechoslovakia, whose governments have signed solemn friendship pacts with the DDR, regard East German travelers with mistrust. A man in Warsaw, Prague or Budapest often prefers the company of a West German to that of an East German, and not only because the West German happens to have money to spend. He is easier to relax with.

The East German people are still paying the bill for the war that Germany launched upon the world in 1939. Everyone pays—the non-Nazis and the ex-Nazis, their children and grandchildren. The price is the absence of political, economic and cultural freedom; despite all talk about "de-Stalinization," the DDR is still far less free than Poland or Hungary. The punishment is twice as hard, considering the fact that East Germans are forced to knuckle under to a totalitarian regime that arouses—in contrast to its Nazi predecessor—little or no enthusiasm. Other than a sentence upon an entire people of life imprisonment, one cannot conceive of a worse, harsher psychological burden than the one the East Germans have to bear. They pay with everyday unpleasantness to an almighty state bureaucracy. They endure a thousand little difficulties that are part of everyday Communist life: in obligations to participate in party events, or lectures on dialectic materialism, in hours-long lines to receive a few pounds of tomatoes. For some inexplicable reason, black thread is suddenly not available, but white or brown thread is in over-abundance. If you need shoes, for some reason you cannot get the right size; or after an eight-year wait the two-room apartment is denied because you have been caught listening to a Western radio station and are branded "an enemy of the party."

In East German department stores you wait a week for a passport picture that was ready in five minutes in the same store thirty years ago, because here, as in most Communist countries the simplest transactions are incredibly overorganized. There are thousands of examples of this nature. The most passionate German-hater could not have planned such Kafkaesque details. The famous, never-executed American Morgenthau plan, which intended to transform Germany into a "farmland" appears—compared with the fate of the DDR—like the vision of a pastoral idyll.

Every foreigner and most West Germans who own passports and have forty pfennig to spend are allowed to see this for themselves. Forty pfennig pay for a round-trip ticket on the S-Bahn, Berlin's elevated train, from West to East Berlin. It is one of the cheapest and, at the same time, most devastating trips imaginable. Until the building of the Wall in 1961 Berliners from either side could travel to the other. Since 1961 only foreign nationals or West Germans (considered foreigners by the Communists) are permitted to cross. West Berliners are given occasional crossing permits, such as at Christmas or Easter, to visit relatives trapped on the other side. East Berliners may never cross.

What must have been almost a daily event before 1961 is movingly described by a young East German writer, Christa Wolf, in her novel *The Divided Sky*. Its subject is the fate of people living in a divided land. Rita, an East Berlin girl, follows her boyfriend, who has fled to West Berlin. "She stepped up to the ticket counter and asked: '*Zoologischer Garten*' [one of the first S-Bahn stops in West Berlin]. A yellow ticket was calmly pushed toward her across the counter. 'Twenty pfennigs,' the woman behind the glass pane said. 'And if I want to come back?' Rita asked timidly. 'Forty then,' the woman said, retrieved the card and shoved another through the little opening. This one difference distinguished this city from all other cities in the world; for forty pfennigs she held the choice between two different lives in her hand."

I entered the S-Bahn at *Zoologischer Garten* station in the heart of West Berlin, and traveled in the opposite direction from Christa Wolf's heroine Rita. The trip has three stops and takes only five and a half minutes. It rolls over roofs and gaping ruins at the border area, over the Spree River with its protruding barbed wire, and finally over the Wall, and the grey, levelled areas where houses still stood a few years ago but which are now mined, past searchlights and machine guns. Aeneas entered the underworld through a more inviting gate than this.

The first station in the East is *Friedrichstrasse*. A young, vigorously built East German border guard stood on the empty platform. He was wearing a grey-green, somewhat shabby uniform of Russian cut. In his right hand, shining in the glare, was a freshly oiled submachine gun. He used it briefly to point the way down a dark shaft that leads to the ground floor. "To the checkpoint," he said. "Chin up," said a young Englishman whom I met in the long, practically empty train on my way from West Berlin. Above our heads, high up in the steel framework that supports the roof, two other soldiers squatted on a narrow gangway. Stubby submachine guns were slung over their shoulders. Bending forward slightly, they inspected our train.

We walked down the stairs and entered a sparsely lit hall. Placards on the walls announce your entrance into the "First German Peace and Freedom State." Another poster denounced Heinrich Lübke, the president of West Germany, as a Nazi; and General Trettner, chief of the West German army, as a war criminal responsible for the destruction of Rotterdam and Florence.

We made a right turn. A single light bulb was burning at the distant end of a long, narrow corridor, shedding its meager light on a crudely built wooden table laden with documents. We walked through the corridor, light bulb and table became larger with every step, as in a classic scene of Orson Well's film "*The Trial*."—Four men, armed with pistols, stood to the left and right of the table.

The first man reached for our passports. He took his time leafing through them as if faced with an exceedingly difficult and serious task. Studying the photos, he raised his eyes, comparing them with the originals. We filled out forms in three carbon copies. Meanwhile, a second man inspected the passports. Again every detail was carefully examined with a concentration suitable to a laboratory that handles poisonous substances. A third man took our forms, then shoved them immediately back. We had not written out —in word form—the sum of money in our possession. (Figures alone are not enough.) Then passports and forms disappeared through a slot in the wall. Around the corner on long wooden benches about fifteen people were waiting, watched over by two uniformed men with holstered pistols. Some had been waiting for half an hour. "Be seated. You will be called." Prussian bureaucracy, the young Englishman said, combined with the Russian capacity for infinite delay: Gogol in Potsdam.

An hour later we finally stood outside on the East Berlin *Friedrichstrasse*. It was shortly after eleven in the morning and there were few people on the street, a half dozen cars on the shoddy pavement. An old woman was selling matches from a wooden bench in front of a wall.

A traveler's first impression of the DDR is one of oppressive, universal shabbiness. It seems as though the war had ended only the day before yesterday. We walked along *Friedrichstrasse* and crossed *Unter den Linden*. Here a few new office buildings, contrasted with surrounding giant ruins. Large fields of rubble covered with garbage and overgrown with weeds peep out behind red, wooden placard-covered Potemkin walls that read: OUR STRENGTH FOR SOCIALISM. IT SECURES PEACE AND PROSPERITY.

Prosperity? There was pitifully little to see of prosperity as one knows it in the West and would undoubtedly have seen here, too, had the military occupation zones been differently charted. The people were poorly dressed, the men in cheap suits of the same strange Italian cut which Khrushchev introduced into Eastern Europe. A few women kept their throats and hands warm in old fur collars and muffs. An old man was pulling a creaking cart loaded with coals or potatoes along that grand boulevard of the twenties, *Unter den Linden*. A lean, tough-looking man alighted from an ancient, wheezing bus. Startled, we looked at him; it was as if a ghost had appeared. He was a caricature of the Nazi storm-trooper man in World War II movies. He was wearing a leather coat that reached to his ankles, and an insignia in his buttonhole betrayed him as a party functionary. The long leather coat, a singularly ugly garment, associated with torchlight parades and street battles of the early thirties, is still very much in fashion in East Germany. It adds to the feeling that time has stopped.

Twenty-five or thirty people were waiting in front of a grocery store. They were standing patiently in line, exuding an eloquent silence. We asked a young brunette what they were waiting for. She had an open, sympathetic face and shining blue eyes, was wearing a fleecy winter coat made of synthetic fiber. She smiled. In East Germany foreigners are as easily spotted by their clothes as Jews once were by the yellow star. Also perhaps by the questions they ask. "For butter," the girl said. Is this customary? "Oh yes," she replied, "standing in line is part of our way of life." What was it the last time? "Ach, it was rice. We have no acute shortages," the young girl said. "Everything has gotten much better recently. But there is always something you can't get, and it is always what you happen to need most." Then she laughed, "There are worse things!"

We walked on, between two ruins, one formerly a theater, the other a church. *Wilhelmstrasse*—here was the heart of the Third Reich. Today it is called *Otto Grotewohlstrasse*, in memory of the late (1965) chairman of the DDR's Council of Ministers. Between the few remaining official buildings where the DDR is governed, lie fragments of vanished ruins. Red flags and banners wave from Herman Göring's Air Ministry. It is today the DDR's "House of the Ministries" and accommodates East German government offices. As we passed, a detachment of armed militiamen was guarding the colossal building as though it contained some frightful secret. Diagonally across the street a red banner announced the coming "Woman's Day": THE REPUBLIC NEEDS EVERY WOMAN. EVERY WOMAN NEEDS THE REPUBLIC.

We came upon a high wire fence fronting a field overgrown with weeds. Here was Hitler's former chancellory; underneath is the so-called Führer bunker, where Hitler spent the last hours before he committed suicide. Parts of the bunker have been blown up, and others walled up. A somewhat round concrete hill protrudes from the weeds like a prehistoric burial mound. Hitler's ashes must be scattered somewhere around here. Under this bush? Next to a mine? The field lies close to the West Berlin border, in a no-man's land between the two worlds. No one is allowed to enter the area. Large, multilingual signs also prohibit photographing.

Our destination, the East German press and propaganda office, was nearby. It is housed in, of all places, the torso of Goebbel's Ministry of Propaganda. In the hall of the former *Reichspressekonferenz*, where the "line" for the Nazi press used to be given out each day, a party "line" is still put out daily for East German editors and reporters. As we waited for Herr Müller, a government press officer, we stood between long glass display cases that were filled with information about the DDR.

"Welcome to Berlin, capital of the DDR," Herr Müller began. East German functionaries rarely pronounce the name Berlin without adding the designation "capital of the DDR."

Herr Müller went on to say how much he hoped that we would

soon see how different, how infinitely superior the DDR was to its image in the West. "We have really done a thorough job in getting rid of Fascism," Herr Müller said. "We have created a state that will never start a war." The Berlin Wall—he called it a "protective dam"—had of course created "unhappy human problems"; but it was, unfortunately, necessary to protect the DDR against Western saboteurs and agents.

We asked why there were still so many ruins in East Berlin. City construction was outside his field of competence, Herr Müller said, "yet I would imagine the DDR has more important things to do. . . . You see, we started with the construction of Socialism. That was closer to our heart than esthetics. We started with industrialization, and collectivization of agriculture.

"This was the poorest part of Germany, the most backward in every respect. Today the DDR is the second strongest industrial power in the Socialist world. In the coming years we will be able to devote ourselves more fully to the well-being of the people than we have been able to until now. Production of consumer goods will be increased, the path will be much easier—in the interest of all 'Peace-loving nations'—if Western countries would recognize the DDR as a state like any other." Herr Müller went on to denounce "the Bonn state, which is governed by warmongers and carries on the Nazi tradition. The DDR has no revanchists demanding a change in the Eastern borders," he added. "No one here demands the return of the so-called stolen Eastern territories. The DDR and the People's Republic of Poland recognize the Oder-Neisse Line as an irrevocable border of peace. This question has never even been raised here."

"That may be so," I said. "But how does one know? There is no freedom of speech here."

"Of course," Herr Müller said. "Of course we don't allow warmongers and militarists any freedom of speech."

On a walk from *Marx-Engels Plaza to Alexanderplatz*, East Berlin seems a bit more lively. *Marx-Engels Plaza* occupies the enormous area of the former Prussian royal palace. The palace, mostly built by the baroque architect Andreas Schlüter, was torn down in the fifties to make more room for giant rallies and state ceremonies. At the edge of the plaza stands Schinkel's "old royal guard house," which the Nazis made into the "Tomb of the Unknown Soldier."

"You are lucky," said a tourist guide leading a group of middle-aged Polish tourists outside the little, chapel-like structure. "The changing of the guards takes place in a few minutes." Shortly soldiers moved in from an adjacent building. Goose-stepping smartly they marched up to the old guardhouse. The goose step has been abolished in West Germany as a "Prussian symbol." Here it has recently been reintroduced. East German soldiers wear the high boots of the old *Wehrmacht* and low-slung grey steel helmets. The Poles watched them in silence. It seemed that this was not what they had come to see.

Crossing the deserted *Marx-Engel Plaza*, I walked a little further up the street toward *Alexanderplatz*. Traffic increased somewhat. Here too, there were ruins everywhere. At *Alexanderplatz* traffic became again about as dense as in a provincial Turkish town. The circular plaza is dominated by a state-owned department store; next to it stands a new multistoried office building. Otherwise, the large plaza remains bare. The new office building is the "House of the Teacher." It is closed to visitors, except by special permit. I asked the uniformed guard how one might be able to obtain such a permit. He was not quite sure, and suggested I try the Ministry of Education.

The regime's new luxury street runs northeast from the *Alexanderplatz*. It is about twice as wide as New York's Park Avenue and what little traffic there is, is lost in its vast expanse. Once upon a time it was called *Frankfurter Allee*, than *Stalinalee* and now *Leninalee*. A young man with whom I had struck up conversation did not know if it was ever called *Hitlerallee*. He was too young, he was an apprentice in a state-owned optical instruments factory. He was going to the movies, wearing the uniform of teen-agers in both East and West: tight-fitting, slightly soiled blue jeans. A yellow brand name on the back pocket revealed its American origin. "Don't you know you are making propaganda for American imperialism with your back pocket," I asked, after we had been talking for a while. He returned a wide-eyed look and said seriously: "Actually not . . . I haven't gotten that far yet, that is, ideologically."

We walked down *Leninallee*. There were huge apartment houses built in the bombastically wasteful, incredibly tasteless style of the Stalin years, with marble façades and useless turrets, spreading like gigantic wedding cakes. The young man stopped in front of a particularly hideous example of Stalinist architecture, a multistoried apartment house adorned with sculptures of heroic workers and muscle-bound women. Giggling, he said: "I know someone who lives here. On the top floor the elevator does not work most of the time...." Façades often are deceptive in East Germany. A peek behind those of *Leninallee* reveals ruins again and old, gloomy, crumbling buildings.

Before travelling to the DDR you generally equip yourself with letters of introduction to relatives and friends of friends, but references are hardly necessary; it is surprisingly easy to enter into intimate conversations. You address complete strangers, in street cars, in the lobby of the opera or in a restaurant. Once the conversation begins, there is no stopping it. It is as if floodgates have been opened, for pent-up hostilities, dislikes, and wishful desires break forth. Impetuously, often for hours, people will pour out their hearts, people with or without party insignia. An Austrian writer once went from door to door in an East Berlin apartment house, rang the bell, introduced himself and announced he only wanted to talk. Not once was he turned away. No one asked him to show his credentials; no one wanted to make sure he was not an agent of the secret police, the SSD.

How melancholy this city is and oddly washed out! How grey the people! Of course it would be ridiculous to claim that people in the DDR don't laugh. But anyone who spends some time in East Berlin, Leipzig or Dresden comes away with that impression. The lack of wit is hard to understand. Where people live in difficult, unpleasant circumstances, political wit allows a release. Through jokes, a people perhaps retains its psychological balance. One thinks of Jean Paul's saying "Wit makes freedom," and of the numerous political anecdotes heard in Moscow, Warsaw or Budapest. Most East German anecdotes I heard in the DDR were merely warmed-up old anti-Nazi jokes.

Here are a few examples: In an insane asylum, the lunatics are crowing in a chorus: Long live Walter Ulbricht, Chairman of the

State Council of the German Democratic Republic! One man watches dumbly, and a visiting party member asks why he is silent. "Sorry" he answers, "I'm not mad. I'm the guard." This joke made the rounds in Viennese cafes in 1936. Ulbricht was Adolf Hitler. Just as shopworn: A foreman, holding portrait of Ulbricht, to worker: "Where shall we put Ulbricht?" Worker: "Shall we hang him or just line him against the wall?"

A rare example of a new kind of joke: A man at a newspaper stand demands the official party organ *Neues Deutschland* (New Germany). It is old out. He asks for the *Freiheit* (Freedom), another party-line sheet. The *Freiheit* is not available either. "Well then, when are you going to get Freedom?" "When we get the New Germany."

A majority of refugees polled in West Germany claims political jokes were much more frequent during the Nazi era than they are today. Of those old enough to compare, only one percent said the DDR has more jokes.

It cannot be the fault of the Communist regime alone that life in the DDR is so cheerless. Anyone who has been in Communist countries in the last few years knows that Prague, Warsaw, Bratislava, Budapest, Moscow or Kiev are veritable models of light-heartedness in comparison with East Berlin, Leipzig or Dresden.

The depressed standard of living does not seem to be the decisive factor either. The average Pole, Czech, Hungarian or Russian is considerably poorer than his East German counterpart. TV sets, ice boxes or washing machines are still almost unobtainable luxury articles for most Poles or Russians. While they are also expensive in East Germany, an average worker can buy such things if he makes the effort. East Germany has the highest living standard in the Socialist world, but the East German evidently lacks something. Is it a feeling of patriotism? A measure of self-assurance to restore psychological balance? Poles and Hungarians are simply proud of what they are. In East Germany the absence of a natural self-confidence, despite the relatively high degree of social security, is remarkable. Unemployment does not exist in the DDR, dismissals for other than political reasons are unthinkable. Children go to primary school, to secondary school and on to the university, regardless of financial status. Medical treatment is free, rents are low. That so much social security is accompanied by a strong measure of personal insecurity is a characteristic of the DDR.

Depression hangs over East Berlin like a thick fog. When I visited the DDR for the first time in winter I thought the bleak mood might be due to the weather. Visiting the country again in spring and midsummer the feeling of depression remained. When night falls and street lamps shed a meager light onto dark streets you feel, regardless of season, almost like shivering. Many streets are as deserted as during an air raid. You hurry to the next elevated train and feel lucky and relieved to own a foreign passport. You can go for a breather to West Berlin, drink a quiet cup of coffee and then slip back under the heavy cloud of melancholy.

I asked many people about this general dejection. An American journalist calls it: "The DDR blues." Even Communists confirm its existence. But what is the reason? Herr Müller of the East German Press Bureau admits that East Berlin's atmosphere has an "oppressive" effect. He blamed the proximity of West Berlin, the shining lights visible in the East, the elegance that East Germans imagine on the other side, the plentiful department stores, the cheerful atmosphere they remember in the entertainment district around *Kurfürstendamm*—all of that must depress those behind the Wall. This will not change, he said "until our economy is up to par."

I suggested to Herr Müller that no other city in the world illustrates as acutely the contrast between what Communism and what capitalism offer the mass of the population.

Herr Müller disagreed and said the prosperity in the West was deceptive, concealing dreadful abuses. "Basically," he said, "people in the East are much happier, as they are not exploited and know that everything belongs to them. And besides, reconstruction of the historic city center of East Berlin—according to new Socialist plans—will begin shortly. A model already exists," he explained.

In a restaurant I met an East Berlin physician. He was about thirty or thirty-two years old and had been a party member for eight years. ("One tries to get along" he said). After we talked a while he invited me to his house for a vodka. He felt the air of dejection had mostly to do with the monotony of everyday life;

it is the feeling of being somehow "stuck" with "no exit." And nothing is worse in life, the young physician said "than to have no alternative." He asked whether I had read the Polish philosopher Leszek Kolakowski, who, he said, strikingly characterized the state of mind typical of many East Germans. I looked it up afterward. In his book *Man Without an Alternative*, Kolakowski writes: "The word 'Marxist' does not mean a person who possesses a firmly circumscribed conception of the world, but one with a definite state of mind. That state of mind is characterized by a willingness to accept opinions that have been confirmed by the authorities. The real content of Marxism is inconsequential—one becomes a Marxist by being constantly prepared to accept the contents of Marxism whatever they may be."

Bertold Brecht's "Berliner Ensemble" still regularly performs the *Three-Penny Opera*. Brecht's widow, Helene Weigel, carries on the legacy of the great "provocateur"; she takes liberties occasionally with the text and direction, but risks no clash with the authorities. Brecht's bitter wit is made to appear directed exclusively against the West; Mack the Knife, says the program, can not be represented as a charming lady-killer nowadays. For, trashy Western literature fosters a dangerously romantic attitude toward crime and exercises a noxious influence on youth. Certain "socially critical" scenes ought to be emphasized instead, like Mack the Knife's close friendship with Tiger Brown, the chief of police. For it is proven that capitalism and prostitution live off each other in the United States, and that the American underworld dominates politics, the police and the unions. . . . The original version of the *Three-Penny Opera*, the program goes on to say, ended as a parody. Mack is saved from the gallows and knighted at the last moment. This end, maintains the program, is precisely the story of present-day West Germany.

During a half dozen or so Brecht plays I watched at the "Ensemble," the audience applauded politely. It laughed when something funny happened and applauded at an unexpected effect. But no one seemed to feel provoked. Brecht is part of the officially sanctioned culture here. I met a young actor after the performance; soon he too began to talk about the East Berlin "depression." He explained it by the fact that the DDR "is unfortunately still a police state. . . . Many things have improved, the pressure is not so strong anymore, the brutal terror is over. Especially for us actors . . . but you can still be arrested for criticizing the Republic in a bar . . . at private parties you're never safe from police informers . . . it is always possible that someone will denounce you . . . so-called colleagues from party district headquarters come to your house, urge you to do something you don't want to do . . . a work detail, a petition. . . ."

The actor's young wife was a commercial artist. She talked of the millions who fled: "We were slowly bleeding to death, anemia produces disturbing psychological symptoms." Until the Wall one felt one could always leave—one only had to want to. That is all over now. Many people see themselves stuck here in this rubble. There's no escaping from it . . . and that is oppressive."

The young actor quoted a poem by the East German poet Stephan Hermlin, who left Frankfurt to move to the DDR in 1947.

> Abandoned by flowers and animals,
> The sea of silence dashes
> Against us. And we freeze
> and are greatly afraid.

"Here in the DDR the Germans have thoroughly lost the war," the young actor added after a while. "And how thoroughly! So thoroughly as you cannot imagine! Its obvious . . . look at the people, even the younger ones."

Late at night I wandered back to my hotel. In bed I thought about what the actor said. The DDR has a sobering effect on those who come to Germany with a bagful of resentments; it even makes one feel guilty. The prosperity in West Germany is dazzling. Somehow as a foreigner and as a Jew you are imbued with a dark, inexplicable, rarely uttered feeling that the fortune bestowed on the West Germans is in some way indecent. Somehow you want to see Germans in hair shirts, barefoot, and covered with ashes. East Germany in its way changes this attitude. You think of the lonely people you meet here, of their perennial despair, of the young people who look so old. You think: for God's sake, enough! It is enough!

8

Old Stupidities from New Antennas

IT IS easier to utter a few intelligent-sounding generalities about the DDR than about its happier, first-born Western twin. To a foreigner, West Germany seems infinitely more complex. It is free, its contradictions are conspicuous.

In the DDR a dictatorship prevents the free exchange of opinion. Political decisions emanate from closed, soundproof rooms. Even controversies among intellectuals—tired mandarins whispering secrets to each other—fall into a code that must first be deciphered. Kafka comes to mind again. It is *The Castle*—not the best way to produce the moral revitalization so necessary to all Germany since

1945. The East Germans tumbled from one totalitarian regime into another. Freedom and human dignity are still wanting.

Economic and political questions are simpler to answer in the DDR. In the twenties, Communists were arguing whether socialism could work when it controlled only a single country. East Germany has gone further: it has tried to establish Socialism in half a country. Relative to other Communist states, it has achieved considerable success. The DDR, say economists, has developed the most rational economic system of any Communist industrial state. Despite the most unfavorable starting point conceivable—the Soviet Union's stripping its industry and agriculture, an enormous national debt, catastrophic misplanning, extravagant misinvestments and mass emigration—despite all these disadvantages, the DDR today is the second greatest industrial producer of the Eastern Bloc, the sixth greatest in Europe.

The fruits of this accomplishment have not yet found their way into East German stomachs. Salaries and wages remain low. For a TV set, a bad-quality sweater, or a pair of mediocre shoes, an East German worker must invest roughly five months', one week's, or three days' wages respectively. His wife joins him in a low-cost vacation at a government-run rest home; but she pays forty East marks ($10) for a pound of poor coffee. Winter fruits—plentiful everywhere in the West—are seen once or twice a year, sold out in a few hours. A single orange costs up to one mark (25 cents) at Christmastime.

The net national income of the DDR grew from 30.3 billion marks in 1950 to 79.7 billion marks in 1963; individual consumption more than doubled. Chemical and metal industries developed enormously in that time and have become a DDR specialty within the Communist bloc. East Germany claims it will soon surpass West Germany in per capita production. While this is hardly conceivable, comparisons with neighboring Communist states are more appropriate. The DDR is not yet a model of Socialism in action, but one day it just may be so. Stalin was probably wrong when he said that Communism would fit the Germans as silk stockings fit a cow. It seems to fit the East Germans better than the Poles.

The success is relative, but impressive enough. One asks oneself, "Why? How?" One conspicuous reason seems to be that qualified technicians and specialists in the DDR vastly outnumber those in the less-developed countries of Eastern Europe. The old tradition of craftsmanship has of course been damaged by Communism, but not obliterated completely. There is know-how in East Germany that does not exist in, say, Hungary or Rumania. Another tempting explanation is the social and political makeup of the Germans. Communism requires a high degree of discipline; Germans, especially East Germans, have always been reproached for excessive obedience to authority—be it Prussian, military, National Socialist or Communist. "The citizen's first duty is to keep the peace," a chief of the Berlin police said during the revolution of 1848. The Communists continue to invoke this dictum even today. There is a greater submissiveness in East Germany than in any other Communist country, with the possible exception of China. Observers of Eastern Europe consider the DDR far less corrupt than other Communist countries. Indeed the DDR seems to have escaped at least the crudest forms of corruption that mark the Polish and Hungarian regimes. Simultaneously, the lack of corruption makes East Germany a much less human place to live and breathe in than Hungary, Czechoslovakia or Poland. In a totalitarian regime, small, illegal mutual favors necessarily make daily life more bearable; they are a conspiracy of humaneness against an unfeeling dictatorship: "I'll get you a car outside the quota and you'll put my name a little further up on the new apartment list;" "I'll 'organize' an electric razor for you from the export firm where I work, if you bring me a crate of oranges from the import firm where you work." This sort of thing is much less likely in the DDR than in Poland, Hungary or Czechoslovakia.

This apparent incorruptibility of the East Germans can be met on the lowest level. Every tourist who goes to Eastern Europe knows that most parking-lot attendants in Budapest or Prague take special care if offered a pack of Western cigarettes rather than the pittance charged. In the DDR, attendants often insist on their twenty pfennigs—nothing more, if you please. Elevator operators and waiters refuse gratuities in Western currency that their colleagues in Warsaw or Prague have come to expect. Most East Germans would rather receive no tip at all. "It is *verboten*" is a common explanation. "I can't take this to the bank." Their colleagues in

Prague or Warsaw would not dream of exchanging Western currency at the official bank rate.

Politically, the DDR is a state. It is a police state, to be sure, but not so very different from many other countries with a voice in world politics, wooed by both East and West. It is a state like many others, with borders and its own currency. The currency has a low exchange rate, this also is not unusual. It has a government, cabinet ministers and dignitaries with high-sounding titles; ambassadors maintain relations with thirteen Communist states, including Cuba. Since official West German policy is to sever diplomatic relations with any country that recognizes East Germany, the DDR must find unique ways to escape possible isolation. A "minister extraordinary with ambassadorial rank" substitutes in Egypt; consul-generals represent East Germany in Indonesia, Iraq, Yemen, Cambodia and Ceylon. Despite protests and economic pressure from West Germany, such special arrangements increase from year to year. "Trade missions" keep the DDR in contact with seven other Afro-Asian countries and Finland. Back-door arrangements also exist with Brazil, Colombia and Uruguay through agreements between state banks. Other substitutes are agencies of the East German Chamber of Foreign Trade, in France, Great Britain, Belgium, Denmark, Italy, Austria and Sweden. Regular channels might work more simply, certainly better. But it works this way too.

In 1967 the DDR was eighteen years old, the same age as the Federal Republic of West Germany. It had already outlived by four years the Weimar Republic, existed six years longer than the Third Reich. Eighteen years is not inconsequential in a world with so many young states. At least a dozen others have come into being through the partition of larger ethnic or national units. If political stability and effective control of a government over its territory are the criteria for international recognition, as the British and French, even the West Germans, maintain they are—then the DDR should long since have ceased to be a pariah state. But after eighteen years it is still looked upon as an outlaw, an invidious situation not solely due to its dictatorial government, for this makes it no different from many other states in the world.

There is but a single reason for the international isolation of the DDR: West German policies. West Germany is so important to its Western Allies that even General DeGaulle, who wanted to divide Germany into four, not two states, after the war, now pays at least lip service to West German demands for reunification. It has even been claimed that President Kennedy was ready to upgrade the international status of the DDR if this could prepare the way for better understanding between Moscow and Washington. In West Germany there are many who hope an easing in the DDR's diplomatic isolation will further internal liberalization. Such hopes are heard, (privately) from members of the Social-Democratic opposition and of the small coalition Free Democratic Party. Even Chancellor Erhard, it seems, is beginning to realize that present policies are leading nowhere: neither to reunification nor to an improvement of living conditions for people on the other side of the barbed wire. Governments, by nature, move very slowly and so far no practical steps toward a new policy have been taken.

Some aspects of the DDR exhibit a dismaying resemblance to the Third Reich. This statement calls for a reservation. The DDR is certainly not a Nazi state in a new guise. The very origins of East German Communism differ from those of the Nazis. East German Communism finds its intellectual origins in eighteenth century rationalism whereas the National Socialists were rooted in the romanticism of the nineteenth century. East German leaders are guided by domestic issues rather than foreign political ambitions. Their lust for power is not motivated by racial hatred but by fanatical self-righteousness in economic policies. When I speak of a "resemblance," I mean traits peculiar to most totalitarian regimes. The Romans adopted rites and even divinities of the peoples they subjugated without simultaneously succumbing to their barbarism; thus East Germany has assumed some of the Nazi ritual. It is too early to judge whether these remnants are merely a reaction to West German pressure, a desperate attempt to hold together a state which "must not exist," or whether terror and pressure are the very nature of a system forced upon a population that resisted it from the very start.

The DDR calls itself the "First Peace-loving German State." It claims to have completely extirpated the Nazi's inhuman methods. But reliable estimates maintain the DDR has roughly twelve thousand political prisoners. In East Germany policemen and soldiers still "obey orders" to shoot and kill. Every known shooting in East Germany is carefully documented by a West German legal agency in Salzgitter. Files on suspected East German soldiers and officers have been assembled, investigations even begun. Does this mean, in the event of reunification, a series of trials similar to those today in West German cities against Nazi murderers who also were "only obeying orders"? If such trials should ever take place, can we expect the defendants to appeal to a 1964 edition of the East German People's Police Handbook: "To shoot no matter what the circumstances, yes indeed, that too is part of being a good soldier."

East German border guards are granted special leaves and similar considerations for shooting—be the victims women, children and old people trying to cross the Berlin Wall or other sections of the 880-mile long border. They are severely punished if they intentionally miss their target. Most Nazi offenders—whether henchmen or university professors—today justify themselves with the defense that what they did was "customary back then." What is "customary today" may not be so awful; there are certainly fewer crimes. But is humaneness a matter of quantity?

Nazism and East German Communism share a common claim for the absolute validity of their view of life. In both cases this claim extends into all reaches of life, state, society and family, and art, as well as the administration of justice. "Legal terror" against political nonconformists is an instrument of the East German Communists as it was of the Nazis. The present legal terror fortunately destroys fewer lives than its National Socialist predecessor. Is justice also a matter of quantity?

Under the National Socialism the Führer's will was supreme law. Until very recently in East Germany, the will of the Party was supreme. On paper, East Germany is the very essence of democracy. A seemingly progressive constitution pays high-sounding lip service to freedom and dignity of the individual. In practice, the administration of justice is determined by party dictum. It is neither bound by constitution, nor obliged to account to a free public. Bearing in mind the substantive differences between the two systems, it is interesting to compare a few Nazi texts with contemporary East German commentaries. Justice is a party affair under both systems. The Judge pronounces not justice, but party policy. He executes decisions reached by the rulers:

Source: Freisler, "The Coming German Criminal Proceeding" in *German Justice*, 1938, Volume II, page 1253.

> We commit ourselves to a penal law that is customarily called voluntary penal law. . . . Particularly such a voluntary penal law demands a clear recognition of the personality of the culprit, of his attitude toward the community of the people inasmuch as it is determined by his heredity, his self-education and education by others, by his strength, capacity or incapacity to influence and change the future deevlopment of his attitude. . . .

Source: Decision of the State Council of the DDR about the further development of the administration of justice, January 30, 1961.

> In its fight against criminality the state invokes its laws in all their severity when it is dealing with enemies of the Worker's and Farmer's state who commit serious crimes under order or influence of Imperialist Agencies. In the case of persons who commit crimes that contradict their normal behavior, the cause for these crimes need be carefully examined and the complexity of the development of the individual's consciousness has to be considered. One of the things that has to be determined during the criminal proceedings therefore is to ascertain the concrete conditions that lead to a punishable act, the state of the individual's consciousness and the educational power of his collective.

Source: *German Justice*, 1937, Volume II, page 1084 and 1939, Volume I, page 899.

> Every judge must be an exemplary National Socialist. Only then is he in the position to search for the German people's right to live. . . .

> . . . in every verdict a judge reaches he has to be the immediate promulgator of the Führer's will.

Source: Law about the constitution of the Courts of the DDR of April 17, 1963: No. 45.

> 1. The judges and jurors must provide a guarantee with their personality and activity that they will execute their function in accordance with the principles of the constitution, work in behalf of Socialism and are loyal to the Worker's and Farmer's state.

Source: Melsheimer, "Socialist Legality in Criminal Proceedings," in *New Justice*, 1956, page 289.

. . . the judges' verdicts must reflect their readiness to execute the decisions of the Party of the working class and of the Government.

Source: Order of the *Reichspräsident* for the protection of the people and the state, of February 2, 1933. No. 1, *German Justice*, 1934, Volume I, page 58.

. . . restrictions of the personal freedom of the right of free expression, including the freedom of the press, the right of assembly and to form associations . . . of property, also outside of the usual legal limits, [are] permissible.

It is not only permitted to impose protective custody* on active enemies of the state but also, for educational reasons, against critics of the Government of the national seizure of power, against gripers etc.

Source: Order about residence limitations of August 24, 1961.

1. When someone is sentenced to imprisonment or in the case of a conditional sentence the court is entitled to impose additional restrictions upon the condemned person's freedom of movement.
2. . . . on the basis of the verdict (restrictions of movement) the organs of the state are entitled to obligate the condemned to take up a particular kind of work.
3. Upon demand of the local organs of the state, the district court can order persons who are uneager to work to undergo work education.

Source: *German Justice*, 1939, Volume I, page 495.

It is known that certain foreign stations are disseminating falsehoods about the German Reich, thereby intending to harm the well-being of the Reich and the Reich government . . . Anyone who disseminates foreign news . . . will be punished with up to two years in prison.

Source: *Young World* of 21/22 October, 1961

It is forbidden in our country to make propaganda with the help of NATO stations and West TV. For example, if someone is walk-

* The designation "protective custody" concealed the concentration camps.

ing along the street with a portable radio and turns on one of the NATO-poison stations, he breaks the law and makes himself liable to punishment. Nor does anyone have the right to turn on the Western TV in a public place, thereby enabling the enemy to inject his poison propaganda into the DDR.

The West Berlin *Ausschuss Freitheitlicher Juristen* (Committee of Liberal Lawyers) has been collecting and publishing East German court verdicts for several years. What happens to people the regime considers politically harmful, has been well documented by them:

• A man was sentenced to life imprisonment because he "agitated for a boycott." His crime: he had distributed West German Social-Democratic Party pamphlets to his colleagues.

• Another man (1961) was sentenced to five years in prison for listening to "enemy broadcasts."

• A man who turned on West German TV while he had guests in his apartment was sentenced to two-and-a-half years in prison. He is guilty of "propaganda and agitation endangering the security of the state."

• A shopkeeper who told a customer that a toothpaste manufactured by a state-owned firm was "useless" and allegedly said: "would sell you a better brand but I don't have one, it's not our fault," was sentenced to two years for "slandering the state."

• Speaking drunkenly against state or party becomes a case of "criminal drunkenness"; hard sentences have been meted out. In vino non est veritas.

• In 1963 a court sentenced a young worker to nine months imprisonment on grounds of "agitating for a boycott against democratic institutions and organizations;" he had made a few sarcastic remarks about Party boss Walter Ulbricht.

• In 1954 a man was sentenced to four years because of "instigating hatred among peoples." On the very day on which "every decent worker was filled with deep sorrow over the death of Stalin," he testified to his hatred of other peoples by singing an "ambiguous hit tune."

To get caught comparing Nazi and Communist methods is a nasty crime in East Berlin. The district attorney asked for a two-year sentence against a man because "during a discussion in a tobacco store the defendant said: "Things aren't any better than under the Nazis—we still have concentration camps today." (A lenient court gave him only one year.)

Like the Third Reich, the DDR gives "training courses" to its young, preserving the Nazi name *"Schulungskurse"* for this activity. Every few months teachers ask their eight- or nine-year-old charges to draft militant resolutions about some international political problem. They will ask the President of the United States to stop his warmongering, or send petitions to the Secretary General of the United Nations. East German boys and girls are also marching again—or still—in step, dressed in uniforms, with drums beating. They shout "Friendship, Friendship, Friendship" as their parents shouted "Heil" on the Nuremberg Party grounds. Quite by chance I participated in a school celebration in Halle. It was the end of the school term and three hundred children were assembled in the school yard. A giant portrait of the East German Chief of State, Walter Ulbricht, dominated the scene. A loudspeaker amplified the voice of a twelve-year-old girl reciting a poem:

> Comrade Ulbricht,
> you hold Ernst Thälmann's* legacy
> in loyal hands.
> Those who disparage you
> blaspheme us,
> the Party and our class.
> There is no "But"
> and there is no "If,"
> it simply means you have to understand,
> or drag along
> stupid and blind
> in the wake of the Enemy.
> You stand
> at the pinnacle of our Party,
> you gave it all you had.
> She was and she is
> your Heart, your Blood. . . .

A few years ago, a kindergarten teacher discussed a class project in an article in a pedagogic journal entitled *New Education In The Kindergarten*. She called her article "Everyone Loves Walter"

* German Communist leader before the war, killed by the Nazis.

118

Objective: The children become acquainted with the picture of Walter Ulbricht, the Chairman of the State Counil. They pronounce the name correctly, they listen carefully when I tell them his story and are supposed to feel that he is a good person.

Subject: We look at the picture of the Chairman of our State Council.

Method: Look at the picture, pronounce the name. I recount: Walter Ulbricht is a good person, he was a worker. Berni's father Angela's mother, Frau M., I and all other good persons like him, he takes care of us. Practice the pronunciation of the name. (Some children say . . . Ullrich!) Hang his portrait above the classroom closet, put flowers into the vase next to it.

Point out to the children that we always want to put flowers in front of the picture of this good person.

Evaluation: The children listened very closely to me. All of them, except for one boy, pronounced his name correctly. I also had the impression that my stories evoked the first positive feelings in them toward Walter Ulbricht.

The National Socialist use of language was discussed shortly after the war by Professor Dolf Sternberg of Heidelberg in a now well-known study *Wörterbuch des Unmenschen* (Dictionary of the Inhuman). Sternberg showed how military jargon dominates under totalitarianism, how words are deployed like troops, and public consciousness is manipulated, and people incited to perform unheard-of deeds. There are parallels between the pseudo-messianic, militant, bombastic style of the Nazis' functionaries and the language of East German Communists. In the East German press appear such derogatory designations as "democratism." East German schoolchildren are taught to hate the *"Klassenfeind"* (class enemy) as they were once taught to hate the *"Rassenfeind"'* (enemy of the race). The two words sound similar, very similar, particularly when shouted by a mass chorus. You begin to feel that a new heresy is using the temple of an older, suppressed, vanished cult.

In 1965 a Professor Helmut Stolz complained in the East Berlin literary magazine *Sonntag* about West German "warmongers": "It is deplorable that they teach the West German population to hate the inhabitants of the DDR." His complaint was apparently considered ideologically dubious. In a footnote the editors remarked: "It is known to our youth that hatred can also be a very positive category." In the same journal a twenty-one-year-old student wrote about his life's goal: "I want to raise high the banner of hatred. Yes, hatred! Hatred which we require as one of our passions. Knowledge itself is not good, we also have to feel; hatred is part of feeling."

Nazi words crop up in West Germany because people are forgetful, incorrigible or tactless. In East Germany such words wear official uniforms; they are the linguistic tools of a policy. In the official vocabulary of the DDR there still exist "*volksfeindliche Elemente*" (enemies of the people) "healthy" and "decadent" art, "conspiracies of international financial circles," "*Grosskundgebungen*" (mass proclamations), or "*Feindsender*" (enemy radio stations)—all concepts that once were part of the Third Reich vocabulary and have survived its collapse. The word "party" has retained the pseudo-sacred quality it had before 1945. An East German Party song, in frequent use as recently as 1960, goes like this:

> She has given us everything,
> The sun, the wind and she was never stingy.
> Where she was, was our life
> What we are, we are because of her.
> The Party, the Party, She is always right
> and, Comrade, let it stay that way
> For if you fight for what is right, you are always right,
> against lies and exploitation.

Language leads its own mysterious existence. The old Bolsheviks in Russia so hated the name "police" (*policia*) that in 1912 they called their own police "militia." The Nazis called their police "People's Police," an appellation employed by the present regime. The German poet and playwright Bertold Brecht did not write a great deal after he returned from emigration to settle in the DDR. However, the following poem was found among his literary remains:

> The new ages do not begin at once
> My grandfather already lived in the new age
> My nephew probably will still live in the old one.
> The new meat is eaten with the old forks.
> The old stupidities came from the new antennas.
> Wisdom was handed from mouth to mouth.

This posthumously published poem could serve as a motto for the DDR.

9

The Disconnected Past

Ɔ N West Germany a vociferous minority makes strenuous attempts to settle accounts with the nation's past. Writers and teachers, clergymen and scholars seek—as they call it—to "overcome the past." It's an endeavor that gives the Federal Republic a peculiar intellectual fascination. Where else would a prosecuting attorney cite an obligation to disobey authority and its laws while at the same time a free defense attorney invokes this very authority to reduce his client's guilt? Elsewhere, these roles are usually reversed.

The literature of no other Western country is involved as intensively as the West German with events of the most recent past. In the better schools West German children learn about the Nazi era. Others find out about it only through TV. And inevitably, some ask their parents what they did during that time. West German literature continually mirrors and discusses this conflict between the generations.

Not so in the DDR. At first glance it would seem that this part of Germany has no problem at all with its past. Some former Nazis do occupy important positions, but none hold cabinet rank as has been the case in Bonn. The East German Chief of State has no close advisers who wrote official commentaries on the notorious Nuremberg racial laws, as Adenauer had in Hans Globke. East Germans claim total disassociation with the Nazi past. They may have retained the Prussian goose step but they have a new national anthem. It begins with the words:

> Risen from the ruins
> And turned toward the future,
> Let us serve your good cause,
> Germany, united Fatherland!
> . . . If we stand fraternally united,
> We will defeat the people's enemy.

As a symbol, it is certainly a less insufferable hymn than "*Deutschland, Deutschland über alles, über alles in der Welt*" that still longs for the old *Reich* and Nazi borders.

East Germany, like every Communist country, pays particular attention to children. In its efforts to raise the level of education, the DDR surpasses its much wealthier sister state. Tenth-grade education will soon be compulsory in East Germany. The normal education in West Germany still ends in the eighth-grade, and far too many children still attend village schools in which all eight grades are crammed into one room. The percentage of students attending universities is almost twice as high in the DDR as in West Germany. Fraternities and student confederations—once hotbeds of nationalism and racial delusions—have been abolished in the DDR; in West Germany they are up to much of their old mischief again.

As part of its official line, the DDR tries to acquaint young people with the crimes of the Nazi regime—bluntly, unadorned by legends and omissions as is sometimes the case in West Germany. In West Germany, children are occasionally told that "horror propaganda" should not be accepted at face value—things were not as bad as all that. In the DDR, instruction about the Nazi era begins in the lowest grades, sometimes as soon as kindergarten. It continued through primary and secondary school. This is incomparably more time than is devoted to the subject in West Germany.

Thus one would think that East Germany would easily "overcome." Yet the past has become hopelessly entangled in a doctrinaire thicket of Marxism. The mirror held up to the East Germans indeed reflects a much larger image than that presented to the West Germans. But it is a distorted mirror; the reflected image is not very believable.

There are many layers to a nation's past. East Germany has not even begun to face its most recent legacy—the blood-red Stalinist period—a process of cleansing comparatively well advanced in other Communist countries. Solzhenitsyn's novel about a Stalinist concentration camp (*One Day In the Life of Ivan Dennisovich*) is read everywhere in the Soviet Union, Poland, Hungary and Czechoslovakia, but not in the DDR. Perhaps because the old Stalinist clique is still in power here, Solzhenitsyn is considered too risqué for East German readers.

East German schoolbooks about Nazism bulge with superficial, misleading Party jargon: The "Junkers" and "industrial magnates" bear all responsibility. The Gestapo is the creation of "powerful financial circles"; Auschwitz and Treblinka are instruments of the Ruhr industry. An innocent reader would have to conclude that the bankers had converted Hitler and his cronies to racism in order to corner the stock exchange. Texts follow their analysis of the Nazi era with smug accolades to the East German regime for the happy state of present affairs. Since the Junkers have been chased out of West Prussia and Brandenburg, and banks have been nationalized, any possibility of reverting to Nazism is said to be averted once and for all.

I visited a high school in the East German city of Halle. The history teacher showed me the official "guideline" for the teaching of history. Page four reads: "The students should be imbued with firm convictions and precise knowledge of the inevitability of the transition from capitalism to Socialism and the decline of imperialism." I attended an eight-grade lesson on "fascistic dictatorship in Germany." Nine school hours a week have been reserved for this subject. The teacher, an ash-blonde woman roughly forty years old and wearing party insignia on the lapel of her smartly designed wool suit, summarized the events of 1933 somewhat like this: Ruhr industrialists, who nowadays determine the policies of Bonn, met in secret session with aristocratic officers in Berlin to discuss launching an aggressive war against the Soviet Union. They introduced a fascistic reign of terror "to prevent peace-loving workers and farmers from coming into power."

Question: Where in Germany are the workers and farmers in power nowadays?

Answer: In the German Democratic Republic.

Question: Where are the aristocrats and bankers governing?

Answer: In West Germany.

Question: What do they want?

Answer: War.

Later I spent a few hours in another school in a small Saxony district town. The school, made of brick grey with age, had been built during Kaiser Wilhelm's time. From the outside it looked as gloomy as the adjacent police barracks and prison, constructed at about the same time.

Twenty-one boys and girls sat at worn-out, narrow wooden desks. To the right of the blackboard hung a portrait of Walter Ulbricht in a gold frame, with the same small bouquet of flowers one finds before the images of saints in Catholic regions. I was allowed to ask questions.

Some looked curious, others laughed stiffly. Yes, they answered, I was the first Jew they had ever met.

No wonder! The DDR is almost "*judenrein*" (free of Jews). According to the head of the nearby Leipzig Jewish community, the last Jewish inhabitant of this little town had died three years ago. The DDR's only rabbi was busy elsewhere at the time, and since a Jewish burial service is no longer available, the dead man was interred by municipal gravediggers.

I asked the students if they knew what had happened to the Jews who lived here before the war.

"Many emigrated," one boy replied. "Others were killed in the war.'

But who killed them? "The Fascists."

Well, who were these Fascists? Germans? Spaniards? Did they come from the moon? Did anybody from this city have anything to do with it?

At this point the teacher interjected: "How did the Hitler dictatorship come into being?" Many hands were raised. A stocky boy with strikingly blue eyes began to recite a text, seemingly by heart:

> The fascistic terror regime in Germany started on January 30, 1933. Imperialistic elements of capitalism joined with *Wehrmacht* officers to exterminate the German Communist Party. They murdered many workers and Jews in the concentration camps. The people suffered terribly. Several attempts were made to shoot Hitler. But he was too well guarded.

One of the most astonishing discoveries you make on a trip through the DDR is that, in spite of candid treatment of Nazi atrocities in the schools and state-controlled youth movements, fewer people than in West Germany are prepared to confess even indirect guilt or responsibility. In the case of young people, this is, of course, a natural feeling. It is the attitude, real or professed, of older people and educators that shocks an observer from abroad. They claim to be the founders of a new social ethos. And yet a peculiar displacement of ideas seems to have occurred in their minds. Talking to them, one is struck with the impression that the DDR was an occupied country during the war, like Poland or France with an—it goes without saying, Communist—underground resistance pinpointing Allied bombers to Nazi objectives and blowing up military trains.*

East German Party functionaries regard the DDR as an entirely new state, totally unrelated to a past that continues to exist only in the West. "It is very simple. We take the future and leave the

---

* The Auschwitz Museum in Poland not only has Polish, Czech or Jewish pavilions but also a DDR pavilion. A Polish tourist guide on the Auschwitz Museum grounds, when asked about the DDR pavilion, turned pink with anger, "What nerve!" he said. Then, shrugging his shoulders, he added: "Orders from Warsaw. It's a crazy world, you know."

past to Bonn," is the answer of a DDR functionary when asked how East Berlin will celebrate an anniversary of the war's end.

Ordinary people in East Germany, usually so skeptical of all official propaganda, seem to take comfort in sharing this viewpoint. It frees them of all qualms of conscience. In fact here may be the regime's greatest propaganda victory.

An old Social-Democrat in Leipzig, dismayed by this elimination of historical consciousness, which he regards as morally false and politically dangerous, comments: "Young people in West Germany think of the Hitler era as something far in the past. Hitler is almost as much a part of history as Napoleon. That is understandable. But here the subject is treated as a Congo massacre, planned and executed by the same imperialist capitalists. That is both incomprehensible and inexcusable. This massacre has nothing to do with us personally—with the history of our country, our fathers, uncles, cousins, mothers, aunts and nieces. Not flesh and blood was responsible for Auschwitz, we are told, but an anonymous system which still exists in Bonn. No DDR citizen ever belonged to this system—that is, until he flees to the West. Then he becomes a Nazi too."

The Nazi era is relatively infrequently mentioned even in private conversation among intellectuals in the DDR. In stark contrast to West German literature, few East German novels, plays or poems do more than scratch the surface in mentioning the Nazi era. Novels such as Heinrich Böll's *Billiards at Half Past Ten* and *The Clown* or Günter Grass' *The Tin Drum* and *Dog Years*, all deeply involved with the problems of German guilt, simply do not exist in the DDR. In the DDR it is rare to encounter that peculiar sense of guilt which is characteristic of many West German intellectuals.

An exception which East German literateurs cite to refute this argument, in Franz Fühmann's *Das Judenauto*, a collection of probably autobiographical short stories. The title story gives a penetrating description of the psychopathological atmosphere among teen-aged students in a village school, that has produced a hysterical anti-Jewish outburst. The usual clichés of materialistic dialectics are conspicuously absent. Unfortunately only the title story lacks clichés; the other stories in this slim volume are well written but unequivocally doctrinaire Party tracts in the style of Ilya Ehrenburg's war stories.

With but few exceptions young East German writers avoid coming to terms with their historical legacy. Every second young West German writer tackles the subject in some way or other. DDR authors commit most of their energies to the fight for abstract art and Kafka—a fight long since won in Poland—and against *Socialist realism* the Party orders them to practice. The convenient sidestepping of historical issues perhaps explains why East German postwar literature is generally poor, compared with postwar literature in Poland and Hungary. No single truly great book has come out of the DDR since the death of Bertold Brecht. And even Brecht wrote nothing of importance following his return to East Berlin. The same is true of other writers who returned to East Germany after the war: Ludwig Renn and Arnold Zweig, Anna Seghers or Johannes R. Becher. The hope that masterpieces have been tucked away in desk drawers becomes increasingly unlikely. The DDR compares in this respect to Austria, where novelists have also gone silent. Austrians too have sought to sidestep their historical responsibility. Though there were more Nazis per square mile in Austria than in Germany most Austrians today look back on themselves as "victims of fascism." Art cannot thrive on lies.

The venerable novelist Arnold Zweig, whom I knew as a child in Israel during World War II, now lives in a pleasant little villa in a section of East Berlin that, for the most part, houses prominent personalities. He is a member of the People's Chamber (parliament) Zweig said: "Here in the DDR we have no historical legacy to overcome. The past goes on living in the West. But here we are all done with it. We didn't overcome it. We puked it out."

I asked Herr Zweig how.

"The big companies were dissolved and the Junkers thrown out. There are no Nazis left at the top here as over there. Yes, they say even Heinrich Lübke was one!"

"Please, don't get excited," Frau Zweig soothed the old man.

"But here too there are former Nazis in the army, police and government bureaucracy," I said.

"Certainly, but they have realized the political mistakes of their past," Herr Zweig replied.

"Can't that be true in Bonn, too?"

"Impossible," Herr Zweig retorted. "Nothing has changed over there. The same industrialists are back in power. It is a new form of Nazism."

A revealing little story is told by *Zeit* editor R. W. Leonhardt. Leonhardt visited the former concentration camp Buchenwald, near Weimar, East Germany. With his guide, Leonhardt viewed lampshades of human skin, manufactured at the order of the notorious camp commander Ilse Koch. The guide explained: "And that is what the spiritual legacy of West Germany looks like."

Why not the DDR's legacy too? Leonhardt sardonically makes the point that West Germany accuses the DDR of Nazi methods while the DDR villifies West Germany as a Nazi state. Summarizing he says: "If I were an outsider, a Martian or even a man from Madagascar, I would have difficulty warding off the impression that here are two siblings trying to evade the responsibility for a family disgrace in far too casual a manner—two brothers with little reason to love their father and shouting at one another: that was *your* daddy."

It is not surprising that Nazi victims receive no compensation from a state that considers itself free of guilt. A so-called victim of Fascism still living in the DDR does receive a priority in living quarters and can retire to a meager old age on a pension of about 450 marks at the age of fifty-five instead of the usual sixty. There are no other concessions, no payment as by West Germany, for stolen fortunes, for "aryanized" property, nor for time spent in concentration camps, for professional injuries or the like. A letter of protest from Dr. Nahum Goldman, the president of the Jewish World Congress, to the government of the DDR has remained unanswered since 1952.

The East German government makes it difficult for foreign Jews to claim restitution from West Germany. Provincial authorities are not allowed to verify the pre-war status of former Jewish inhabitants of East Germany; they are not allowed to provide the necessary documents and deeds which West German authorities demand prior to paying restitution. No leading Party member with whom I spoke could offer a satisfactory explanation for this heartless obstruction.

"Indemnification has to be paid where the crimes were committed and where the criminals are still today, namely in West Germany," declared Otto Winzer, the East German foreign minister, who claims Jewish descent himself. He was probably mindful of the fate of another Jewish member of the Politburo, Paul Merker, who was imprisoned in 1953 on charges of having planned a "dislocation of the property of the German people." The crime? Years before, as a refugee in Mexico, he had written: "The compensation for damages inflicted on Jewish citizens should be made to those who choose to return as well as to those who choose not to." Veteran Communist Erich Jungmann, the Jewish editor-in-chief of the Party journal *Volkswacht*, lost his post at the same time. He too had demanded that "all damages the German people have inflicted on the German Jews be compensated, in preference to all other damages.'"

A functionary in the East Berlin propaganda office gave me two reasons for the DDR's refusal to pay restitution. "First of all: In contrast to Bonn, we are not prepared to give the Jews [he said "Jews," not Israel] money to make arms deals with Bonn. . . . Second: We don't have to. We have eradicated Fascism in this part of Germany; a new society has come into existence. We offer this moral accomplishment to the victims of Fascism; it outweighs any material compensation."

Nor is it surprising in a country which evinces such lack of guilt that the Ulbrich visits to Cairo in the spring of 1965 should have occasioned a campaign of hate against Israel. Twenty years after Hitler's death it was very strange to hear, as I did, the East German Minister for Foreign Trade and Internal German Trade, Julius Balkow, state at a press conference in Leipzig that Israel is nothing but a "colonialist beachhead" planted by the United States amidst the peace-loving Arab world. There was no mention of the fact that Israel provided sanctuary for over a million refugees and surviving victims of Nazism.

Around the same time in Cairo, East German Prime Minister Willy Stoph called it "outrageous" that West Germany was furnishing Israel with arms. He saw nothing wrong with West German missile technicians developing intermediate-range rockets for Egypt. When a journalist reminded Stoph of the Nazi past of some of these missile technicians, Stoph called the question a brazen provocation, which "I must reject in the sharpest possible manner as an insult to the United Arab Republic."

Of the eighteen hundred-odd Jews remaining in the DDR, about sixteen hundred are members of the state-supported Jewish community. In 1946 there were almost twice as many. A few hundred escaped to the West, others died. The head of the Jewish community, an East Berlin official named Schenk, breaks down the community into age groups: 90 percent of all East German Jews are over fifty, 60 percent are sixty or more, and only 8 percent are under twenty.

Herr Hennig, chairman of the Leipzig Jewish community, gives the following count: before the War, 18,000 Jews lived in Leipzig, only 115 are left today—69 of them above sixty, 11 under thirty. The "final solution of the Jewish problem" will soon be completely realized, at least in this part of Germany.

10

The World of Yesterday

EAST BERLIN is open to foreign travelers from West Berlin. It is not so easy to enter other parts of the German Democratic Republic. The DDR is not so hermetically sealed off as China or Albania, but it is still less accessible than other European Communist countries. Several East European Communist countries now boast not only of abstract art, but also of tourists. Foreigners nowadays move about more or less freely in the Soviet Union, in Hungary, Rumania, Yugoslavia, Bulgaria and Czechoslovakia. Czechoslovakia and Austria have even reestablished a "limited frontier traffic." Citizens of some Western states receive visas right at the border. Rumania and Bulgaria have practically abolished visas altogether.

The DDR has not yet joined this trend. A series of new tourist hotels has been constructed there recently but tourism as it flourishes in Hungary, Bulgaria, Rumania, Yugoslavia or Czechoslovakia does not exist. Hotels are often half empty but it is possible to be turned away because they are "officially" booked up. This is one of the mysteries of a centrally directed economy; also, some rooms are permanently reserved for traveling functionaries and "delegations." Perhaps this will change one day, but at present it is impossible for a private person to travel through the DDR as through Hungary or Rumania. You must be "invited" or go as a businessman who wants to buy optical instruments in Jena or furs in Leipzig. Normally you must take a "guided tour" and thus enjoy the "privileges"—that is, restrictions—of a "delegation." Hotels must be booked and paid for in advance.

A laborious process enables West German citizens to visit their relatives in the DDR; the East German relative must apply for permission at his local police station. After a few weeks his application is either granted or refused. If granted, the relative in the West received his visa by mail. It is limited to a certain city or district, the route to and from the destination is exactly prescribed. Departure from the prescribed course requires special permission. If you are in Leipzig and want to go to nearby Dresden or Halle for the day you must first ask the police to put a special stamp in your passport. This is not always given.

Newspapermen have an even more difficult time. Many are forced to wait months for their visas. Some never get it. A special authority in East Berlin (Visitors Bureau) handles these cases, and applying for a ten-day visit at times is as intricate as negotiating an international treaty. Relationships with such foreigners seem to be matters of great import which can either help or endanger the state. Once finally in possession of a visa, journalists must travel with an official "guide" along a predetermined route with precisely fixed stops.

Until two or three years ago the guides were officials of the state security organizations. Now they are likely to be nice young writers and teachers who somehow get assigned to this duty in lieu of a regular job. It is even entirely possible sometimes to elude them, especially at night. Only then can you enter into conversation with willing, open people. Otherwise, the guide follows like a shadow. He is present at every interview and visit to every factory or city hall. He holds seemingly urgent telephone conversations with a central office in East Berlin. Unbelievable complications ensue if you ask for a small program change once on the way —if, for example, you want to visit a kindergarten or factory instead of paying scheduled visits to the public school and power plant. Journalists are discouraged from bringing a car; the central authority prefers to bind the traveler to rented car and chauffeur. This way the first guide also has a guide.

When I think of my two trips through the DDR—in February, 1965 (with guide) and in July of the same year as a tourist—I am immediately filled with dismal recollections. Frequent visitors to the DDR in the last few years report constant improvement in conditions of life. They say there is less pressure from above, more freedom and a new freer economic system. On a first visit, however, the DDR is a very sad place. I remember a strange desolation; also sudden police checks on lightly traveled roads. Heavily armed, slightly embarrassed young men halt the car, demand to see papers, know our destination. I remember main streets in Leipzig or Dresden that are almost deserted shortly after sundown; and sleepy provinical towns that look like yellowed picture postcards of the twenties. Most of the people you meet seem to live in a state of resignation to an irrevocable fate. They talk about the regime, about the almighty Party as of the weather. There are lonely people everywhere; nowhere have they affected me as in East Germany.

Most East Germans express vague hopes for reunification with West Germany. But at the same time they do not believe in it, perhaps once they did, but not any longer. A young couple was sitting next to me at the smooth wooden table in Auerbach's beer cellar in Leipzig, the cellar that provided Goethe with the setting for a famous scene in *Faust*. The young man was a chemist. The yearly spring fair was just taking place in Leipzig, and I asked him if that is why he was here.

"No," the young man replied, "I live in Leipzig."

"In that case all this noise must get on your nerves."

The young man said no, no it did not; in fact, he always looked forward to the fair even though he must sublet his living room for the duration because of lack of hotels. He looked at his girl and asked: "Should I tell him why I look forward to the fair?" "Better not," the girl answered. "I'm going to anyway," the young man said. "Look, my fiancée here lives in Nuremberg. She went over to the other side a few weeks before the Wall. Now we see each other only twice a year: once when we both can vacation in Hungary or Czechoslovakia, and here during the fair when its easy for her to get a visa."

In the old university town of Jena I struck up an acquaintance with a twenty-year-old student. He was a child of the new era. He complained bitterly about what the DDR lacks: intellectual freedom, modern literature and music, free elections, independent judges. I asked him how he reached such opinions, as he only knows the DDR and as his father, he admitted, had been a Nazi (today his father is a Communist). He looked surprised, "From books, of course," he replied. Which books? "Oh, Albert Camus or John F. Kennedy." Kennedy or Camus are not for sale in the DDR, but a few copies are always circulating among students. (It is said there are students who copy hard-to-obtain books in longhand, as in the Middle Ages.) Meeting in the home of a fellow student in private seminars, one student lectures about Camus, another about George Orwell or about the *nouveau roman*. A discussion will follow. "We are among friends, everybody knows one another, so there is no danger of being denounced. We speak openly," the student explained.

What happens if someone informs the police?

"It isn't as bad as it used to be. There was a time you could be brought to trial for agitating against the State. Sometimes it brought a prison term. It is still theoretically possible, but actually the worst thing that happens today is that you lose your scholarship, or that you're not allowed to register for the next semester, they just say there is no room. A commission of faculty members, labor union functionaries and Young Communists decides who may study and who may not.

"Intellectual freedom is not our only problem" he went on. "There are other things too. Students are constantly asked to 'volunteer' for industrial or agricultural work. Such work is supposed to strengthen the contact bewteen the intelligentsia and the working people. You help with the harvest or must work for a week in a tire factory. Of course this isn't so bad. The so-called political actions are much worse. When the Berlin Wall went up every student had to sign a promise to defend the frontiers of the DDR with his own blood. Several friends and I refused to sign."

Why? "Well, because I didn't believe in it. That 'blood' business repelled me. And what happened? Nothing at first. Then we were presented with a new declaration. We were simply asked to pledge to defend the DDR, this time without blood and so forth. We signed. Two months later we were suddenly told that this was not enough, we had to sign the first declaration as well. They threatened to expel us from the university. So we signed."

I asked the young man what he thought of reunification. He was personally for it but did not believe that it will ever happen. At least not during his lifetime. Why not? "Because as long as the two governments cannot communicate with each other any form of reunification is impossible. Each feeds on its hatred for the other." Nor did he think he would see a liberalization of living conditions inside the DDR. "It is possible in Hungary or Poland . . . those are not divided countries." The young man's pessimism struck me as indicative of the resignation you encounter frequently among young intellectuals in the DDR. He belongs to a different breed of men than that which mounted the barricades in Budapest in 1956. In front of the main building of Jena's Friedrich Schiller University we shook hands as we said good-bye. He hesitated a moment. "Don't think too badly of us," he finally said. "People here aren't bad. Only the regime is."

"How marvelous! These washing machines, and so cheap!" a Russian engineer whom I met in a Halle hotel, exclaimed. He spoke fairly good English. "Excellent *Autobahns!* I wish we had such roads in the Soviet Union." This engineer, who was visiting the DDR for the first time, was full of enthusiasm. He came from Smolensk where he supervised a power plant. He found the DDR ultramodern, was glad to be here and hoped to be able to come back soon.

But anyone who comes to the DDR from the West is overcome by the peculiar feeling that the calendar has been turned back thirty or forty years. Hazy pictures, vaguely remembered from old magazines, come to mind. A sense of *déjà vu* alternately touches or haunts you. West Germans, after a visit to the DDR will exclaim: "Oh yes, oh yes, that's how everything looked at one time." The reaction of *Zeit* editor Marion Dönhoff is typical of West Germans who revisit the DDR after twenty or thirty years. In a travelogue (*Journey to a Distant Land*) she speaks of "old Germany," which she rediscovered here of all places. The "Americanization," that is, the social and technical progress of West Germany is missing, she notes. "Sometimes you have the feeling "as though you were living (in the DDR) in a pretechnical age— not with respect to industrial equipment, which is in part very modern, but with respect to everyday life." The telephone book of Weimar (65,000 inhabitants) contains eleven pages. A West German city of the same size will list five times as many telephones.

Leaving the *Autobahn,* which was built during Hitler's time, one drives across the land on narrow country roads, passing through towns that seem to have last expanded in the twenties. Whitewashed suburban developments, as in the West, are almost completely missing. City and country are more sharply divided than in the West. Fewer urban conglomerations clutter the landscape, not because town and country planning is better but because construction of new buildings proceeds at a much slower rate. Heavy, old-fashioned horse-carts, laden with hay or passengers, clatter slowly over the cobblestone roads.

Small provincial towns can be cozy, as in France; picturesque, as in southern England or Italy; the little towns of Thüringia and Mecklenburg are neither. The houses, which don't belong to any one, are dilapidated because they belong to everyone; plaster is crumbling off the façades, courtyards and stairwells have a run-down look. An ancient streetcar dawdles along the main street of Eisenach. It was built around the turn of the century and elsewhere would be a museum piece by now. Zwickau, considered a "metropolis" with its 140,000 inhabitants, possesses hardly a bright streetlight. On the main street of Karl-Marxstadt (the former Chemnitz, 287,00 inhabitants) you find a few privately owned shops adorned with faded business signs of prewar vintage. A few old watches or radios are displayed in the small shop windows, pink, carefully folded lingerie, wretched-looking men's shoes and the like.

"Old-fashioned" too is the so-called Stalinist architectural style. A Soviet Union import, it was the building style prevailing in the DDR until the middle of the 1950's; it prediminates in many cities rebuilt after the war.

In his youth, Stalin must have subscribed to the German magazine *Gartenlaube*, which reflected the taste of the German *petit-bourgeois* before 1914. The similarities in style between that period and Stalin's time, between the Battle of Leipzig memorial and the pompous Red Army memorial in Berlin are striking. No matter which you stand in front of, you momentarily expect a torchlight parade or the grand entrance of a popular Wagnerian prima donna.

You see these hollow pompous edifices everywhere, blown up, disfigured, crenelated, adorned with towers and massive, ostentatious stone façades. It is the style in East Berlin, in Leipzig, in Halle, in the center of Magdeburg or in Dresden.

Herder, the philosopher, once called Dresden "Florence on the Elbe." In the broad Elbe valley bordered by gentle hills, Duke August the Strong of Saxony, also King of Poland, built a proud residence. In a single night in 1945, several weeks before the end of the war, the city sank into ruins. Large parts of Dresden are covered with ruins even today.

The number of deaths that night and the extent of the destruction are often compared with Hiroshima. East German propagandists use Dresden as their example of the "murderous cruelty" of Western imperialism.

The air attack on Dresden was the largest and most intensive conventional bombing attack in history. As time passes and tempers cool down, the military objective of the raid on Dresden appears more and more dubious. Tens of thousands of explosive and incendiary bombs were dropped here within a few hours. Between 36,000 and 130,000 people died. The exact figure can never be ascertained; thousands of refugees were in the city at that time. David Irving in a recent book, *The Destruction of Dresden*, talks about thousands of people sucked into the firestorms, cremated at one thousand degrees centigrade; after the attack the dead were found melted with the asphalt into a single pulp. Charred people lay in the cellars. Weeks after, corpses were still burned on huge funeral pyres. It was ten weeks before the end of the war when the survivors of Dresden tasted the same sweet stench of burning human flesh which Auschwitz survivors report hovered for years above their camp.

The Western side today claims the air attack was meant to support advancing Soviet troops, only seventy-five miles from Dresden at the time. The Eastern side replies that the attack on Dresden was meant to destroy an all-important railroad center and thus prevent the further advance of the Red Army toward the West.

The physical destruction of Dresden probably was not more extensive that that of Cologne or Hamburg. But contrary to Cologne or Hamburg, Dresden is still not rebuilt. Whereas the old part of Warsaw, which resembled that of Dresden in some respects, has been lovingly restored by the Poles, reconstructed Dresden looks ugly and dull.

Today Dresden has some 100,000 fewer inhabitants than before the war (503,859). Huge areas in the heart of the city and around the famous *Prager Strasse* are still uninhabited.

A red banner is attached to the façade of the city hall which was built in 1903, destroyed in 1945 and reconstructed in 1952: OUR FRIENDSHIP TREATY WITH THE USSR HELPS PREVENT ANOTHER DESTRUCTION OF DRESDEN. The office of Dresden's deputy mayor is stuffed with construction plans and models. In addition three different portraits of Ulbricht adorn the walls. "We haven't had it so easy as over there in the Federal Republic," he said, somewhat nettled (West Germans often accuse Dresden of having failed in its reconstruction.) "We've had a more difficult time . . . everything here was destroyed, nothing was leftover, literally nothing. . . . We first had to build factories to give people work, and housing, housing and more housing. At the same time, he said, the West had tried to undermine reconstruction, "they tried to steal our boys away from the Technical Institute so that we wouldn't have any engnieers." The Wall (he said "Protective" Wall) had improved matters.

As a souvenir of Dresden, the Deputy Mayor offered me an illustrated essay *The Dresden Inferno* by former Mayor Walter Weidauer. Weidauer is particularly eager to allay the suspicion that Dresden was destroyed on request of the Russians. On the contrary, he writes, Dresden was destroyed in order not to fall "undamaged into Russian hands." The attack was an Anglo-American sabotage of the Soviet offensive to liberate Germany. Weidauer also claims Dresden had originally been designated as a target for the first American atomic bomb. Delays in Los Alamos, he says, thwarted this plan at the last minute.*

"Dresdeners know what an atomic war means," the Deputy Mayor said. "People in the West only talk about 'megadeath' and 'overkill' but people in Dresden have already experienced it. That is why people are for peace and disarmament here."

I asked what the reaction of the population of Dresden was when the Soviets broke the voluntary atomic test ban in 1962 and exploded huge megaton bombs.

The Deputy Mayor straightened up in his chair. "Of course it was widely discussed" he said. The city administration even organized a few discussion evenings. How were the megaton explo-

---

* The German Nobel Prize winner Werner Heisenberg (today in Munich), who participated in the German atomic bomb project, reports that Field Marshal Göring asked him in the summer of 1944 whether an atomic attack on Dresden was possible. The reason for Göring's inquiry was a report from Lisbon to the effect that an American officer had warned a German agent that an atomic bomb would be dropped on Dresden unless Germany capitulated at once. Göring wanted to know whether Heisenberg considered this possible; the question caused Heisenberg a great deal of worry. On the one hand, Heisenberg was an opponent of the Nazis and looked forward to the defeat of Germany; at the same time he was one of the few people in Germany who had an inkling of the dreadful consequences of an atomic attack. He had no way of knowing precisely how far advanced the American preparations were. Had he said "No," and the attack taken place, he would have felt responsible for the loss of human lives; if he had affirmed the possibility and the attack not taken place, the Nazis would probably have thrown him into a concentration camp or murdered him as a saboteur. Heisenberg answered evasively. There is material here for a modern drama.

sions explained? "We made an attempt to make it clear to all comrades that in this case objectives had to be taken into account. The Soviets were testing nuclear weapons for the defense of peace."

The center of the city, which was most heavily destroyed during the air attack, is now scheduled to be rebuilt by 1970. I was told that huge apartment houses and hotels surrounded by green belts with underpasses for traffic are planned. The style will be "modern" from now on, not Stalinist, with a great deal of glass and prefabricated material. A model in the Mayor's office looked like a Marxist Miami.

Dresden's most famous building, the old *Zwinger*, has already been rebuilt. The magnificent baroque building was restored according to photographs and Canaletto paintings; the original plans had been lost. The restored *Zwinger* sits majestically along the Elbe embankment; surrounded by nothing but weed-covered ruins. It again contains the famous Semper Gallery, one of the most important European art collections. The Russians took the collection in 1945, returned it in 1958. It includes Raphael's *Sistine Madonna* and the *Madonna* of Holbein the Younger, Corregio's *Holy Night* and *St. George's Madonna*, Titian's *Venus*, Ruben's *Boar Hunt* and Del Sarto's *Abraham's Sacrifice*. Museums in Communist countries are normally crowded; those in the DDR are no exception. As I walked through the *Zwinger*, factory workers and farmers from nearby agriculture communes were guided from picture to picture. "With these wealthy, distinguished hunters, the painter is protesting against the unjust class differences of his time," was the museum guide's comment on a painting by Rubens. Or, ". . . As you can see, the master even painted his saints as full-blooded, healthy, vigorous men." To prevent a group of Magdeburg workers from getting too favorable an impression of the aristocracy, the museum guide added: "But August the Strong didn't hold the paintbrush in his hand, or the chisel, he was not the one who created these marvelous works of art, but skilled craftsmen and master painters who were rooted in the people."

Dresden's second best-known landmark, the Old Market, has also been reconstructed, but in contrast to the *Zwinger* no one can be proud of it today. Here the Communist puritans buried the old magnificence and, sadly, it is still visible as it was only in the great paintings of Dresden by Canaletto. Today, Dresden's Old Market lies beneath a jaundiced mixture of Nazi *Führer* balconies and petit-bourgeois pseudo-gothic. Even the guide finds it "horrible." Grotesque façades surround the huge plaza like backdrops of a bad comedy. The day I was there a long banner announced in white letters on a red background: WORKERS IN THE BRIGADES AND COMMUNES OF SOCIALIST WORK! BE PIONEERS IN THE FIGHT FOR HIGHEST SCIENTIFIC-TECHNICAL STANDARDS! WORK, LEARN AND LIVE SOCIALISTICALLY!

Dresden ruined or rebuilt is a kind of open-air museum. As Geoffrey Scott has observed: "The history of civilization leaves its truest, because most unconscious, traces in architecture." First there are the magnificent buildings of the two Augusts, sensual baroque lords, whose gaze was directed southward to Italy, to the "land where the lemon trees bloom." Then there are the grey-black colossi of the 1870's and 1880's that still dominate many quarters, and the stigma of the industrial revolution: dark, narrow long blocks of flats with gloomy, filthy courtyards. The tenements of Dresden must have played a significant role in the development of nineteenth-century Germany Socialist thought. Marxists began to feel then all construction would have to be nationalized and landlords dispossessed if workers were to receive decent housing.

Then the Hitler period begins in Dresden. Its greatest showpiece that has remained intact is the main office of the *Deutsche Reichsbahn:* a great stone box with massive cement pillars at the corners, decorated with runic letters. Ferocious-looking Imperial Eagles hover above fortress-like embrasures. Beneath a row of firing slits hangs another banner: FIGHT FOR THE SIGNING OF A PEACE TREATY. A second one: ALL OUR STRENGTH IN THE FIGHT FOR SOCIALISM. The exhortation "fight" is used surprisingly often in the "First German Peace State." What do the words "fight" or "peace" mean? After the tower of Babel was built people no longer understood each other because the same things had different names. Today we seem to misunderstand one another because different things have the same names. Five hundred years before Christ, Confucius said:

If something is wrong with the language, what is said is not what is meant; if what is said is not what is meant, works are not created, and morality and art do not flourish; if morality and art do not flourish, justice is not appropriate; if justice is inappropriate, the people do not know where to put hand and foot.

On through history's museum, through rubble fields, ruins heaped upon ruins like receipts in a transcendental clearing house. Eventually you reach the new southern suburb, Housing Installation II. Housing Installation II dates from the "time of the personality cult," my guide somewhat apologetically explained. "Time of the personality cult" is a euphemism for the Stalin era. It is used in many ways. One says "personality cult in the police" and means terror; "personality cult in industry" means misplanning; there are even references to the "personality cult in small livestock breeding" or in road building. The richly sculptured façades of Housing Installation II are reminiscent of Moscow subway stations; it would be difficult to choose in which of the two you would prefer to live. Symbolic figures crouch beneath gabled roofs, but plaster is crumbling as in the ruins, the floors are buckling, the stairs are either broken or already worn. A young girl was coming up from the cellar with a bucketful of coal. There was no central heating, but expensive mosaics decorated the lobby.

The tour of inspection ends in the Socialist borough of Striesen, the most recently constructed part of town. It is evident that many things have indeed improved during the last few years. We looked at a beautiful new whitewashed building with large windows and wide balconies. A tall, seventeen-year-old boy was taking his small motor bike apart. He told us his father was employed in a soap factory, his mother as a cleaning woman in City Hall. He will receive his baccalaureate the same year. Then, "if everything goes well," he said, he will go on to study chemistry. His older brother was already studying at the Dresden Technical University. We talked a while, then he mounted his motor bike and putt-putted off down the tree-lined street. Proudly the guide said: "These are are new young people. They are well off."

The more one is exposed to drab, everyday life in the DDR, the more pleasant it is to flee into remote periods of the past, to islands of culture that lie in the muddy sea of party uniforms, banner signs and "Ernst Thälmann Housing Installations." These scattered islands remind you that it was in this part of the divided country that some of Germany's greatest cultural achievements were attained.

In Leipzig's St. Thomas Church a few fresh flowers lie on the simple stone slab marking the grave of Johann Sebastian Bach. Upstairs in the gallery stands the large organ on which he played the the music that will be heard when all Party songs of the past and present will have been forgotten. The church is overcrowded when the St. Thomas choir sings Bach's cantatas in the evening. Outside, the heavy back limousines of the East Germany's "new elite" drive past; high functionaries are being chauffeured to a gala reception at the Leipzig Spring Fair. Comfortably, the mighty repose in their back seats, their stony faces half hidden behind curtained windows.

In Jena one drives past Schiller's house, a rather modest building compared to Goethe's home in nearby Weimar. Schiller, Germany's "national poet," is still misused by nationalists, though it was he who warned his countrymen against being super-patriotic. Patriotism, as he put it, was "seemly only for primitive people"; it was the German's duty to "do the necessary and humane through exercising the power of reason." Not far from Schiller's house is Jena University, where he taught history. The subject of his first lecture was: "What is the meaning of, and what is the end of universal history?" Later, Karl Marx was to receive his doctorate at this school.

At Wartburg castle, high above the city of Eisenach, one can inspect the cell where Luther translated the Bible. In Wittenberg, halfway between Leipzig and Berlin, is the large palace church against whose door he nailed his "fifty-nine theses." "The church was spared by the war," recounted a resident, an older, vigorously built man wearing a dark topcoat. He himself was away in the army, but "people told me afterward what it had been like. Luckily the Russians bypassed the town." I asked him where he had spent the war. "I had the honor of serving the Fatherland as a soldier in both World Wars," he replied. "Surely you are being sarcastic when you mention honor?" I asked. "But no, not at all," the man answered, "you are too young to understand that."

"People still support the church," the sexton said. Do many

children come to confirmation? Or do they prefer the Communist attempt at a substitute "youth initiation?" "One can refuse the youth initiation," he answered. What happens then? "Nothing."

Why don't more people refuse to be initiated if that is possible?

"Well, you see, that always seems to be the problem in Germany," the sexton replied.

In Weimar, in front of the theater, Privy Councillor Goethe and unsalaried History Professor Schiller stand bronze hand in bronze hand on a stone pedestal. Behind the statues, on the left and the right sides of the theater entrance are two plaques. The one on the right commemorates the unfortunate Weimar Republic that was proclaimed in this building in 1919; the one on the left is dedicated to the DDR whose task it is to find the way "to true, wise forms of humanity."

In Goethe's home at *Frauenplatz* ("the place a noble man set foot on is consecrated") I followed a large group of Bulgarian Kolkhos members who were here to learn about the "progressive bard" of the German bourgeoisie. Gothe's house was hit during an air attack on February 9, 1945. The restored building was reinaugurated in 1949. The front of the house holds the poet's stately reception rooms, decorated with plaster casts of antique sculptures. In the back part is his simple, spartan working room: grey, undecorated walls, a wooden standing desk at which he wrote *Faust*. The house also contains his large collection of art and rare objects. Was there anything this universal genius was not interested in? Here are frescoes, fossils, paintings, seeds and flowers, optical instruments, astronomic tables, copies of old sculptures, engravings, and five thousand volumes of his private library; German, English and French books, books written in Hebrew, Greek and Sanskrit. From Paris, the first edition of the Great Encyclopedia, from London, *Childe Harold's Pilgrimage*. One senses how unified Europe must once have been and the extent to which East Germany had been a part of it.

Today it says on plaques in the Goethe house: ". . . *Faust* mirrors the entire history . . . of the bourgeois emancipation during the Goethe era." The object of *Faust* is "to describe the life of different classes and their struggles during the transition from feudalism to

144

capitalism . . . it is a picture of the social and ideological struggles of his time."

Another plaque tells us that Goethe, in *Werther*, meant to "defend the bourgeois against the arrogance of the nobility who wasted the meager income from the land on feasts and hunts." Goethe, whose well-known servility towards the aristocracy was not his most attractive trait, is represented here as a pioneer of the common people. The fact that he himself made great efforts to be raised to the nobility, is not mentioned.*

Goethe as one of Duke Carl August of Weimar's ministers, is pictured as a kind of forerunner of Bertrand Russell: a man relentlessly working on behalf of disarmament, to reduce the Duke's army from 532 to 293 men. But "his reforms were thwarted by the opposition of the nobility."

The poet fled to Italy. Why? Because "his insight into irreconcilable class conflicts forced him to flee Weimar."

Upon his return to Weimar, "problems of the bourgeois Capitalist society" become the "center of his creative work." . . . In *Elective Affinities* "marriage problems are viewed in the light of emerging capitalist tendencies.". . . In *Wilhelm Meister's Wanderjahre*, Goethe discusses his "conflict with capitalist society, its schism between intellectual and physical labor."

The Goethe museum gives a room-by-room chronological presentation of the poet's life. By the twenty-third room Goethe has finally progressed to where he is "ideologically ready" to write *Faust*. This work, we learn, "anticipated the DDR as a society free of the insoluble conflicts" of capitalism and feudalism.

Responsible for all this nonsense is a "Socialist study group of scholars" who supervise the house and the museum by order of the government. The study group goes about its tasks "from a viewpoint of historical and dialectical materialism." There is a saying that no committee has ever written a sonnet. Goethe himself on the same subject (in a conversation with Heinrich Luden in December, 1813, a difficult time for German freedom): "I have often felt acute pain at the thought of the German people, who are so

---

* In the *Gentle Epigrams* of 1825 Goethe wrote: The common people are a burden to me, / they're never of one mind, / because they hate the nobles, / they think they are right.

worthy as individuals and so wretched as a whole." (This quotation, underlined in pencil, is on display in Room 19.)

By car it is only a few minutes from Goethe's house to the former concentration camp Buchenwald. Between the two rises a huge barracks complex of the Soviet Army. The close proximity of Goethe, Soviet Army and Buchenwald displays in one cosy valley the dismal situation into which the Germans have maneuvered themselves and Europe during the last thirty years.

Of the quarter million people imprisoned at Buchenwald, fifty-six thousand died. Here is a small brick building with a high chimney; inside is a rectangular room. Here the prisoners were placed face forward against the wall, told that their height was to be measured. Instead they received a shot in the neck. Right around the corner was the crematorium.

A few steps further on is a storage room used for the SS personnel kitchen. Outside can be seen the charred trunk of an oak. When the tree still stood, it was called "Goethe oak" because the poet liked to rest and meditate there during his walks. A little plaque in the middle of the former concentration camp reminds you of this. "I can conceive of no crime I could not have committed," Goethe once said and probably did not know what he was saying.

The International Buchenwald Committee built a small museum here during the 1950's. It is visited by many schoolchildren from the DDR. Previously, between 1945 and 1950, Buchenwald served as a concentration camp for opponents of the Communist regime. The exhibition hall displays some of the tools of the torturers: whips and thumbscrews, sticks and meat hooks on which corpses were hung up like slaughtered cattle. There are letters from various cities competing with Weimar for the honor of having the concentration camp in their immediate proximity. Another Nazi document shows the value of camp inmates; their worth dead and alive:

Average daily wage	RM 6.00
minus food	RM .60
minus clothing amortization	RM .10
	RM 5.30
average life span	
9 months = 270 Days =	RM1,431

Proceeds from the rational utilization of corpses:

1. Gold teeth
2. Clothing
3. Valuables
4. Money

minus cremation costs	RM 2.
average net income	RM 200
total income after 9 months	RM 1,631
plus proceeds from bones	
and utilization of ashes	

Lamp shades of human skin, manufactured by order of woman SS Commandant Ilse Koch, are another show piece of the Buchenwald museum.

A fifty-meter-tall bell tower stands on the slope above the museum; the bells toll during memorial services given by the International Buchenwald Committee. A cast-iron, old main gate of the concentration camp reads: "TO EACH HIS OWN," a counterpart to the Auschwitz gate with its inscription "WORK MAKES FREE," Eighteen inscribed pillars stand along an "Avenue of the Nations," leading to three mass graves. I walked down the Avenue with a former prisoner who now is an employee of the "National Memorial," past the reliefs depicting resistance in the camp. He recounted the story of a three-year-old child who came into the camp with its father in 1944; he was hidden in the clothing storage room by prisoners and saved.

After the liberation, traces of father and son had been lost. Their names were Zacharias and Stefan-Jerzy Zweig. Subsequently their story became known through Bruno Apitz's novel and movie *Naked Among Wolves*. In 1964 both were found in Israel, where the child, Stefan-Jerzy, had grown into a vigorous, tall all-star player on the national handball team. In February, 1964 a touching reunion was arranged in Buchenwald between the young man and former prisoners who had hidden him and loved him like their own child.

The next day I took the train back to West Germany. The soft hills of Thüringia slowly rolled by. Frail old men and women crowded the train. They too were traveling to the West. A few weeks earlier the DDR had given permission to its pensioners, most in financial strain anyway, to visit their relatives in West Germany. Everyone had to debark at the border. Foreign passports were quickly inspected. The old men and women were carefully searched; one elderly man and a hard-of-hearing woman were taken in for a physical inspection. Paltry cardboard valises and baskets were emptied out, wristwatches duly registered to prevent people from selling them in the West. Then the train rumbled across a steel bridge. Barbed wire, machine guns, booted guards came into sight. We were inside the death-strip. Then, rolling corn fields, farmhouses, shining new cars. The West German border control takes only a few minutes.

11

Old and New on the Rhine

ROLANDSECK is a picturesque little hamlet on the Rhine, dominated by an ivy-covered legendary medieval ruin. Here the river curves and flows dirty and evil smelling toward the West. "Foolishness grows on the Rhine," Heine wrote; he meant the heady wine that grows "on green hills" along the riverbanks.

This was early in the nineteenth century; the river was not yet the prime object of a singularly pseudoreligious, superpatriotic folly. But as the century wore on and some of the roots of Nazism were planted in the poetry, education and politics of the age, the Rhine was to become almost as "sacred" to Germans as the Ganges is to religious Indians. It was "Germany's river," not just Germany's border with France.

Sixty or seventy years ago Germans spoke of "Father Rhine" the way Americans speak of "Old Glory." A wet idol, calling for sacrifice of "blood and life." Germany was said to be "as rich in heroes' blood as is the Rhine in water's flood." Germans once sang:

> A rousing call like thunder
> like the changing of swords and the clashing of waves
> At the Rhine, the Rhine, the German Rhine.

In poetry, the "proud, beautiful, woman Germania" stood at the Rhine, "her body boldly bent forward"; beyond the river's bank, "every man's name was Enemy."

A long section of the river—entirely German between 1890 and 1918 and again between 1940 and 1944 forms the frontier with France. German nationalists who continue to demand a revision of postwar borders in the East, seem to have accepted, for the time being at least, the loss of Alsace-Lorraine. Today the Rhine is Europe's longest sewer. West Germany's booming industrial cities empty foul-smelling sewage into the once-sacred stream; the few fish that still live in the Rhine taste of phenol. Cement factories, quarries, refineries and railway lines disfigure long stretches of the river bank.

Urbanization and industrialization are altering the picture post-card quality of the Rhine landscape. Yet at Rolandseck, on the so-called middle-Rhine, there still are stretches of that same landscape which has enchanted poets ever since the onset of romanticism. Byron's "blending of all beauties, streams, and dells/Fruits, foliage, crag, wood, cornfield, mountain vine/and chiefless castles breathing stern farewells." Romantic ruins perch on crazy ridges, vigorous cliffs descend steeply to the water. A delicious wine is grown along the banks and here and there snuggles an intimate little town, a cluster of cozy wood-frame houses and old trees, as though transplanted from a fairly tale.

It is a landscape pregnant with legends. The ridges on the bank opposite Rolandseck are called *Siebengebirge* (Seven Hills), the setting for Grimm's *Snow White*. Downstream a bit on the right river bank, a dark bulky cliff juts three hundred and nineteen meters up above the hazy river. This is *Drachenfels* (Dragon's Rock), one of the most frequently climbed mountains in Germany (3 million visitors per year). Here Siegfried allegedly killed the dreadful dragon, bathing his body in the monster's blood, thus becoming invulnerable (except for that one place on which a linden leaf had settled down). Today visitors munch curry sausages, drink beer, buy funny straw hats made in Italy, and have their pictures taken in front of a stone likeness of the dragon. Little Dragons made in Hong Kong are on sale diagonally across from the *Drachenfels*—this unfortunately is no legend—at a resort called Godesberg where Hitler and Chamberlain met in 1938, before signing the Munich Agreement. Here the fate of Czechoslovakia was sealed and Hitler encouraged to new adventures. From the Hotel Dreesen at Godesberg, Chamberlain looked out at the *Drachenfels*. "What a wonderful view!" he is said to have exclaimed. The Dreesen still exists today; the view from the hotel terrace is still wonderful. It is a favorite place for foreign ambassadors to Bonn to hold cocktail parties, in the midst of a fairy-tale landscape.

Today new housing developments sprout up almost next door to the Dreesen; northward toward Bonn proper their monotonus functionalism presses hard upon the dignified villas of nineteenth-century industrialists and rentiers who wanted only to retire on the banks of the Rhine. A few whitewashed new office buildings fly the black-red-gold flag of the Federal Republic of Germany. Godesberg blends into Bonn, the old university town on the Rhine, at present the capital city of West Germany. The heart of the old city, which was destroyed during the war, has been completely rebuilt; there is a beautiful small city hall on the market square, a few narrow, crooked alleys, a lovely church, an old palace that today belongs to the university. In the *Bonngasse* there stands a narrow-chested house in which Ludwig van Beethoven was born in 1770.

On the embankment a few cannons from the Franco-Prussian war of 1870 aim outwards to the Rhine; close by there is a memorial to the Bonn professor and poet Ernst Moritz Arndt. Arndt was the author of a famous poem: "The God who let iron grow did not want slaves." Arndt, though a humanist, unwillingly served the worst of causes. His emotional outpourings helped prepare the way for Hitler:

What is the German's fatherland?
Is it: Prussia or the Swabian's land?
Is it where the grape glows in the Rhine?
Where the seagulls skim the Baltic brine?
Oh no, more grand
Must be the German's fatherland!

What is the German's fatherland?
Bavaria, or the Styrian's land?
Is it where the Master's cattle graze?
Is it the Mark where forges blaze?
Oh no, more grand
Must be the German's fatherland!

What is the German's fatherland?
Now name for me the mighty land!
Ah, Austria surely it must be,
So rich in fame and victory.
Oh no, more grand
Must be the German's fatherland!

What is the German's fatherland?
Now name at least that mighty land!
"Where'er resounds the German tongue
Where'er hymns to God are sung!"
That is the land
Brave German, that thy fatherland!

That is the German's fatherland!
Where binds like oak the clasped hand,
Where truth shines clearly from the eyes,
And in the heart affection lies,
Brave German, this thy fatherland!

That is the German's fatherland
Where scorn shall foreign triflers brand,
Where all are foes whose deeds offend
Where every noble soul's a friend:
Be this thy land
All Germany shall be the land!

Bonn's young lovers meet after dark at Arndt's memorial near the old cannons. Arndt's home serves as a museum, but it is generally empty. That is about the extent of historical sites and sights of this city.

Bonn has been the political capital of West Germany since 1948. But West Germany has several capitals. Economy, finance, art, press and society each have one or several centers—in Düsseldorf, Frankfurt, Munich, Hamburg or Stuttgart—all larger than Bonn in both area and population. Bonn is the center of the federal administration. That is not quite right either. Some administrative and judicial national headquarters are located elsewhere, such as the Federal Supreme Court (Karlsruhe) or the Federal Bureau of Investigation (Cologne). Bonn, to be quite exact, is the seat of federal ministries and the legislature.

Bonn's career as a federal capital began on September 1, 1948. On that day the new (West) German Parliament was inaugurated —for lack of a place more suitable—in the Bonn zoological museum. Surrounded by enormous skeletons, stuffed bears, monkeys and Siberian wolves, members of the new parliamentary council took their seats. They gathered to codify a democracy introduced shortly before on Allied bayonets, like the monarchy into France after the fall of Napoleon. They came from all Western zones of occupation and called themselves "the German people in the states of Baden, Bavaria, Bremen, Hamburg, Hessen, Lower Saxony, Northrhine-Westphalia, Rheinland-Pfalz, Schleswig-Holstein, Würtemberg-Baden and Würtemberg-Hohenzollern." This underlined the confederate character of the new state and counteracted the old centralist concept of the Reich. The founding fathers of West Germany agreed upon "a new order" but for a "time of transition" only, until the day of reunification with the Soviet-occupied zone, later the DDR, took place.*

The Bonn inauguration of September 1, 1948, though solemn in the extreme, was in many respects an amusing improvisation. Today participants smile even as they recall it. The mammoth skele-

* The provisional character of the West German state is deliberately built into the Constitution drawn up at that time. Article 146 states: "This Basic Law becomes invalid on the day on which a constitution, freely decided upon by the entire German people, goes into effect."

tons in the hall of the zoological museum had been scantily clad in brown wrapping paper, a stuffed giraffe was hidden behind sheets. An orchestra played Beethoven's *Leonora Overture*. There was much pathos, very little pomp and circumstance at the premiere of of a new state.

Nor is Bonn very different today, nineteen years later. Politicians and higher officials no longer take a streetcar to their offices, but are deposited by chauffeurs in black liveries and heavy limousines. The Alexander-König-Museum again serves the study of zoology; Parliament has its own building. But the face of the small Rhenish provincial city has not changed much. This little residential town that rules a modern industrial and military power of almost sixty million inhabitants, is one of the oddest, most improbable capitals imaginable. With less than 150,000 inhabitants (at least thirty-five West German cities are larger) Bonn is smaller than Sofia, duller than Helsinki; it is as if San Remo was the capital of Italy or Bath the capital of Great Britain. It is one of the ironies of history that Bonn resembles Vichy, to which the victorious Germans banished the French Government in 1940. Bonn like Vichy is a spa.

Bonn is sometimes compared with The Hague. But the comparison is not appropriate. The Hague lies at the sea, it inhales the great wide world. Bonn exhales the air of provincialism and has less of an international flavor than any other European capital. Perhaps this is why Bonn's views of the world at times seem so detached from reality. Huge maps hanging on the lobby walls of Parliament give the impression that nothing has changed in Europe since 1937; territories east of the Oder-Neisse line are still part of Germany, merely noted as under temporary "Polish administration." Nor can the Berlin Wall be found. The second German postwar state is simply called "Soviet-occupied zone." Alsace-Lorraine, at least, is unequivocally recognizable as belonging to France.

The Cold War atmosphere in Bonn is a departure from other NATO capitals. The Cold War, as a holy crusade against the "Bolshevik Anti-Christ," waning in Washington even during John Foster Dulles lifetime, is still very much alive here. One reason for this of course, is that Germany is the only NATO country

154

where the Cold War is also a civil war. Germany is a divided country. Dulles' demand to "roll back the Iron Curtain" naturally has greater meaning to Germany than in France, Italy or England.

Thus, Bonn was and still is considerably slower than other Western capitals to notice the decline of Stalinism and gradual evolution of a decentralized group of nations in Eastern Europe, nations that are increasingly asserting their independence from the Soviet Union. It is still difficult for many Bonn officials and politicians to understand the profound and historically well-founded mistrust of Poles or Czechs toward Germany—especially a mighty, reunited one. Rather than allay this mistrust, and thus to encourage Warsaw or Prague to exercise a greater degree of independence from the Soviet Union, the policy of Bonn has at times intensified it. Some officials have even talked themselves into believing that the government of Poland is not really interested in a formal recognition by Germany of the finality of the present border, for fear that peace on the German front might undermine the Communist government's hold over the people. It is not that Bonn politicians are aggressive or malicious; they are rather insensitive, unimaginative and narrow minded. Bonn hesitated to ratify the atomic test ban treaty in 1963, not because Bonn—like China—wanted to test but because the DDR, which cannot be acknowledged in any manner or form, was among the signatories of the treaty.

In 1965 Bonn sought to make the international nuclear agreement dependent on "progress" in the solution of the German question. The West German government felt misunderstood and deceived when the Western allies refused to accept this formula in dealing with the Soviet Union. Twenty-two years after the war, West Germany is still, in a very profound sense, alone in the world.

Bonn was honestly surprised when the first West German Ambassador to Israel was met by demonstrators—weeping former concentration camp inmates who had last heard the German national anthem in Auschwitz. When these same demonstrators rose in protest against the playing of the same German hymn in front of the President's house in Jerusalem, West German

Vice-Chancellor Erich Mende called it "Fascist-Bolshevist methods." Bonn was just as astonished and disconcerted when Israel only reluctantly accepted a former Wehrmacht officer and Knight's Cross recipient as first ambassador of a new, different Germany—even though he had not been a Nazi himself. These instances do not show a maliciousness, but more an estrangement from the world, a lack of sensitivity and political intelligence which dumbfounds foreigners in Bonn. Instead of the arrogance and megalomania of old Prussia, the Bonn government nowadays merely displays a certain tactlessness. The leading emotion in Bonn is probably self-pity. Officials continually regret that the world shows so little understanding of the "difficulty" in prolonging the statute of limitations for Nazi war criminals. What seemed obvious to most outsiders was seen by Bonn officials as an unjustified demand.

Bonn has none of the famous "champagne air" of old Berlin. Sitting in the ditch of the Rhine plain, it has the oppressive, exhausting climate of a laundry. That is why so many of its inhabitants are said to suffer from circulatory ailments, apathy and tiredness. One hears constant complaint of headaches or dizziness.

As a capital, Bonn remains a product of embarrassment, of chance and of improvisation: a modern power center grafted upon a small university and pensioners' town. Government, town and university lead neatly separated lives in three different social ghettos. Politicians and those that surround them know very little about the city, frequently less than about Stuttgart or Berlin from whence they came ten or fifteen years before. Students and citizens are not much better informed about the goings on in Parliament. It is something like Washington in this respect, but Washington, while grafted onto a province, was at least planned as a capital.

In this peculiar capital on the Rhine, sheep and lambs graze on meadows between the huge buildings of Parliament and the Chancellor's modest villa. Sitting in the Parliament restaurant, engrossed in high politics—one can suddenly hear a rooster crowing. The London *Times* once described the nearby British embassy as "Her Majesty's only mission in a wheatfield."

Trains stop for only one or two minutes at the modest Bonn railroad station. Express trains usually do not stop at all in small cities; they stop in Bonn seemingly to honor it as the capital.

The railroad tracks divide the city. Grade-crossing gates go up and down one hundred and twenty-eight times a day, each time stopping all traffic. *Time* magazine once figured out that the gates are closed for twenty out of every sixty minutes; the worst possible traffic jams naturally result. The railroad station at which the West German president occasionally must receive foreign dignitaries had only a single porter until recently, a veteran with one hand.

Army barracks and other inadequate buildings still—nineteen years after creation of the Federal Republic—"provisionally" house many government offices. Since Bonn with its total area of 7,731 acres is too small, its ministries and foreign embassies are scattered over the surrounding area. Over half of the more than eighty foreign missions are located outside of the capital, mostly in the little neighboring town of Bad Godesberg. The Swiss Embassy is housed as far away as Cologne; the Ministry of the Interior and Ministry of Housing are almost sixteen miles apart from one another.

The capital has only three Class "A" hotels, of which two are hardly more than "better family boarding houses." One—the Stern hotel—is in the marketplace. When the president's official car comes to fetch a newly arrived ambassador for the presentation of credentials at the presidential villa, it must make its way between fruit and vegetable stands. The president receives visitors at the Villa Hammerschmidt, a small pretty house on the bank of the Rhine, built in the classical style and surrounded by well-groomed flowerbeds. A single policeman stands at the gate. The villa is really only for receiving, and not too many at once. West Germany is one of the world's wealthiest countries, but the president cannot invite more than sixteen guests to a banquet. There is no room for the president to live; he resides in an apartment on the nearby Venusberg and drives every morning to his office.

After nine or ten o'clock in the evening, Bonn is as deserted as its counterpart, East Berlin. Night life is confined to one concert hall, one theater, fourteen movies houses and two or three little bars whose chief attractions are a few strip-tease acts. A local joke has the *Bundeshaus* doormen replying to a delegate's query about Bonn night life: "Sorry, the lady is in Cologne tonight."

These provincial airs astonish the foreigner, drive the local bureaucrats to despair and provide the political cabarets (Bonn

itself, of course, has none) with an inexhaustible stream of anecdotes. Improvisations—such as housing the *Bundestag* in an awk-
wardly rebuilt women's seminary seem to be intentional;—they
emphasize the "provisional" quality of this capital, a caretaker for
Berlin. In 1948 three other cities—Stuttgart, Frankfurt and Kassel
—campaigned for the new government seat. But something too
lasting might have been interpreted as writing off Berlin (in many
eyes an act bordering on high treason). Bonn's advantage was that
it could never give this impression. For years, Parliament refused
to appropriate money to enlarge ministerial buildings or even the
Bundestag (Parliament). Each modernization or new office building must not appear as an "immortalization" of Bonn, as the capital;
the result, of course, reflects this attitude.

Personal reasons also apparently played a role in Bonn's selection.
Just as a swampland on the Potomac became the capital of the
newly created United States of America because the first President
had an estate in nearby Mount Vernon, the proximity of Bonn to
Rhöndorf, West German Chancellor Konrad Adenauer's home is
said to have been a factor in choosing the little university town as
the seat of the Federal Government. Finally, Bonn was much less a
stronghold of the Social-Democratic opposition than, for example,
Frankfurt or Kassel.

Looking back, it seems doubtful that Adenauer ever regarded
Bonn as only provisional. He seems to have worked consciously to
move the political center of gravity from the Protestant East to the
Catholic West. As early as 1946 he advised against picking Berlin
as a capital whether East Germany was Communist or not, whether
Berlin would be partitioned or not. In an interview on November
30, 1946, Adenauer claimed that Berlin was too Prussian. "We in
the West reject the Prussian spirit . . . the German capital should
rather lie in the southwest than so far east in Berlin; the new capital
should be in the vicinity of the river Main, where Germany's windows are wide open to the West. If Berlin becomes the new capital,
we will never be able to still the suspicions of the rest of the world.
He who makes the new capital in Berlin revives the spirit of
Prussia." Sometime later Adenauer again said the new German capital ought to be situated "among vineyards."

Vineyards indeed surround Bonn. Adenauer's objectives are

realized, at least for the time being. It is not entirely disadvantageous; there are benefits as well. The choice of Bonn has spread the postwar development of Germany more evenly. Other West German cities—Munich, Hamburg, Düsseldorf and Stuttgart—have developed as cultural, social and political centers. There is no single center, no almighty metropolitan magnet attracting every name and talent, leaving the country as a whole a cultural desert. The decline of Berlin, and the absence of a substitute, permits relatively small cities to have first-class theaters, permits opera houses or symphony orchestras, scientific institutes, ballet or even the political cabarets normally found only in capitals. The loss of Berlin has, in a sense, restored Germany to the conditions of the eighteenth century, to the era of flourishing self-sufficient principalities. The leading West German literary critic, Marcel Reich-Ranicki (he lives far away from the capital in Hamburg—which would have been unthinkable before the war), feels that decentralization has always been a prerequisite for a flourishing cultural life in Germany.

A second advantage of Bonn's selection is its very lack of grandeur. Bonn so far has no magnificent buildings from which the majesty of the state extends itself to a loyal and obedient people. It has no glorious streets for extravagant parades or plazas for mass assemblies. Bonn in this respect is significantly different from the other German postwar capital, East Berlin. Magnificent streets and parade grounds may seem a normal aspect of capital life, not even worth mentioning, but they become a factor in a country where only a few decades ago mobs with flaming torches, ran screaming with enthusiasm after a screeching Pied Piper. The future Pied Piper will have to make a less ceremonial start if he should ever appear again.

12

A Working Democracy

𝕿HE NEW Bonn Republic, meanwhile, seems to have become more stable, peaceful and democratic than many people—inside and outside of Germany—had assumed in 1949.

At that time, not only former victims of the Nazi regime—Poles, Dutchmen, Jews—but hordes of others were seized with fears. Germans too, who saw Hitler not as an accident of history but the evil result of long social and intellectual processes, viewed the creation of a new German state with extreme skepticism. The new army, commanded by old generals, had a disconcerting effect. But so far, these fears have found little basis in fact.

The Bonn Republic is better than its reputation, despite its built-in provisional quality or vague longings for the re-establishment of the Reich within its old borders. It is still no pleasant experience to anyone sensitive to the German past, for in this country you can never be sure whose hand you are shaking. But for the first time in history, democracy is a reality here.

It has its weaknesses and susceptibilities like any other democracy. History is full of surprises and not all of them are unpleasant. The tragedy of Weimar has not been repeated. The new Bonn Republic seems to have finally made democracy palatable to the Germans. The Kaiser allowed no democracy. The Weimar Republic was a democracy but it was rejected by the people. In 1965, 81 percent of West Germans, according to a public poll, thought democracy the best form of government. Since the new Bonn democracy owes its existence more to Allied than German initiative, this figure is of some significance. It was the Western Allies who—not without opposition—forced the federal structure upon Germany, decentralized the mass media, and introduced the present system of "checks and balances" which, especially in the case of the Supreme Court, is patterned after the United States. Today the majority of Germans do not seem to question the underlying principles of this new republic. Young Germans simply accept these principles without much thought.

The electorate, still so conservative that it almost panics at the thought of "experiment" or "change," has kept the Christian Democratic government party in power since 1949. But the trend is toward a two-party system, a trend that is accompanied by the decline of extremist groups, both right and left.

Much of the Republic's stability is due to the development of political parties. The day of the purely ideological party often considered a particularly German phenomenon, is past. Two major parties CDU/CSU (Christian-Social Democratic Union) and SPD (the Social-Democrats), receive more than 90 percent of the national vote. Both parties are developing along American lines. Both of them are de-ideologized power organizations, loose coalitions of interest groups, associations and lobbies of a modern industrial and welfare society. Pollsters, not ideologues, determine tactics, help formulate election slogans. There are, of course, nuances, and contrasting accents; but as the Republican and Democratic parties in the United States are coalitions of big business and labor, liberals and conservatives, men, women and minorities, so the two German parties seek representation in all camps, from farmers to refugees, from former Nazis to liberal intellectuals. Party programs are almost indistinguishable; younger party leaders seem interchangeable, a familiar phenomenon in other mass democracies. Here, as elsewhere, a modern industrial welfare society requires a type of party that serves as many groups and interests as possible.

The Social-Democratic Party—the only holdover party from Weimar—is no longer the party of the poor or of the workers. Its leaders emulate the memory of President Kennedy, not of Karl Marx. The Christian Democratic Union—a postwar creation and meeting ground of the old "bourgeoisie"—conversely becomes more and more "democratic," and less and less "Christian." Each CDU government has boasted a union leader in its cabinet. Foreign policy—on reunification or Eastern borders—is bipartisan. This was not the case during the Weimar era. Unanimity among the parties has caused public discussion to move from the parliamentary arena to the press, thus prolonging the life of many national illusions and taboos.

The Bonn Republic has been spared perhaps the worst curse of the Weimar Republic: the bickering about the responsibility for the last defeat. Bonn has not two camps, one accusing the other of "having stabbed the nation in the back." This may have resulted from the Allied demand for unconditional surrender during the late War. It is often said that Allied insistence on unconditional surrender discouraged Germans from conspiring against Hitler. Had one of the conspiracies against Hitler succeeded, would there have been a new "stab in the back legend" plaguing German politics?

Today every political party affirms the democratic constitution. This was not so during the Weimar Republic, when a voter's choice was not between democratic alternatives. The bourgoisie had no proper concept of democracy, and few democrats had any proper concept of the use of power. Opposition in many eyes was tantamount to treason. Today, West Germans are beginning to accept that oppositions can play a positive and necessary role within the "system." The first postwar chancellor, Konrad Adenauer, did little to help them to this realization. On the contrary, he repeatedly announced that the "Social-Democrats are Germany's downfall."*

The West German electorate is not yet confident enough to throw one party out of national office and occasionally hand government power to the opposition.**

Constitutions are what people make of them. "A piece of paper," wrote Metternich, "does not make a constitution. Time alone does." Nonetheless, the unexpected stability of the Bonn Republic is due in part to its constitution. It is, in many ways, a constitution based on the lessons of the past. "The ghost of the Weimar Republic stood at its cradle," commented West German jurist F. K. Fromme. In its fourteen years of existence the Weimar Republic had no less than seventeen government crises, seventeen Chancellors, seventeen cabinets. Finally, Parliament and democracy were completely discredited; no further obstacles stood in Hitler's way. Bonn has had more luck.

The new constitution confesses a certain mistrust of the people; it eliminates the plebiscite. In contrast to the Weimar Republic, the President of the Federal Republic is not elected directly by the people. His powers are clearly defined, narrowly confined to almost entirely a representative nature. He is no surrogate kaiser like Hindenburg. Conversely the constitution strengthens the

* A few statements by former German rulers on the role of the opposition:
  Friedrich Wilhelm IV: "I love a principled opposition." Wilhelm II: "I no longer know any parties. I only know Germans." Hitler: "We will educate our people to fight against the idiocy of democracy, and again realize the necessity of authority and leadership."
** When the Social-Democratic opposition lost its fifth successive federal election in 1965, its candidate for chancellor and party chairman, West Berlin Mayor Willy Brandt, bitterly said that not the party but he personally had been rejected by the people. Brandt is an illegitimate child. His origin is blemished in more than one sense. He spent the war abroad fighting Germany as a Norwegian partisan and soldier. That this should be held against him is a further example of the moral schizophrenia of West Germans. In the eyes of a large majority of the electorate, it is still no moral achievement to have fought against Hitler, even though it is almost universally acknowledge that Hitler was a disaster for Germany. During the campaign, Brandt was constantly reminded of his past, and even Chancellor Erhard obliquely referred to it.

federal chancellor as head of the executive branch. The chancellor alone—advised by his cabinet—determines the "guidelines of policy." The chancellor and the government cannot be overthrown at the drop of a hat (the plague of the Weimar Republic). According to Article 67 of the constitution, chancellor and government can only be removed from office by means of a "constructive vote of no confidence," that is, only after Parliament has agreed upon a successor. That this has not occurred so far proves, on one hand, the Republic's stability and, on the other, suggests that its gravest tests are still to come.

As late as 1955 a public opinion poll indicated the mass of people thought almost as highly of Hitler's dictatorship with its atrocities as of democracy!

"Would you say that Hitler would have been one of Germany's greatest statesmen if he had not started the war?" was answered "yes" by 48 percent of those asked. In 1959 the percentage was 41; by 1960 it had sunk to 34. In 1961, 30 percent (!) replied "yes" to this question.

The *Institut für Demoskopie* in Allensbach regularly asks a cross section of West Germans: "In your opinion, what was the best time for Germany during the past century?" In 1951, 42 percent still regarded the Hitler era as Germany's "best time," a figure that seemed to justify the mistrust of the people on the part of the authors of the constitution. During the course of twelve years, from 1951 to 1963, there occurred a dramatic change in emotional attitudes, as the following table shows:

Germany's Best Time	1951	1959	1963
Now, today	2%	42%	62%
Between 1933 and 1939	42%	18%	11%
During the Weimar era	7%	4%	5%
Before 1914, under the Kaiser	45%	28%	16%
No opinion	4%	8%	6%

Another polltaker, *Institut für Demoskopie* in Bielefeld, concluded in 1953 that 15 percent would still vote "for a man like Hitler." By 1958, this percentage had fallen to 10 percent. Since 1960, it hovers around 5 percent—a residue of malcontents that most states probably have to digest.

In 1949, freedom of speech was considered the most basic freedom by only 26 percent. By 1963, the figure had grown to 56 percent.

Parliament, once derided as a "chatterbox" by extremists of the Weimar Republic, is gradually rising in public esteem. There are relapses and times of stagnation. But election results and polls prove that by-and-large respect of the parliamentary system is on the increase.

A questionnaire regularly sent by the Allensbach Institute refers to the Bonn Parliament:

"Do you believe that one must be very talented in order to become a Bundestag representative in Bonn?"

	1952	1953	1954	1957	1959	1961	1964
Yes	39%	46%	49%	45%	58%	61%	54%
No	40%	31%	34%	38%	27%	22%	28%
No opinion	21%	23%	17%	17%	15%	17%	18%

"If you sent a letter to the delegate who represented your election district, what do you believe would happen to the letter?"

	1951	1957	1962
Read by the delegate	32%	49%	47%
It would not reach him or would remain unread	49%	30%	22%
Don't know; it depends	19%	21%	31%

"Should several people determine the policies of a country or should the power of government be entrusted to one 'capable' politician?"

	1955	1960	1962
Several people should determine it	55%	62%	66%
A single man at the helm	31%	21%	18%
Don't know	14%	17%	16%

"Is it better for a country to have several parties or only one party, to achieve the greatest possible unity?"

	1951	1955	1961
Several parties	61%	74%	73%
A single party	22%	14%	10%
Don't know	12%	10%	16%
No parties at all	5%	2%	1%

More searching questions often reveal a comparatively high degree of political ignorance. Approximately two-thirds of those questioned misunderstood the meaning of often-used words—"opposition," "coalition" and the like. A poll taken in England in the middle of the fifties showed that 67 percent of those asked knew the name of their Member of Parliament. A similar investigation in West Germany disclosed that only 28 percent of those asked knew the name of their representative.

In themselves, these figures do not necessarily mean much. And yet, it seems, they reflect an atmosphere. This atmosphere gains in importance when seen against the background of other attitudes and relationships. The attitude of important social elements toward democracy as a working political system has changed considerably.

Before Hitler's rise to power in 1933, state bureaucracy and army, social and financial elites, schools, churches and universities, combined to undermine the young democracy. Just about every law lecture debunked democracy, says Professor Theodor Eschenburg, a political scientist at Tübingen, who attended the university during the Weimar era. Pro-democratic professors of law and of German philology were the exception. Today no prince of the Church, no editorial writer, no professor, no general staff member, no banker agitates against democracy. On the contrary! To profess your belief in democracy is the fashion; everyone does it.

No irony is meant here. Democracy is the most difficult form of government. It must be anchored in the minds, emotions and speech of a people. Democracy is in a precarious situation everywhere; it must survive a daily struggle between reason and passion, between judgment and prejudice, patience and perfectionistic haste. The United States of America—next to Ethiopa, the oldest political system in today's world—is in the 190th year of a fight between democratic *façons de parler* and racist *façons de discrimination*. Little more than half of those entitled to vote avail themselves of this right, and a frighteningly large number of citizens were prepared to endure a McCarthy or voted for a Goldwater. The most comforting quality of American democracy is that government and intellectuals, churches and unions, the best politicians of both parties and numerous citizens, are prepared to commit themselves to the daily struggle for freedom. That is also the most comforting quality of the young Bonn democracy.

Adjusting to the responsibilities of democracy is not an easy task. The Germans have submitted to strict authority over a longer period than other European peoples. More than other peoples they have been taught to respect authority, any authority. Love of freedom has been alien to a "spirit of subservience." In West Germany one inevitably looks for remnants of this subservience that have survived the calamities of the last fifty years. Still missing is a pride of citizenship so familiar in an Anglo-Saxon democracy. In West Germany, some citizens still react to government like Catholic priests to the Pope. To one who comes from a more relaxed atmosphere, it is amusing to hear the way government officials are addressed here: "If Herr *Ministerialrat* permits, I will admit Herr Schmidt," "If Herr *Ministerialdirektor* will allow me to, I will make an effort to restate my request."

The old spirit of submissiveness continues to flourish in officially tended and preserved sanctuaries. The phenomenal democratic development of West Germany during the last twenty years seems not to have reached the padded doors of a few higher officials. Behind those doors, the free air that blows through Parliament and the Americanized metropolitan postwar society has not yet penetrated. There, the feudal arrogance of a vanished era has been conserved. Many bureaucrats survived the collapse of the *Kaiserreich*, of the Weimar Republic and the Third Reich. They were raised in the world of the university dueling clubs; not infrequently will you encounter a ministry director in Bonn with a face lacerated by dueling scars—like the breast of an African chieftain. Some officials give off a peculiar air of self-possession; one rarely has the feeling that they are humanely approachable. In an incorruptible but ice-cold manner, they manage the new Republic and democracy with the same sense of duty and remote efficiency they once managed death under Hitler. Some must have incredibly split personalities, having solemnly sworn allegiance to three or even four regimes and constitutions during the course of their career, one Kaiser, one Führer and three Presidents. They live in their own world and sign the most inconsequential letters with "i.A." (*im Auftrag*—by order).

Fewer Germans voted for Chancellor Adenauer than Frenchmen for President de Gaulle. But the General hardly engenders the same kind of enthusiasm among habitués of French bars as does the retired Chancellor in German beer halls, or even as does former Defense Minister Franz Josef Strauss in his home state of Bavaria. Strauss is a good case in point. He is praised for having "political talent," for being a "hell of a guy" with whom you can go "through thick and thin." Many West Germans consider "craftiness" the distinguishing quality of a "thoroughbred politician," a trait deserving respect. According to Professor Bracher of Bonn University, the author of a study about the Weimar Republic, this is an old German character trait. "Hegel already said that history is made by ruthless men."

Occasionally one sees little signs dangling from key rings with the inscription "Buddy, duck down!" Duck down for what? Characteristically, the German language must use foreign words to designate many of the basic qualities of a free society. A good example is "*Zivilcourage*." The German word "*Mut*" is a different kind of courage. *Heldenmut* (heroic courage) is expected in certain situations and is honored. But *Zivilcourage* signifies the courage to oppose the opinion of the majority, to violate taboos. For this kind of courage there has never been an Iron Cross in Germany. West Germany, while permitting the wearing of medals from the Nazi era on official occasions, still has no medal honoring active resistance to Nazism.

Everyday speech reflects a politeness approaching the servile. West Germans are not more polite than other peoples, but as far back as 1810, Madame de Staël noted that the Germans, whose books are so bold, make an uncommonly servile and unfree impression in conversation—due to many empty formulas they employ. "If I may express my gratitude," "If I may say good-bye," "If I may say the following" or "and please let me state with perhaps shocking candor." Postwar Germans have created the cumbersome, even grotesque, "*meinungsfreudig*" to mean "the joy of having one's own opinion." Titles are so abundant here, one wonders how they maintain their aura. Former princes are still addressed as "Imperial" or "Royal Highness," even at official events. In this Republic newspaper bylines such as "by Count H. W. von Finkenstein," reporting a debate in parliament, are not uncommon. The chairman of a CDU youth convention in Koblentz greeted Chancellor Erhard in December, 1964 with the following words: "You, my *Herr Bundeskanzler*, crown this convention with your presence." In 1964, during a visit of the West German President Lübke in Hollstadt an der Saale, the schoolgirl Gertrud Schmitt recited the following:

> O great day! Herr President!
> that we may see you in person . . .
> O benevolent ruler! Respectfully we thank you!
> O noble Sir! Your heart is only filled with love.

Protestant seminary students have long ago caught on to what questions will embarrass their teacher. "What is your position on murdering a tyrant? What is your position on the famous letter of the Apostle Paul to the Romans, in which it says: '*Jedermann sei untertan der Obrigkeit, die Gewalt über ihn hat. Denn es ist keine Obrigkeit ohne von Gott; wo aber Obrigkeit ist die ist von Gott verordnet'?*" (13:1)

It is interesting to compare the English or French translation of this biblical text, which has been so often politically misused, with the German translation by Martin Luther just quoted. The English translation (King James Version) goes like this: "Let every soul be subject to higher powers, for there is no power but from God." "Higher powers" (in the plural!) stand for something different than the German concept of "*Obrigkeit*" (political authority). The French translation by Louis Segond: "*Que toute personne soit soumise aux autorité supérieures; cah il n'y a point d'autorité qui ne vienne de Dieu.*" "*Autorités supérieures*" is also something different than "authority" in the singular. It is interesting that German pre-Luther Bibles make no mention of the "*Obrigkeit*," but speak of "*höheren Gewalten*" (higher powers).

Several years ago a great discussion arose in West Germany about this Bible passage. Despite St. Paul, a Christian is not obligated to obey a totalitarian state, the chairman of the Council of Protestant Churches in Germany, Berlin's Bishop Otto Dibelius, wrote in a privately printed pamphlet criticizing Luther's extremist "authoritarianism." The pamphlet was written as a birthday present for the Protestant Bishop of Hannover, Dr. Hanns Lilje. Yet, the recipient replied: "I cannot share Dibelius' views. Authority is authority." This happened in 1959!

The discussion still goes on. The Bishop of Berlin, who had been so severely attacked in 1959, later published a pocket book on the same subject, in which he sought to give theological foundation to his thesis. The simple epilogue by the Bishop is the most effective part of the book. Dibelius describes a meeting he had during the war with the mysterious Kurt Gerstein, the famous prototype of the priest in Rolf Hochhuth's drama *The Deputy*. Gerstein, a faithful Christian who voluntarily joined the SS and led a "dangerous, almost suicidal double life," visited Dibelius in 1942. He described to him at great length the mass exterminations in the concentration camps. "He literally screamed," Dibelius writes, 'You must help! The world must know it. There is no other way to stop this unbelievable hideousness.' I was deeply shocked. Should I have said to him 'Gerstein, but you are Christian, you know Romans 13:1? Why didn't you tell these poor people? These SS men happen to be your authority. I tell *you* in the name of Jesus Christ. Why didn't you tell them: 'All authority has been instituted by God, for your own good! You have to obey it voluntarily, for the sake of your conscience!' Why didn't you tell that to the people?' "

"That was not what I said," Dibelius writes (actually he had immediately transmitted Gerstein's news to the Bishop of Upsala). "That was not what I said. I was not able to bring a blasphemy over my lips. But later on, when theologian friends of mine said to me, 'All authority is from God. All, *Herr* Bishop, all!'—I turned away not entirely without bitterness. I had gone through a different theological school."

Protestantism, which began in Germany as resistance to papal degeneration, developed along different lines here than in Switzerland or the Anglo-Saxon countries. German Protestantism soon reconciled throne and altar. The religiously buttressed traditions of the authoritarian state are difficult to cast off. Less than a hundred years ago these authoritarian traditions were celebrated by the "liberal" German novelist and poet Theodor Fontane as the "best, most comfortable . . . and also the most agreeable by far to free spirits." Even Thomas Mann praised them as late as 1917. The war had to be fought, Mann wrote in *Betrachtungen eines Unpolitischen*, for "German culture and against the democratic, political civilization of the [Anglo-Saxon and French] West." In a recently published letter written on August 22, 1914, Mann wrote to the publisher Samuel Fischer about the "great victories of the German troops in Lorraine. . . . It is the German spirit . . . German culture and training that is winning there and thus people like me have no need to despise themselves now." A few years later, of course, Mann gave unreserved allegiance to the Weimar Republic and repudiated his wartime writings. In his great novel written during World War II, *Doktor Faustus*, he portrayed the German soul complete with its romantic emotional haze and unloosed demons, those very aspects that provided the origins of Nazism.

The case of the young Thomas Mann would show that not only Prussian militarists, churchmen or Junkers paid homage to the authoritarian idea. There is no telling how much of this spirit is left in Germany today. But its political effectiveness is probably finished. The political avalanches of the last fifty years have uprooted too many of its practitioners. The modern industrial society requires more complicated processes of thought than those of the old authoritarian state. The old spirit still evidences itself occasionally, as in the attitude of many of his colleagues toward Chancellor Erhard. Erhard differs greatly from his authoritarian predecessor, Dr. Konrad Adenauer, who at times treated the constitution lightly, or Parliament with disrespect. Erhard likes to call himself a "people's Chancellor"; he grants Parliament a role it did not play under Adenauer. This relaxation meets with the greatest disapproval in Erhard's own party. Some CDU members say "He is too good for his office." They mean: "He is too weak."

Does this mean that the "strong man complex" has not been eradicated completely? Does it prove the overestimation of "order" at the expense of liberty, the fateful tendency to expect all political impulses from above instead of generating them below? The Germans are not without a leader under Erhard, but indeed are a step ahead of Adenauer's one-man rule. Erhard represents a healthy phase in the dissolution of this nation's undemocratic belief in a Führer.

In West Germany one still hears of incidents which reflect an older authoritarian tradition, incidents which are much rarer elsewhere. One story is told about Franz Josef Strauss, the right-wing chairman of the Bavarian wing of the government party. One day, when he was still minister of defense, the traffic cop at the busiest Bonn intersection stopped the ministerial limousine to let the other traffic pass. Strauss, infuriated by this *lèse-majesté*, ordered his chauffeur to drive on; his limousine avoided collision with a streetcar by a hairsbreadth.

Less well-known is the story Terrence Prittie, former Bonn correspondent of the *Manchester Guardian*, tells of a small-town citizen who sued the Mayor because the latter had called him an "idiot." His lawsuit rejected, his attorney made a last appeal to the judge. "Wouldn't you feel insulted, your Honor, if I would call you an idiot?" The judge was, and promptly sentenced the attorney to a prison term without option of a fine.

Impulsive Franz Josef Strauss may be a unique example in present-day German politics. And yet there are frequent complaints, publicly filed by politicians who have not been saluted by policemen with sufficient respect or are not given special treatment on the *Autobahn*.

In 1965, Vice-Chancellor Erich Mende officially complained that a detachment of traffic policemen had not let his car pass through a blocked-off street. Even Chancellor Erhard once protested, when met at the airport by a representative of the Berlin Senate dressed in a mere business suit. Morning coats are in order. Public criticism—a by-product of public life—is also anathema to some German politicians. West German courts are overburdened with libel suits that leading politicians, cabinet members and delegates have filed against colleagues, journalists, clowns and even cartoonists and cabaretists. In 1965, Federal Minister of Transportation Dr. Hans Christoph Seebohm brought slander charges against a political satirist who, in a radio broadcast, had sarcastically "refused" to differentiate between him and a donkey. Seebohm, as the leader of the Sudeten Germans and supporter of the Munich agreement, often embarrasses the Bonn government. Seebohm's lawyers demanded three thousand marks in damages. The trial, which discussed at length and in all seriousness whether a donkey is really stupid, lasted one week. The verdict: two thousand marks or one day in prison for every hundred marks. The convicted clown was ready to carry his appeal to the Federal Supreme Court. Fortunately a lower Court of Appeal dismissed the first verdict outright.

Bundestag Administrative officer Hans Trossmann proved himself just as humorless and hypersensitive. In 1965 he brought action against Hans Hermann Köper, editor of *Twen*, a journal for teenagers, for having "libeled the Federal Parliament." At the instigation of the well-known German parodist, Robert Neumann, Köper had planted fictitious marriage advertisements in several newspapers. Such ads are a regular feature of most German newspapers. Neumann planned to use the replies for amusing "social analysis." One such announcement read: "Bundestag deputy (Gov. Coalition) would like to meet gentleman (industry/big business) with marriageable daughter/sister, who would welcome bond with very busy, ambitious politician with spotless private and political past, affectionate, as lover and sportsman."

The editors waited for Miss Krupp, but instead the police responded. Köper was summoned to a special hearing; after explaining the ruse, he was told by the investigating judge it was a serious case, "the *Bundestag* is behind it." Investigation continued and the magistrate set a day for a trial. Köper leaked the story to the press; another deputy threatened to raise a question in Parliament. The trial was called off.

The massive, spontaneous reaction to the arrest of the *Spiegel* editors belongs to the credit side of this balance sheet. It was the first nationwide protest movement for freedom of speech in German history. The demonstrators were mainly young intellectuals, students and professors—children of the postwar era. This, too, reflected a change, for during the Weimar era, German students had organized *autos-da-fé* and flung "unpatriotic" books onto the pyres. Now they came out into the streets for a better cause. The popular reaction to the *Spiegel* affair has sometimes been called a "turning point" of German democracy. The future will show whether this is the case.

A Shattered Trumpet

TOWARD the end of the nineteen-forties the distinguished British historian, Sir Lewis Namier, observed the re-establishment of the national state in West Germany. It had taken half a generation, Namier wrote, for a new aggressive nationalism to arise in Germany after 1918. If history permitted analogies, the next critical period in Germany would begin about 1959. At this point a new generation would have grown up, a generation which knew the humiliating defeat of 1945 but not the horrors of war. This generation, Namier felt, might well be capable of producing a new Hitler.

Almost twenty years have passed since this gloomy forecast. The new generation has come of age. There is no evidence of a new, aggressive nationalism. But can it not grow? The temptations are still great. There is no lack of clever enticers, or of emotionally loaded slogans and resentments. And yet, it is safe to say that a decisive quality of nationalism, which exists elsewhere, is lacking.

The Munich historian Joseph Othmar Zöller, in a fascinating analysis of contemporary West German "patriotic feelings," *Rückblick auf die Gegenwart* (Looking Back at the Present), writes: "Older Germans are helpless because they have experienced 'too much of Germany,' younger Germans because they have experienced 'too little.'" The more you discuss concepts like "nation," "Volk," or "patriotism," with younger Germans, the truer this strikes. The ruins have been rebuilt; but one realizes that Hitler destroyed much more in Germany than houses and human lives.

Long after leaving Germany, the impression lingers that, as a nation in the traditional sense, West Germany is somehow emasculated. A national self-assurance—not necessarily political—has been destroyed. One misses a national self-assurance that evolves out of the continuity of history, a feeling of homogeneity of a people in harmony with itself. Even political leaders give the impression—despite frequently forced outbursts of patriotism—that they are incapable of genuine, unself-conscious patriotic feelings.

The Weimar Republic still possessed this self-assurance. The Bonn Republic does not, perhaps because it was meant to be a "provisional" state. The encouragement of an independent West German patriotism was and still is "prohibited;" this might sap the desire for reunification.

The Bonn Republic gave itself a good constitution, but it was never imbued with a great idea, such as the concept of freedom that dominated the founding of the United States and even today is still the strongest link among Americans. The Bonn Republic also lacks an ancient religious-national tradition of the kind to which the new "artificial" State of Israel, created at approximately the same time as the Bonn Republic, has recourse.

For years the Cold War contributed more to the Bonn Republic's "sense of being a state" than anything else. Probably neither the Federal Republic nor the DDR would have come into being —such as they did—had it not been for the Cold War. This explains the relatively primitive vehemence of anti-Communism in West

Germany as well as its counterpart, the equally primitive anti-capitalism of the East Germans. A 1961 to 1963 poll of high school students in West Germany exhibited a peculiar result of all the anti-Communist propaganda. The Frankfurt Institute for Educational Research asked students about the historical origins of the persecution of the Jews. Almost 20 percent of the male students and 25.3 percent of the females in the twelfth grade cited as the cause Karl Marx's "recommendation" to set fire to Jewish synagogues, burn Jewish books and prohibit rabbis from teaching.

An Englishman once called the Federal Republic an "economic system in search of a state." There is certainly a search for some identity. But which? In no West European country is the idea of a united Europe as popular as here, nowhere do as many people prefer to be "Europeans." Either they are ashamed to be Germans, or they are suspicious of nationalism or no fresh nationalism has as yet arisen. The "spirit of Europe" is evident in everyday life; nowhere do you see as many cars sporting the blue placard of the European Council next to the national code-letter "D." The chief of the European Economic community regularly opens the most important West German industrial fair in Hannover. Nowhere in Europe has John F. Kennedy's concept of an "Atlantic Community" been received more enthusiastically. These are outward signs; one senses a mood, too. How much longer will it last?

We still know relatively little of the subconscious forces that can intensify the self-assurance of a people to a degree which the German writer Kurt Tucholsky once called "national drunkenness." But if a lack of national self-conceit contributes something toward peace, if the rejection of an inflated "self-image" is a prerequisite for greater European unity, if the national state can give way to a greater idea only when "my country right or wrong" is no longer the rule—if all this is true, then the West Germans are several years ahead of their neighbors.

The people of every country have a certain image of themselves, and often attribute an opposite image to other peoples. Images express themselves in clichés: courage, loyalty, cleanliness, industriousness, spirituality, devoutness, humor, frugality, proficiency in love are qualities of one's own people; corresponding opposites are ascribed to others.

It is an irony of history that the former "Master Race" now has the most self-effacing image of itself among the European nations, according to polls taken in 1963 in seven European countries, by the international edition of *Reader's Digest*. Results showed that the way an average German sees himself practically coincides with foreign views of Germans, which are still considerably negative. An Englishman recently wrote that the Germans were "Europe's new Jews." They are called the same things: "insolent and without manners" and simultaneously, "wily businessmen."

At the instigation of *Reader's Digest*, pollsters in six countries asked for "positive qualities" of one nation in the eyes of the other. This was made equivalent to 100. Next, "positive" qualities of a nation in its own eyes were counted. The positive self-image of the West Germans was roughly 105, not much higher than the image of Germany entertained by critical foreigners (100). The self-image of modest Englishmen or Dutchmen each stood at 122 points. Belgians rated 135; Italians, 203; Frenchmen appeared to have the highest opinion of themselves in all of Europe—their self-image scored as high as 284 points.*

Insecure as they are, Germans are eager to be loved. Every visitor to West Germany meets an overwhelming demand for praise. Even in the DDR, where people carry no torch for the regime, sharp opponents of the regime will expect a foreigner to show enthusiasm in acknowledging economic and educational accomplishments. Every ambassador who arrives in Bonn or leaves after a tour of office is given a solemn attestation, to wit, he is a friend of Germany and loves it very much. Against this background it is easier to understand the extraordinary response of the German masses when General De Gaulle in 1962 told them "*Sie sind ein grosses Volk*" (You are a great people), or the euphoria that overcame them when an American magazine a year later discovered the "Fräuleinwunder," announcing to an astonished people that its young girls were sexy and attractive. For years no one had been that nice to Germans.

Whether the Germans respect themselves or not, are they pre-

* To disparage themselves, while adoring foreigners, has once before been a German characteristic. In 1849, Bismarck complained self-effacement was a "political malady confined to German territory."

pared to do for their country (or for reunification) what they occasionally demand of their allies? Georges Clemenceau said in 1928 that the German had "made a pact with death ... [he] meets death as though it were his beloved." Later, Churchill talked of the Germans' "passion for death." In 1964 the *Allensbacher Institut für Demoskopie* asked: "In your opinion is there anything in this world worth sacrificing everything for, even your own life?"

More than half of those polled answered "no," there was nothing worth sacrificing everything for. Forty-nine percent said "yes." But when asked what for, only 1 percent stated that they were prepared to sacrifice their life for "my country." In 1960, 89 percent of all polled West German university students stated they knew an idea worth dying for. But only 6 percent regarded *Heimat* (homeland) as being that idea, although the majority (59 percent) favored the retention of the West German army. In 1954, 38 percent of those asked still believed that Germany would be one of the "mightiest" states in the world one day. Only 19 percent still entertained such hopes in 1962.

The older forms of "national arrogance," "patriotism" and "nationalism" seem to be waning in all of Western Europe and in North America. Just as the exhaustion resulting from the European religious wars led to a separation of religion and politics, we may be observing the first signs of a similar separation of nationalism and politics. Truly passionate nationalism probably flourishes only among the new African and Asian states. Nonetheless, there is a difference between most Germans and most other Europeans one meets. An Englishman or a Swede can be "proud" of his country without an accompanying intoxication with "patriotism." West Germans, of course, are just as happy as Frenchmen or Englishmen when their international soccer team wins. Yet a foreign observer in Germany misses a natural sense of belonging together, a sense one takes for granted among Frenchmen or Americans.

Members of other nations discuss their national past with much less restraint. The past is a closed chapter, a digested experience that can even be joked about. You find West Germans uneasy even about events that lie far in the past, such as the Wars of Liberation against Napoleon I or the era of the Kaiser. At a West

German masked ball it is rarer than, say in England, to find some one costumed as an historical German personage. An English student imitating Queen Victoria in a black lace dress is likely to be a great success. "Kaiser Wilhelm" at a West German masked ball would likely be considered in bad taste. West Germany has almost no romantic historical novels, such as the many novels about the Civil War in the United States. Are the Germans tumbling from one extreme into the other? Do you have them "either at your throat or at your feet," as Churchill claimed in a speech before the United States Congress? I had a different impression. An extensive wasteland, left behind by the fires of nationalism, separates many people here from their national past.

Nationalistic movements have not yet occurred in any European country without some intellectual underpinning. Popular speakers have never been enough; poets are also needed and flaming literati. Nationalistic poets were plentiful before 1933. Today you have to look hard to find them. Except for an aging minority, West German intellectuals are less nationalistic than their colleagues in other European nations. In no European country are the so-called intellectuals as "alienated" from the state as here. Nowhere are they so frequently accused of living apart from the community or even of "having lost all contact with reality." The younger West German writers share a disgust for everything that smells of nationalism or *Vaterland*. Many intellectuals will say *hierzulande* (in this country) in order to avoid the word "Germany." A poem by the West German writer Hans Magnus Enzensberger (born 1929), expresses a widespread mood:

Native Tongue

What have I lost here,
In this country,
Into which my elders have brought me
through lack of guile?
native yet unconsoled,
absent I am here
domiciled in the comfortable misery,
in the pleasant satisfied ditch.

What do I have here? and what am I doing here,
in this slaughter bowl, this land of milk and honey,
where things go upward and not forward,
where disgust bites into the embroidered misery,
where poverty, white as chalk, croaks with a choked voice
out of the whipped cream in the delicatessen shops and shouts:
things are going upward.

What am I doing here? and what am I to say?
In what language? and to whom?

. . . this country . . .
Germany, my land, unholy heart of nations,
usually in bad repute
among all ordinary people:

my two countries and I, we are divorced,
and yet I am here in earnest,
in ashes and sackcloth and ask myself:
what have I lost here?
that is what I have lost here,
what hovers at the tip of my tongue,
something else, the whole,
that jokes fearlessly with the whole world
and doesn't drown in this puddle . . .

. . . exemplary land
murder-ditch, into which I am cordially flung
my body halfways alive,
that's where I will stay,
I quarrel but I won't budge,
that's where I will stay a while,
until I take leave and go to other people,
and rest in a very ordinary land,
not here,
not here.

"No great love of country can exist in a land that has been divided for centuries and where, almost always at the instigation of
foreign powers, Germans have been fighting Germans; nor can
the love of glory be very vigorous in a country without a center,

without a capital and without society." Thus wrote Germaine de Staël, in her book *De L'Allemagne* (1810). Her comment was never more valid than in the partitioned, decentralized Germany of today.

The intellectual's rejection of nationalism is shared by only a few active politicians. There are those who are not satisfied to seek their luck within given borders. The trumpet of nationalism lies battered on the ground; some try to solder it together, hoping to strike up old tunes. It has a hollow, artificial sound, but a sound nonetheless. The trumpeters are not only old Nazis.

It is again becoming fashionable for politicians to complain about lack of super-patriotic feelings—a dearth that the same people were quite proud of until recently. A series of factors contributes to this turnabout. Chief among them is the example of Gaullist France. Ever since the Napoleonic wars, the French have had a great influence on German national consciousness.

West German politicians who bemoan the lack of national spirit do not necessarily entertain evil designs. They are mostly old-fashioned people who consider "patriotism" a moral value, much as religion, or family. They frequently lament the evaporation of national feeling in the same breath with which they complain about high divorce rates or free sex life. They have returned to a conservatism that was once admirable but also served as a fountainhead for Nazism. New ideas do not occur to them so they recite old litanies. They claim that concepts like "nation" or "nationalism" are wholesome and real; that without "national spirit" there exists no human solidarity. In a confusing and complex new world they latch on to old oversimplifications. Sometimes one suspects that the yearning for a new patriotism points to a lack of will, or to an incapacity to deal with the difficult contemporary problems, in education, city planning, transportation, old age pensions or leisure. There is still a defensive note in these appeals to national sentiments. Politicians do not generally demand "patriotism" as such, but "purified patriotism." But even a purified patriotism needs shining examples—the somewhat comical efforts of several leading West German politicians to "rehabilitate" Bismarck indicate the problem. In 1965, Parliament met in special session to attempt "rehabilitation" of Bismarck on the occasion of his 150th birthday. Young West Germans, who until then had been told that certain logical developments led from Bismarck to Hitler, were to be presented with a newly polished Bismarck image: a Bismarck without laws against the unions and without forged telegrams, without desire for hegemony and without "*Kulturkampf*," without the famous dictum: "The great questions are not solved by means of speeches and majority decisions—but through iron and blood." The "new" Bismarck, would be a "pioneer of the striving for a united Europe."

Bundestag President Dr. Eugen Gerstenmaier's efforts toward a new patriotism are characteristic. He has launched such hazy concepts as: "Germany has a claim to our love," or "Fatherland is still fascinating." The chairman of the CDU faction in the *Bundestag*, Rainer Barzel, demanded in a speech: "We must be someone in politics again." *Bundespräsident* Lübke asked the younger generation to sing more "patriotic songs." No primer of European patriotic songs is so imbued with "blood," "clanging of swords" and the hatred of foreigners as the songs that originated in Germany in the nineteenth century. Lübke regretted that too many young people regard these songs as "antiquated and passé." As far as he was concerned, "nation" was an equivalent of "art." He said: "A people that loses its power to give artistic expression to its nationalism also stands in danger of being deprived of its political right of existence."

The Bavarian leader Franz Joseph Strauss has gone several steps further. He demanded West Germany's participation in an atomic force and warned the world of a "new Hitler" if Germany is left out. At the same time he declared: "Anyone who renounces Breslau and Stettin (today parts of Poland) today will renounce Leipzig and Magdeburg (today part of East Germany) tomorrow—next he will renounce Berlin. All for the sake of sweet and lazy peace."

This impetuous outburst, so typical of Strauss, points to the potential sources of a new German nationalism: reunification with the DDR and settlement of the Eastern borders with Poland. The conflict with Czechoslovakia over the right of "self-determination" for former German inhabitants of the Sudetenland constitutes a side issue. All three problems are potentially explosive.

Every political party, and just about every leading politician, constantly emphasizes the national necessity "to complete Germany," to unite West Germany and East Germany into a single, powerful, Great Germany. "Unification" is described as almost heavenly ordained; much less is said about more personal freedom, security and a higher living standard for East Germans. Warnings like one given by Vice-Chancellor Erich Mende in 1965 sound ominous: "If the world powers do not steer the will for reunification, it will break out like an unchained natural force into a huge political avalanche. . . ."

Almost daily, politicians will admonish people not to accept affluence and personal security as a matter of course, sounding as though partition endangers affluence and personal security. Thus said *Bundespräsident* Lübke in December, 1964 to members of a jingoist organization known as "Indivisible Germany": "The long duration of this [partition], as well as the convenience and seeming security of an affluent and satisfied life, make us forget all too easily. The salutary concern that motivates us for the future of our nation can be lost so quickly." There is not only uneasiness in freedom, as noted in the previous chapter; there is also uneasiness in affluence.

The old German territories of East Prussia, Silesia and Pomerania lie on the other side of the rivers Oder and Neisse. These territories, lost in 1945, have become the focal point for a jingoistic agitation of the kind that has triggered wars in the past. Oddly enough, it is not a question of West Germany's border with Poland but of the border between Poland and East Germany. All West German political parties and almost all politicians refuse to recognize the present Western borders of Poland. None is willing to grant it permanence. Every West German cabinet since 1949 has adopted a similar position, promising at the same time to refrain from the use of force. "The German people have begun to atone for the hideous crimes committed under the leadership of those of whom it approved openly during the hour of success and whom it obeyed blindly" —thus begins the section dealing with Germany in the 1945 Agreement of Potsdam, where the United States, the Soviet Union and Britain decided to expel the German population from the East and resettle it in the West.

No West German party, no political leader will publicly recognize this forcible resettlement now twenty years old, for what it was: a sad but inevitable result of a war started by Germany. In intimate unquotable conversations, politicians may retract these views. But nationalistic passions are fomented in public; they are not reduced through private retractions of public declarations.*

All parties and most politicians publicly support the right of the resettled to return to the old homeland, which has been the homeland of millions of Poles and Czechs since the end of the war. They also publicly renounce any use of force. Yet it is hard to believe that returning refugees (if any can be found who really want to return) will be prepared to live as Polish citizens on the other side of the rivers Oder and Neisse. "Self-determination" in the old homeland means simply the right to make the lost Eastern areas a part of Germany again. The possible fate of millions of Poles and Russians settled in these areas since 1945 is left vague.

Approximately nine million Germans lost their ancestral home east of the rivers Oder and Neisse after the war. The figure has increased to include refugee children born after the expulsion. The political, economic and social absorption of the refugees into West Germany is almost complete. Their successful integration represents the second German miracle (the first of course is economic). Yet refugees—to be more exact, a vociferous group of professional functionaries—inject and continue to inject nationalistic passions into the political structure, the popular press and even into the educational system.

Refugee organizations press constantly to see that "Germany's mission" in the East and Germany's "inalienable right to the stolen territories" is not forgotten in West German public schools. Refugee "study institutes" maintain contact with thousands of teachers. Since almost no leading politician wants to be suspected of being a "*Verzichtspolitiker*" (a politcian who renounces all claims to the Eastern territories), refugee institutes enjoy financial and

---

* Chancellor Erhard in a speech of March 22, 1964: "We certainly are not demanding foreign territory. But, faced as we are with responsibility to the German people and to history—we are not renouncing and cannot renounce the ancestral homeland of so many of our German brothers and sisters."

184

often ideological support from federal and state authorities. For example, in 1965 a refugee organization disseminated to approximately three thousand schools a pamphlet with the imposing title *"Wegweiser durch das Schrifttum und die Lehrmittel zur Ostkundlichen Unterrichtsgestaltung."** According to the author of this pamphlet, West Germany—unnaturally overcrowded—needs all of its Eastern areas back; otherwise there will be more than seven million unemployed during the next economic crisis. In such a crisis West Germany could "hardly survive a few months" without the "graneries of East Prussia, Pomerania and Silesia."

The object of this guidebook is not only to relate German history in Eastern Europe but to "keep alive the claim to the territories, which cannot be given up, and prepare German youth for a new thrust East, in the name of Europe," according to the editor, a Dr. Ernst Lehmann. Such notions, along with slogans about "blond Germans" facing "Slavic intruders," are aimed at primary school children. Another recommended book (*The German National Consciousness* by Herbert Cysarz) offers the conclusion that Hitler did indeed permit crimes but "the crimes of the leadership should not confuse what was in itself a good cause, a pure motive and an unconditional sacrifice."

An outraged report in the Hamburg *Zeit* in April, 1965 exposed this refugee pressure group's "educational" activity. Unfortunately only a small number of such cases are publicized. A liberal *Bundestag* Deputy, Dr. Oswald Kohut, one of the few West German politicians who refuse to be intimidated by the nationalist taboo of the Oder-Neisse line, queried the government about refugee literature distributed to public schools. Vice-Chancellor Erich Mende confirmed the fact that the *Wegweiser* was indeed subsidized indirectly by the Federal Government. But, in his opinion, the editors did not propose "any political objectives that would hinder the efforts of the Federal Government in behalf of a better relationship to the East European states." The expression "German youth should be prepared for a new thrust East " was nothing "but an Eastward extension of the European idea."

How effective is the propaganda disseminated by refugee or-

* This totally untranslatable title tells us this is a guide to literature and educational means conducive to creating a proper awareness of the East.

ganizations? While many young people who can remember the horrors of the war reject the "dangerous nonsense" of the refugees, still younger people are being taken in. No one knows how many of them there are, but they are beginning to make their weight felt in public life.

These young people—twenty, twenty-five or thirty years old —do not feel responsible for Hitler's crimes. As innocent victims, and in the name of a "historical claim," they demand the return, or at least the partial return, of those Eastern territories that were lost as a direct result of the wars against Poland and Russia. They dress in what Bismarck once called the "gown of offended innocence." Amnesia is a sign of schizophrenia. Young people such as these, can they be blamed for it, living, as they do, in a country whose leading politicians affirm in public and deny in private? A country where World War II officers, who went on fighting for a demented dictator to the very end, are now considered just as "honorable" as those who participated in the July 20, 1944 conspiracy against Hitler?

Such young people—it is surprising that there are not many more of them—notice that West Germany again matters to the world and is wooed by other countries. Some succumb to the demagoguery of a Gerhard Frey, others applaud cabinet ministers who urge them to stoke fires of *heilige Deutsche Unruhe*. (This untranslatable phrase again reflects the pseudo-religious character of German political language. It says as much as "sacred stirrings of the German soul.") They are told that "twenty years of suffering are enough" and "one must finally think of Germany's true interests." They still avoid old-fashioned hypernationalistic slogans. Rather, they assume a worldly wise air and try to strike a balance between Nazi crimes and so-called Allied crimes. Dresden is like Treblinka, Auschwitz like Hiroshima, the persecution of Jews like the expulsion of Germans from East Prussia, East Pomerania and Silesia: "That's the way the world is; we do not hold anything against anyone, let no one hold anything against us." A young man named Conrad Bund writes a letter to the Hamburg *Zeit:*

> I belong to the young generation not responsible for all that. I feel that the Polish and German nation have nothing left to reproach

each other with after the horrors 1939 to 1945 in Poland and of 1945 to 1947 in [Polish] East Germany. We must go forward into areas beyond guilt and together draw the poison out of the Polish-German relations."

Whatever its feasibility, the goal is commendable. But how can it be achieved? This young West German has a ready answer. He demands the return of Lower Silesia, East Brandenburg and Pomerania in exchange for economic compensations and demilitarization. For the situation "demands sacrifices from both sides." Since West Germany has no common border with Poland (the DDR has recognized its present border with Poland as a "border of peace"), it can be assumed that Herr Bund assumes reunification with the DDR as one Polish concession for the sweetening of relations with Germany.

Such young people are like the sons of a ruined gambler. Twenty years after their father's suicidal bankruptcy, they demand the return of his squandered property, giving as their reason: we ourselves had nothing to do with it, we don't drink alcohol, we attend church regularly and never go to a casino.

The self-conscious philo-semitism, which has been preached to excess since 1945, has produced a peculiar reaction among some sons of the refugees. Some compare themselves to the Jews who remained faithful to their promised land until they returned two thousand years after expulsion. If the Jews were able to wait for two thousand years, they say, then they too can wait a few years more before returning to their "ancestral homeland."

The Union of Refugees consists of two million active members, organized in thirty thousand local branches. This is an impressive organizational achievement, and takes the steady work of three hundred full-time organizers. But some local branches often are little more than clubs aiming to preserve the folklore of the lost territories.

Conventions of affiliated associations and the yearly demonstrations of the parent League of Refugees are mass assemblies of major proportions. Beneath gaily patterned coats of arms—East Prussia, Pomerania, Silesia, or Bohemia, Danzig or Memel—flutter banners screaming "Silesia, Germany's East," "Germany's Memel," "East Prussia: German and Free." They are the only mass political demonstrations in West Germany with uniformed youths standing in formations, beating drums to hail each leader and each speaker. Speakers love to modify Arndt's poem:

> For not the Federal Republic alone—
> It's all of Germany we want!

Listening to refugee speakers at their mass demonstrations, wading through mountains of publications (in part printed and distributed with state funds) one notices a remarkable similarity between these outbursts and the rhetoric and journalism of the twenties. Most speakers are bitter, critical of everything but themselves, and full of unshakable self-righteousness. They have always done the right thing and everything would have turned out well if only the Allies had recognized the danger of Bolshevism in good time. The Nazis prior to 1933 had cried that shirkers, traitors and Jews had stabbed the nation in the back in 1918; refugee leaders hold today that Communist leaders in the Roosevelt administration at least are partially responsible for the loss of the Eastern territories to Poland and Russia. The nomenclature is new, the spirit the same.

The president of the League of Refugees, Wenzel Jaksch, is a Social-Democrat. He prudently condemns Hitler's crimes yet feels that German opponents of Hitler "put up much more decisive resistance than the appeasers in the West and the governments in Warsaw and Prague. . . ." In a 1965 interview, Jaksch stated that it was wrong to burden the German people with the entire guilt. When asked what should happen to millions of Poles who now live in Germany's lost territories, Herr Jaksch was deliberately vague and snide. "Perhaps many Poles who today sit in Silesia would prefer to work in Northern France and vice versa. . . ."

The Sudetan Germans of Czechoslovakia are a special category of refugees. They are the classic representatives of borderland *Germanism*. A peculiarity of these borderland Germans is constant dissatisfaction. Until World War II they wanted to come "home into the Reich"; now that they are inside they press to go back to their ancestral homeland. Sudeten Germans too renounce the use of force but clamor at the same time to return to

Czechoslovakia. And after they get back they plan a "free demo-cratic election" to determine the political future of the Sudeten-land. All of this has a nice ring of "democracy" about it; it is merely a repetition by legal means of the union of 1938 forced by Hitler under the threat of war.

Almost two hundred thousand people attend the annual conven-tion of the Sudeten Germans in Stuttgart. "We Sudeten Germans reject revenge and commit ourselves to Europe . . . but we want to return into our Sudeten homeland, and not as a tolerated minority," declared Sudeten German Association Chairman Dr. Franz Böhm at the 1965 convention. The previous year, Federal Minister for Transportation, Hans Christoph Seebohm endorsed the 1938 Munich agreement. It was still binding, he claimed. In 1965 Chan-cellor Erhard sent a message to the convention confirming the right of the Sudetan Germans to their homeland and self-determination as "inviolable."

It is part of Bonn political ritual that both the government party and the opposition must lend public support to the refugee cause. This is especially surprising since the absorption in West Ger-many of the expelled Sudeten Germans, Pomeranians, Silesians or East Prussians is about effected. Polls of refugees usually show that the majority would go back only under completely unthinkable conditions. Even they do not believe such conditions can ever be fulfilled. In 1958, 40 percent of the refugees still wanted to return; five years later only 25 percent were interested. In 1965, only 10 percent were prepared to return to a Communist-governed Poland, 17 percent if Poland should revert to capitalism. If Poland should cede the controversial areas to Germany, 44 percent would return to their old homeland; only 18 percent agreed to go if the present Polish population remains. These polls seem to show that spokes-men of government-financed refugee associations do not neces-sarily speak for the refugees.

West German politicians often say that it is better to "embrace" refugee leaders than to make extremists out of them by renouncing the Eastern territories. More convincing an argument would be an attempt to satisfy the refugees' valid demands for compensation. The burden of Eastern territorial loss was not equally distributed; refugees have been paid only a fraction of the value of their lost possessions. Should a former Silesian peasant pay more for Hitler's lost war than an inhabitant of Hamburg or Munich? A high government official in Bonn has said that full payment for property lost in the East would be impossible, not only because of financial reasons but also due to "weighty political considerations," that is, it would be the equivalent of an official renunciation. The West Germans have taken an easy road; they have saved money and simultaneosuly conserved a nationalistic hotbed.

Refugee organizations and their spokesmen are not taken really seriously in Bonn; they serve another purpose entirely. Some political leaders hope eventually to be able to negotiatae reunification with the DDR, offering the Soviet Union recognition of the Oder-Neisse line as their part of the bargain. The public activities of the refugee organizations can be of some help toward this end. If the refugee organizations did not exist, West Germany's case at such negotiations would be weakened. The same Bonn politicians maintain these associations present no internal political threat. They are looked upon as a lunatic fringe. But others remember with fear that only a small minority took the Nazis seriously in the twenties. In the 1924 *Reichstag*, the Nazis controlled thirty-two delegates, in 1928, only twelve. Many Germans went to Hitler's assemblies in the spirit of enjoying grotesque sideshows. Lunatic fringes can turn into broad bands.

Watching the refugees at their mass meetings, shouting and ranting, one appreciates the blessing that is West Germany's economic miracle: it stands like a protective dam between millions of Germans and radicalism. If West Germany were not as prosperous and Bonn continued to "embrace" the refugees—into what mad adventure could these people plunge the country?

One view of history suggests that the English Channel—in isolating the English from the chaos and wars on the continent—made them into the kind of people they are today, usually relaxed, tolerant, peaceful. The same theory sees the French as fortunate to have found their natural borders and national identity relatively early in their history. As a people they are said to know what, who and where they are. The Germans, accordingly, are the unfortunate "people of the middle." They have never known where their land began and where it ended. Once the border was here, then again over there; sometimes they were united, at other times not, first they pushed, then they were pushed in return.

Today, more than one hundred and fifty years after the German War of Liberation (when Goethe wrote: "Germany, where does it lie?") and one hundred years after Bismarck, the Germans still are not sure of their borders. How many Germanies are there? One or two? Or three—for is Austria "German" too? Three-and-one-third, with the "German" part of Switzerland? This Germany, does it look East or West? Germans are still searching for their country. Will they ever be content?

Anyone who travels through the German states will not find any easy answer. The further he looks, the murkier the view. He meets those who want to remount the battle horses and "ride toward the East," as it says in the old "patriotic" song that refugee organizations distribute to schoolchildren. Others are less militant but continue to grumble: "The Allies have divided us, now they must reunite us."

Will there never be peace in this land? Many do say there is no "German" soil, there is no French or Polish soil. "There is good soil and bad soil, sandy soil, marshy grounds, and so forth," a high school student in Munich replied to a question. At a meeting of refugee Silesians in Hannover a speaker called out: "Silesia's soil is drenched with German blood." A middle-aged man shouted from the back of the hall: "There are better fertilizers."

As recently as 1964, the city council of the old university town Tübingen decided to erect a traffic sign listing distances to "Berlin the Reichshaupstadt" and various other *"Reichstädte"*: Eger, Memel, Königsberg and Breslau, all well outside Germany's new borders. Eger and Memel lie beyond the 1937 borders. Outraged professors and students suggested to add the distance to Auschwitz (1130 kilometers) as well. The sign still lies in the town hall cellar. However, similar signs are posted in many West German cities, especially near the East German border of the DDR.

"What is the Germans' Fatherland?" The West German writer Günter Grass made this his motto in his 1965 election campaign for the Social-Democratic candidate Willy Brandt. Party officials were not terribly happy. Grass grew up in Danzig, to which he has erected a magnificent poetic memorial in his novels. Said Grass in his speeches: "With respect to Silesia, Eastern Pomerania, East Prussia, I—who come from there—gritting my teeth and beating my breast, can only utter the truth: we have squandered these provinces, gambled them away, challenged a world, lost it." Grass continued: "Let us put an end to the costly refugee meetings that fatten the functionaries! In their stead I recommend a serious research of vanishing dialects . . . and the founding of well-planned . . . cities that might be called Neu-Königsberg, Neu-Allenstein, Neu-Breslau . . . and Neu-Danzig. Let us be founders of cities! We have the room. . . ."

Another protest was registered in 1962 by a number of Protestant laymen and theologians who joined to publish the so-called Tübingen *Memorandum of the Eight*. Among them were the Berlin professor Helmuth Becker, Düsseldorf's Joachim Beckmann, the director of the West German Broadcasting Corporation (Cologne) Klaus von Bismarck, the Munich Nobel Prize winner Werner Heisenberg. The "Eight from Tübingen" said:

> The freedom of the people living in Berlin is a right the entire world acknowledges, but the national desire for reunification in freedom cannot be accomplished today . . . and we must consider our claim to sovereignty in the territories east of the Oder-Neisse line as lost.

> We believe that responsible circles in all parties share our views; but, for internal political reasons they are afraid to state them in public. An atmosphere that prevents the political leadership from telling the people the truth is poisonous.

In 1962, these were quite daring words. The authors of the memorandum were immediately accused of "intellectual arrogance," and called traitors who "accept Communist theses." The words of Kant (a citizen of Königsberg and so a favorite among the refugees) were invoked: "All the power of heaven stands on the side of justice."

The Council of Protestant Churches in Germany immediately disassociated itself publicly from its lay leaders. Three years later, however, the Council published its own statement in support of the same opinions from which it had disassociated itself in 1962. The statement entitled "Refugees and the attitude of the Germans to their Eastern neighbors," called for "new approaches." It asked Germans to begin to respect the people of Poland's "right to live" and grant them the "room necessary for their development" in peace. Precisely because of the suffering caused to Poles by the war Germany had started, the present borders of Poland should be respected.

The statement released a political storm of some magnitude. Politicians, who had never opposed nationalistic sermons in the churches, never found fault with priests blessing cannons or celebrating victories by the ringing of church-bells, suddenly protested what they called "unjustified interventions by the church in political matters."

The incident again illustrated a phenomenon characteristic of West Germany: not only a good part of the press but also the churches are ahead of official politics. They fill a vacuum in public life, left—out of fear or complacency, or both—by the political parties.

14

Fathers and Sons

N HIS novel *Dog Years* the West German writer Günter Grass (born in 1929) describes the extraordinary success of an imaginary consumer gimmick, so-called magic spectacles. They were the "hit" of 1955. Ten years after the end of the war the magic spectacles were manufactured "on the basis of most modern market research" and grabbed up within a short time by hundreds of thousands of teen-agers.

It is a description full of macabre comedy. The new-fangled spectacles, also known as "enlightenment glasses" or "Father-un-maskers," manifested their magic only on noses younger than twenty-one years. To young wearers, they disclosed a mysterious new world; they were completely ineffective when looked through by fathers and mothers. For the young, the glasses "reveal, and even worse—unmask" the past of every grown-up thirty years and older.

"After supper," Grass writes, or "during family outings, from the window, while father is running circles with the lawn mower, there are opportune moments to see . . . the parents' past appears in alternating pictures . . . episodes which were kept secret from the growing children for some reason or other, become distinct and tangible." Not only "frightfully many erotic secrets are aired" but also "acts of violence, performed, tolerated, instigated eleven, twelve, thirteen years ago: murder, often a hundredfold. Aiding and abetting of. Cigarette smoking and watching during. Proven, decorated celebrated murderers. Murder motives become leit-motifs. With murderers at a table, in the same boat, bed and casino. Toasts, orders to go into action. Entries into record books. Breathing on a rubber stamp." Sometimes "only signatures and wastepaper baskets . . . recur in the two-fold circle of the father-detection glasses" for "many paths lead to (murder). Words (lead to murder) and keeping silent. Each father has at least one to conceal. Many remain almost as if never committed, buried, cur-tained off, firmly lodged until the magic spectacles come on the market in the eleventh postwar year and expose the culprit."

Günter Grass, a master of social and political parody, not a moralist, summarizes in this scene the hopeless relationship between the generations in West Germany. Hyperbole and simile, fiction and truth, guilt and innocence, hope and irony, intermingle in a tragedy of philistinism. Everywhere the magic spectacles stop the laughter of children. The children let "cakes and packages tied up with gold-colored string" drop to the ground; they "run off, screaming." But then they fall silent. Industrious market researchers stand at movie house entrances and at athletic fields and tirelessly ask: "Tell me, young fellow, what effect did the wearing of our spectacles have on you?" But the young people only reply: "Well, in the case of my old man I can see quite clearly now." And though the market researchers ("in the interest of our customers" and "for the sake of further improvement of the spectacles") would like to have had more specific answers—the young people evade all further questions.

"Available material is kept secret by the sons and daughters just

as the fathers and mothers used to be discreet even in their dreams."
Shame may be an inhibiting factor, Grass writes. "Anyone who
resembles his father outwardly is afraid of conclusions about further similarities."

Secondary school and university students are afraid of interrupt-
ing their studies which are "frequently financed by sacrifices" on
the part of the parents. Thus, there is no "new children's crusade"
nor an "insurrection of the children against the parents." The expected revolution does not take place; it is prevented by "family
considerations, the instinct for self-preservation, cold-blooded
speculation and love of mystery."

An outsider can only guess to what degree the natural conflict
between the generations is magnified in Germany by the past of
the fathers. Every day there must be tense moments in German
homes when children, upon learning something about Hitler and
World War II, ask: "Daddy, what did you do between 1933 and
1945?" Or "Where were you at that time? Were you in the Party?"
How many parents tell the truth? And how many simply snap:
"These are things you don't understand. Don't talk so much and eat
your soup." Whoever wants to investigate this situation in West
Germany will often run into a wall of silence. It is not easy to
persuade fathers or sons to disclose the intimacies of such talks.
Few deny that such conversations do take place. Their content
belongs to a well-guarded private sphere which, understandably,
remains closed to the outsider. Yet the longer you live in Germany
and the closer you become to people, the more you notice a tension between the fathers and sons. It is, as if fathers and sons are
moving in a badly marked minefield, like enemy armies during a
precarious truce.

Especially among college boys, one notices an impatience of demeanor and a peculiar irritability in dealings with the older generation.* This is the more noticeable since parental discipline is
often greater in German families than in their French or English
counterparts. In Germany, more than in other countries, fathers
still play the role of *pater familias*. Publishers and editors agree
that the recent increase in the sale of books dealing with the Nazi

* An important exception are the members of fraternities practicing the
"duel" or wearing "colors." See the next chapters.

196

period is most likely explained by the increasing interest of the younger generation in their parents' concealed past. The same thing could also be said of the huge successes of plays such as Hochhuth's *The Deputy* or Peter Weiss's *The Investigation*.

The Oedipus complex of certain young West German intellectuals is not only a "father" complex or a "Hitler" complex; it is also a "State" complex. This sounds ridiculous in French or English, but in German one talks of "father state," referring to the anonymous state authority. Older West German politicians complain that young people are disrespectful not only toward their fathers but toward any authority, any order, especially that of the state.

There is no telling what lies in the hearts of many young people, even those without "magic spectacles." One receives an inkling, an impression, and that is all. There are occasional revelations. Thus, in February, 1965, *Die Welt* published a poem by nineteen-year-old Hans Leuschner whom the editors introduced as a recent "high school graduate." It was an awkward poem but all the more touching for it. It was dedicated to the twenty-second anniversary of the execution of Hans and Sophie Scholl in Munich. The suicidal, public protest of the Scholls against the National Socialist regime in 1944 was one of the very few spontaneous acts of resistance wholly inspired by moral considerations. Leuschner entitled his poem *Not for the Fathers*.

> This is not addressed to the fathers.
> They don't count.
> They have flopped.
>
> On the 22.2. (the year is known)
> two students,
> Sophie and Hans Scholl,
> were executed in Munich.
> I say no more.
> We learn this in school.
>
> I am still young,
> and the fathers say,
> when they hear me speak,
> that I am not mature.

What is that: to be mature?
When crime hovers
above the heads of the living,
when the land groans
with murder—
to sneak out of the country,
or crawl up to the cross,
to buy absolution?

That is what the fathers call: to be mature!
I would say they just saved their own skins,
or what is worse:
they wanted to have their peace and quiet.

The fathers no longer count.
They have flopped.
I address students,
girls and boys
who think.

Think of Sophie and Hans
on the 22.2.
They were your age.
They had their heads cut off.

On the 22.2.
you should tear the grimaces
off your walls
and look at the Scholls.
and you will not laugh
that day.
And you will never allow that to happen
what your fathers chose.
And will rediscover
(perhaps) that
which your fathers took from you:
your faith.

The editors received an extraordinary number of outraged letters
during the following weeks. Most letters were sent by fathers who
"no longer count." The tone of most letters was even more significant than the content. One writer suggested that the editors

of *Welt* remember it was the fathers who paid subscription fees, not "sons like that who write poems." Another instructed the young poet to be grateful to the fathers whom he despises for having created a new order after the defeat—one which enabled him to publish such poems without endangering himself. A third predicted that the young poet would whisper one day at his father's grave: "Old man, forgive me the nonsense I wrote back then, I was still so foolish at the time." A fourth writer advised young Leuschner to emigrate to East Germany if he didn't like it in the West. Irascibility, anger, bad conscience, hypersensitivity, aggressiveness. condescending moralizing and self-pity characterized most letters. Leuschner had obviously touched a sore spot.

Young West Germans in Stuttgart, Bonn, Bremen, Cologne, Frankfurt and Hamburg in 1965 wrote a class theme on the subject "How do you feel about the concepts 'Fatherland,' 'patriotism' and 'national feeling'?" The essays were written at the same time that several leading politicians were demanding a "new patriotism." The boys and girls were between thirteen and fifteen years old. Some interesting excerpts:

Fatherland is an outdated word. Who today would say "I will give my life for my fatherland?" The word has no meaning for me . . . Their feeling for the fatherland cost our parents dearly. Two absurd world wars have strengthened it or shaken it. (A thirteen-year-old boy.)

I find "patriotism" completely wrong . . . There should be "national feeling," but not too much of it; for the national feelings of the people have been used once before as the foundation for a war which cost millions of lives. (A thirteen-year-old boy.)

Of course you are more closely tied to the country in which you are born . . . , but if you talk about "my Fatherland," there is always the danger that you will forget the other countries that are "Fatherlands" too. (A fourteen-year-old.)

To die for the Fatherland—that is the greatest absurdity. It is much more important to live for the Fatherland. You can serve your country by working, but not by dying for it . . . We Germans, I believe, have a little too much patriotism anyway . . . We immediately feel that our honor has been slighted. That is no way of coming closer to the other countries . . . One should try to serve one's country by bringing it closer to the other countries. (A fourteen-year-old boy.)

Certainly, national feeling can be quite attractive for some people. However, it was this national feeling, supported by many flags, hymns and parades, which cost the lives of millions of people. On the basis of World War II, I strictly reject this feeling. (A fourteen-year-old.)

The "Fatherland" is responsible for many crimes. Since I was unable to select my fatherland, I am not guilty of the crimes of some of my countrymen. Nonetheless, we, the next generation, must show the victims that not all the German people are bad. (A fifteen-year-old girl.)

What is our Fatherland? I have no feeling for a Fatherland. Nothing ties me to "Germany," there is no Germany. If there is anything I honor, it is my town. (A sixteen-year-old boy.)

The concept Fatherland. . . . It is difficult to have to write about concepts you have not really thought about. When I hear the word "Fatherland" I immediately think back to my homeland which I had to leave at the age of seven because my parents wanted to preserve us from Communism. I am still deeply attached to this homeland even today; perhaps because we had a huge piece of property there, with a factory, gardens, woods and houses.

Defeats supposedly provide fertile grounds for lasting hatred. Some years after Japan's defeat in 1945 an anti-American neurosis developed among Japanese high school boys and girls; it still plagues relations between the two countries. This has not been the case in West Germany.

Compared with young people in other Western countries the West German youngsters appear not only less "patriotic," but almost ominously sedate and precociously sober minded. There are no "Mods" or "Rockers" or crazy teen-age fads in West Germany. Despite the availability of money, the relatively great freedom between the sexes and attempts to imitate the life in the neighboring countries, West German youth has not been infected by a *dolce vita.*

The ruinous outbreaks of youthful rowdyism—so common in England, Scandinavia or America—do not generally occur in West Germany, although one might expect exactly the opposite. West German youth grew up in starkly adverse conditions: more than one and a half million children had lost one or both parents in the War; for years afterward, millions of fathers were still prisoners of war. At War's end, 40 percent of all young people were said to suffer from neuroses resulting from war experiences; the crime rate among young people was twice as high as it had been during the twenties; 23 percent of all young people suffered from venereal diseases; prostitution among minors was four times as high as during the prewar period. That plus the destruction of the cities, the lack of heating, the malnutrition. With the "economic miracle," the difficulties vanished. It is perhaps an even greater miracle that the time of deprivation did not leave deeper scars, did not produce worse conflicts among the young.

The 1945 defeat and the subsequent humiliation deepened the split between the generations. The political, moral and military collapse of the older generation in 1945 has destroyed so many traditional values that today young West Germans hardly know what to believe in. One result may be a tendency of West German youth to shun the community and withdraw—almost sulking— to a private sphere. The "Youth Movement," once so vigorous in Germany, has almost totally disappeared. All attempts to revive it after 1945 have failed. Today's youth talks about "*Beruf*" (profession), not about "*Berufung*" (calling). Most political discussion clubs for youths in West Germany are adjuncts of the churches or the parties; they must be supported by the State and would probably fold without subsidies (which allow them sandwiches and beer during meetings).* Even so, very few youngsters participate.

Young West Germans are frequently criticized for this apathy. Snippier older critics call it a "flight into egotistic materialism." Yet such glib and easy phrases do not pinpoint the true causes but simply gloss them over. The Oedipus complex of many young West Germans is also a complex against "community." Consciously or unconsciously, many keep a distance from anything that has a communal smell to it. The noisiest celebrants at the famous Rhenish

* In the same way in which the taxpayer supports political parties, the Federal Government and the states subsidize political youth clubs, student clubs, and educational trips—to France or Israel as part of "operation reconciliation." Education in citizenship is the purpose of all these measures.

carnivals are for the most part middle-aged men and women. Amidst the hooting, drinking, singing, seesawing mass of well-fed citizens one sees younger people looking slightly confused and abashed. At office parties, older employees make merry and strike up hearty folk songs; younger people sit around slightly bored and aloof. It is not their world.

What is their world then? Twenty five years ago, it was the world of the brown shirts. The young were Hitler's most fanatical supporters. Fifteen- and sixteen-year-old boys were the last, most embittered defenders of the Thousand Year Reich in its final hours. An army of teen-agers was preparing to make a final stand in the Bavarian mountains. Even the Scholls "believed" until 1942. Youth had been Nazism's favorite child and Hitler had called it "guarantor of the future." This phrase too died in the smoke of the burning cities; ever since politicians, sociologists and teachers have argued how best to describe the post war youth. It has been called skeptical, sober, sullen, mistrustful, nihilistic, irresponsible, insecure, selfish and lonely. Psychological tests seem to justify all these designations. Most often one hears: "Youngsters are cynical."

Thirty years ago, submissive, loyal young Germans simply could not think that they were governed by a gang of criminals. Today, many youngsters describe the government as just that—although this is not the case. Power has a foul smell to it; even to seek it seems despicable. The younger generation takes a very small part in politics today.

If you consider the developments within the last twenty years, it is astonishing that young people are not even more cynical. From 1945 until 1949 Germany was down and out, arms were a thing of the past. It was a time that future Defense Minister Strauss could say: "Anyone who again picks up a gun—his hand should drop off." The ruins bred a Christian pacifism; *Wehrmacht* generals were condemned at Nuremberg; officers returning from prisoner-of-war camps could not find work (they were considered "tainted").

A few years later rearmament begins. The victorious powers submit to German pressure and release masses of war criminals and former generals from the prisons. Perhaps they want to provide the right atmosphere in which to form a new army, perhaps they are áfraid too few would volunteer otherwise. Former Nazis are hired as state secretaries in the new Bonn ministries, among them Chancellor Adenauer's "right hand," State Secretary Hans Globke, author of the official commentary to the infamous Nuremberg laws. With the beginning of rearmament, the word "pacifist" becomes a term of abuse. The same man who did not even want to pick up a gun again speaks about "expunging" the Soviet Union "from the map," an expression reminiscent of the Nazi past. "We Germans do not want to be the foot soldiers of the American atomic knights," Strauss says. The way leads from "no" weapons to "small' weapons and finally to "atomic weapons."

I know a man from Hamburg who was born in 1924 and was made a captain in the German *Wehrmacht* during the last year of the war. When he returned from a prisoner-of-war camp in 1947 he wanted to study law. Hamburg University turned him away; as a former officer he was a "militarist" and not fit for study. He became a businessman. A few years later, he began to hear from Army authorities, asking him to volunteer for the new *Bundeswehr*. His military experience, they said, was badly needed. Is it any wonder that he is cynical today?

What about the very young? A new generation is now appearing on the scene: the postwar children's children, who never "burnt" their fingers. For them Hitler and his wars are just history.

The *Theolinden-Mittel-und Oberschule* is a girls' primary and high school in a relatively new, upper-middle-class Munich suburb. It is considered by some good, by others far above average. The textbooks in use here treat the Nazi era with noteworthy candor, as is still not the case in many West German schools. But here, textbooks include photographs of extermination camps, schematic representations of the Auschwitz death factory, maps showing the vast network of concentration camps that covered half of Europe, excerpts from authentic diaries and letters of the persecuted.

"Cruelties and atrocities have been part of all wars among peoples," it says in a German history textbook in use here. "War brutalizes human beings . . . yet Heydrich and his successors' systematic extermination undertaking, based on ice-cold calculations, is unequalled in the history of the world." (This is followed

203

by detailed descriptions of the extermination processes.) Then an excerpt from the letter of a Warsaw boy to his younger sister in Palestine:

> Dear Tamara, Where should I begin? I will start with mother. She was taken to Treblinka. Everyday thousands of mothers, fathers and children are being dragged away. Why should our mother be an exception? . . . Do you know how people die in Treblinka? The boxcars are shunted into a special track up to the murder house. . . . Then the people have to undress. *Nagaikas*—submachine guns. Everyone has to put his clothes bundle on a special spot. Then he gets a number. So he is being sent to work, of course. But before he goes to work he has to be deloused (the camp commander usually says: "the most modern delousing plant in Europe"). They go inside. After a minute there suddenly resounds horrible screaming. But only very briefly. A lever is turned once and a huge maw opens and swallows the people that are later burned in the crematorium. The entire process only takes a few minutes. (Friends of Wanda, "good" Germans, say: "What is so horrible about that? Our people are dying at the front. And it doesn't hurt here, either. It's over quickly.") Jews, who have been especially selected beforehand, collect the clothes under the supervision of Ukrainians and load them into wagons. They also take the ash out of the crematorium. And then they too are sent to be "deloused." Sometimes one of them succeeds in hiding under the rags. And someone like that will tell you everything afterward. And so mother has died also."

"After careful calculations," the book goes on to say, "it can be estimated that the National Socialists murdered altogether five million Jews. How quickly this figure is written down! How quickly it is read! When we memorize it do we know what immensities are concealed behind this figure of five million murdered people? An old French proverb says: 'A hundred-thousand corpses is a statistic. But the death of a single human being remains an acute human pain.' "

I cite such a long excerpt from this book because it is one of the best history books in use at West German schools. I will soon discuss the others. Yet even at this model school, the young history teacher complains his instruction is a daily struggle against the prejudices of the home. The parents of these children are mostly upper-middle-class businessmen, doctors, architects and officials.

I sat in on a fourth-grade geography lesson where the subject was "Critical Areas in Asia." Class discussion moved from South Viet Nam via Indonesia to the Near East.

Teacher (at the large map): What are the causes of the Arab-Israeli conflict?

Student: It's about religion. Jews against Mohammedans.

Teacher: That can't be the only reason. Can someone give the national reasons? There are also Jews who are Christians. What do we Germans have to do with the fate of the Jews?

Student: "We Germans" is exaggerated. But Hitler killed thousands of Jews.

Teacher: Thousands?

Student: Yes, one does not exactly know how many.

Second Student: And nobody knows how many Germans were murdered in Siberia. By the Communists. One hasn't been able to estimate that.

Third Student: There was a war on. Everybody murdered.

Fourth Student: It is always like that, everywhere.

Teacher: How did you find that out?

Third Student: My uncle was in the war. He told us all about it.

Teacher: Germany was not at war with the Jews. Why did we make a point of killing the Jews?

Student: The Jews were always persecuted.

Teacher: But here it was worst of all.

Student: No, that's not true.

Teacher: But it is, it is.

Student: The Jews are a bad—perhaps not a bad—but a funny people.

Teacher: Is that any reason to kill them?

Second Student: I believe that the Jews should not always talk about morality.

Here the teacher seemed to be losing control over the situation. He gave a brief lecture about the persecution of the Jews in Europe, which started as religious persecution and culminated under Hitler in the gas chambers.

Student: Yes, but they should not blackmail us.

Later in the morning, the young teacher demonstrated that eleventh-grade students differed significantly from the fourth. The eleventh-grade girls were informed about politics to a degree which would be noteworthy in any country. They knew the Weimar constitution and its weaknesses, discussed the economic background of Hitler's war plans, knew his crimes, even mentioned several leading West German industrialists who they felt got off too easily. I asked them about the basic laws of the Federal Republic and received intelligent answers.

The young teacher accompanied me to the exit. He had reason to be satisfied. Smiling, he said: "The pollsters would say that people do not change, only public opinion."

This was a new school in a new suburb. It is different in schools where teachers belong to an older, more self-conscious generation and where some history books conceal or distort the facts. Roughly half of all active teachers taught under the Hitler regime. In recent years both teachers and textbooks have come under frequent attacks by the West German press and TV.*

Many history books have been rewritten since or even withdrawn. Still, many textbooks leave much to be desired, both in terminology and content. These are still in use in public schools:

1. *Geschichte im Überblick*, IV, Verlag Stalling, Oldenburg: This book is designed for high-school students between the ages of 16 and 19. It has this—and no more—to say about the Nazi terror: "The so-called *Röhm Putsch* had already provided the occasion to murder several hundred personalities of the opposition. . . . The Nürnberg Laws required each official to be of 'Aryan descent.' The measures against the Jews became more and more intense. In November, 1938 synagogues were systematically set afire."

2. *Geschichte der Neusten Zeit*, Verlag Klett, Stuttgart. This is a widely distributed textbook for lower high school students. "In November 1938 there occurred a particularly undignified

---

* A broadcast titled "A Look At Our Youth," by the West German TV reporter Jürgen Neven-Dumont on April 29, 1959 started what seems to be a fashion today and is often cited. Neven-Dumont asked ninety-five students of four Federal states: "Who was Adolf Hitler and what did he do?" He received—and broadcast—answers like: "Hitler had a mustache," "He built the *Autobahns*," "He gave the unemployed work." Only two high school students gave satisfactory answers. It turned out that they had acquired their knowledge on their own initiative and not in school.

event. An emigrée Jew shot a German diplomat in Paris who himself had been anything but an enemy of the Jews. The National Socialists exaggerated this deed out of all proportion and used it as a pretext for an intense persecution of the Jews. Members of the Party organization set fire to the synagogues by order of Goebbels. They also mistreated many Jews and damaged Jewish businesses and houses more or less heavily." Concentration camps are dismissed in two sentences: "The concentration camps were built. Most of the prisoners were followers of the KPD [Communists]."

3. *Lebendige Geschichte*, Part 3, from 1815 to the present, Dummler-Verlag, Bonn, 1960, uses a mere five words to dismiss the extermination camps, calling them "intensified measures against the Jews."

4. *Aus deutscher Vergangenhit*, Part II. Verlag Cassianeum, Dönauwort, 1960: "The Jews were treated as non-Germans and disenfranchised even when they had fought as soldiers for Germany and had completely fulfilled their duties as citizens. Many of them fled the country to escape the persecution. Those that remained behind were robbed of their property, sent into camps where they were inhumanly tortured. Hundreds of thousands of imprisoned Jews lost their lives here, or at least their health."

5. *Geschichte der neuesten Zeit*, Verlag Klett, Stuttgart, 1959: "From the very beginning Hitler's followers contained many dubious elements in addition to well-intentioned idealists. The fact that the followers, who had valuable qualities, were unable to make their influence felt and let themselves be outranked when Party offices were filled, contributed materially to the degeneration and the downfall, for the leadership thus fell into the hands of disreputable toadies and unprincipled adventurers. . . ."

6. *Erbe des Abendlandes, Part IV*, Verlag Schwann, Düsseldorf: "Hitler would have entered history with great honor as the creator of Great Germany if he had now moderated his ambitions." (1940)

7. *Grundzuge der Geschichte von der Frühgeschichte Europas bis zur Weltpolitik der Gegenwart*, Verlag Diesterweg, Frankfurt 1961: "Jews from all over Europe were cruelly murdered in special extermination camps erected by Hitler. However, the German people were informed of the full extent of these atrocities only after the war." Students who use this textbook have not been in-

formed of the full extent even now. It is designed for grades nine and ten.

A widely distributed history book gives the following account of the war in the East:

8. *Geschichte der Neusten Zeit, Part IV*, Verlag Klett, Stuttgart 1959: "On Stalin's order partisan units gathered behind the front. These units later congratulated themselves for having killed more than 300,000 German soldiers and officers. German counter-measures [sic!] also violated international law."

9. *Lesebogen für Geschichte, P IV*, Verlag Klinkhardt, Bad Heilbrunn puts the blame on America: "In [1941] the United States declared war against Japan as well as its two Allies, Germany and Italy. . . ." The same book turns into a spokesman for Hitler's wishful thinking. Discussing conditions in Russia in the fall of 1941, it says: "Moreover, Russia had lost immense masses of war material and roughly four million prisoners of war. It stood at the brink of collapse."

The alliance against Nazi Germany was a "conspiracy" according to:

10. *Der Geschichtsunterricht, Part IV*, Verlag Progel, Ansbach, 1955: "Three men conspired to bring about Hitler's downfall: Churchill, Roosevelt and Stalin. They laid their plans well ahead of time."

The intoxication of the German masses, their ecstatic enthusiasm for Hitler, receives remarkably little mention in most textbooks. This is true even of books that avoid glossing over the disaster. Almost all textbooks contain remarks such as:

11. "Criticism of the rulers could not be voiced, not even when it was felt in wide circles such as during the persecution of the Jews in November, 1938 (*Reichskristallwoche*)." (*Unterrichtswerk für Geschichte*, IV, Lurzverlag, Munich.)

The following attempt at civic education sounds strangely suspicious:

12. "The mass of the German people were incapable of offering any open resistance. The Gestapo persecuted every trace of deviationism. More than a million Germans went through their concentration camps." (Jews are probably being included in this number.) From *Werden und Wirken, Neueste Zeit*, Verlag Braun, Karlsruhe.

Many textbooks give the impression that the National Socialist regime was a three-man show—Hitler, Himmler, Heydrich. *Werden und Wirken* also states that Himmler was responsible for the fact that "the SS was misused to commit crimes."

13. "Only the ruthless pressure of the Party, employing everything at its command to assert itself, could force [sic!] the continuation of the war." We are dealing here with 1941, not, as one might think, the last weeks of the war. (*Grundriss der Geschichte, A IV*, Verlag Klett, Stuttgart, 1960).

Contemporary history is not an isolated subject. It is one subject among many which shape feelings of national identity and educate young citizens to be politically responsible. Dangerous politics have many ways to enter the heart of a nation, as the early history of the Nazi idea proves. One is through literature.

West German critics devote much attention to novels and poems of young postwar writers. The works of Günter Grass, Heinrich Böll, Hans Magnus Enzensberger, Uwe Johnson, Peter Weiss and Ingeborg Bachmann are available in most school libraries, and many students certainly read them. Even more important to students and teachers are the anthologies used as texts in primary grades.

It is in these anthologies that one finds dismaying allusions: The critic and professor of literature at Tübingen University, Walter Jens, called attention to such school anthologies in 1961. In a summary representation of contemporary literature, Jens pointed out that the most important West German school textbooks of literature are not free of the evil spirit of the past. Writers like Erwin Guido Kolbenheyer, a notorious chauvinist and nationalist mystic upon whom the Nazis heaped literary prizes, are sympathetically discussed.

"The Bavarian state textbook publishing house asked Dr. Arno Mulot to write a textbook of literature," Jens writes, "in which Dwinger and Wehner, Busse and Schauwecker are mentioned [all of them literary nonentities but glorifiers of war and worshippers of blood-and-soil, who were particularly honored during the Nazi era]. You look in vain for [liberal or emigrated writers such as] Annette Kolb, René Schickele, Robert Walser and Joseph Roth . . . evidently all deleterious intellectuals, enemies of what is healthy." Mulot's textbook—a best seller—has been published in nine editions so far, five since 1959. The author has been the chairman of an official board of examiners since 1964, and is in a position to decide on the suitability of candidates for teaching positions. The very same Dr. Mulot wrote Nazist literary critiques during the Third Reich.

An example from Mulot's *Soldier in German Writing of Our Time* (1938): "The pacifistic and maliciously-defeatist war books ... were never blood of our blood. They belong into the category of viruses that have been able to throw the mass of people into heavy feverish convulsions but have been thoroughly excreted by the healthy community." Or on another page: "The Führer called the German people out of a state of heinous decadence to fight for the *volksdeutsche* Reich. The brown battalions marched ... [et cetera]." (*The Reich in German Writing*, 1940.)

The Schleswig-Holstein poet Bartels—a notorious Nazi—continues to be held in high esteem in that state. Streets and schools are named after him even today. In a public school in Kassel I overheard a fourteen-year-old girl being asked to recite a poem by the Nazi poet Hans Johst. The poem lauded the "voice of the blood." The girl had never heard of Thomas Mann or Bertoldt Brecht. The middle-aged teacher explained that these writers were too intellectual for this age group. Jens quotes a "classic" West German reference book, now in its eighth edition, that claims that Thomas Mann was "more a juggler of words than a writer."

The widely used literary anthology *Wesen und Werden der Deutschen Dichtung* by Georg Ried (now in its sixteenth edition, 171,000 to 175,000!) glorifies war to a point where literary values are lost. Writer Ernst Penzolt is commended because he recognizes the "ethical impetus of war" and because he wrote the lines (1941!): "Goodnight then,/ and God protect/ all good soldiers of the world." Ried cites at length from the Nazi showpiece novel *People Without Lebensraum* by Hans Grimm. But Heinrich Heine is "derisive," "cold and rational." "Unfortunately Heine mocks and misuses the tone of the people," the effect being a "deleterious" one. Erich Remarque (*All Quiet on the Western Front*) wants to represent the reality of war, but unfortunately his attempt is a "one-sided" one. Remarque, he complains, shows only the "repulsive, miserable" aspect of war.

There are pedagogues and officials in West Germany who believe that the general backwardness of the educational system is more dangerous than such textbooks. The crisis in West German education has been a political issue for some time. Most German children quit school after only eight years of study. As far back as 1955, a member of the government party, *Bundestag* Deputy Erich Peter Neumann, wrote about the quality of the West German primary schools: "Eight obligatory school years create—at best—the type of person who can talk without knowing anything, and can listen without understanding a single word. Such is the material of which you carve dictatorships. And we know how."

Compared to other Western industrial countries, Germany today is educationally underdeveloped. Among numerous reasons for this are the many denominational primary schools and the tiny one-classroom village schools which many politicians want to retain as a valuable "image of real life."* In such village schools, children from six to fourteen learn in the same room, at the same time, from the same teacher. Much of the backwardness of the West German educational system is a result of the Nazi regime and its contempt for learning. During the regime's twelve years, only five schools were built in the entire city of Berlin.

Only 17.6 percent of all West Germans between the ages of 15 and 19 attend school full time. In the United States, the percentage is 66.2; in Canada, 45.9; in France, 30.8; in Norway, 35.7; in the Soviet Union, 48.6; in Holland, 32.8; in Japan, 36.0 percent. The figure for Holland is almost twice as high as that for West Germany. And West German per capita production is more than 20 percent higher than the Dutch per capita production.

In 1965 only 45,000 West Germans graduated from high school. That represents one eighteen-year-old out of every fifteen, half as many as in Sweden, France, Norway or even Greece. France intends to triple its baccalaureate recipients by 1970; Italy and Holland hope to double theirs. West Germany expects an increase of

* A statement by Bavarian Minister of Education Theodor Maunz, in June, 1963. Maunz has since been forced to retire because of his Nazi past.

only 12 percent by 1970. One immediate result will be a severe shortage of school teachers; by 1975, about half of the teaching posts at primary schools may be vacant.

Professor Hellmut Becker, head of the West Berlin Institute for Educational Research, says: "I am afraid of the political consequences of an educational crisis . . . we are the last people in Europe who can afford mass stupification." Professor Becker (son of a liberal Weimar Republic Minister of Education), was one of the signers of Protestant lay memorandum in favor of the recognition of the Oder-Neisse line. Another signer, Heidelberg Professor of Religious Philosophy Georg Picht, has warned the West German public of an impending "educational catastrophe."

The West German government does not share his views. Chancellor Erhard complained in the summer of 1965 that "extraordinary mischief" was being perpetrated with the use of the term "educational emergency." In an anti-intellectual vein so common to German politics, Erhard declared that there exists "an intellectualism which tips over into idiocy when the intellectual only stirs up dissatisfaction without understanding anything about the matter."

15

Teachers and Students

ɔN THE University town of Göttingen a few steps lead from the marketplace down into the old *Rathskeller*. Coats of arms, emblems and flags cover walls blackened with smoke. Above the vaulted entranceway, to this pub, which Heine once praised for its tasty beer, there is the inscription: *Extra Göttingam non est vita.*

Robert Jungk refers to this bold claim in a moving description of Göttingen in the twenties. Many of the great physicists and mathematicians of our time were living here then. "To many members of the university," Jungk writes, "who studied, thought or spent their old age here, it must have seemed that the statement was daily confirmed anew." This was in the "beautiful years" before 1933. Göttingen was still world famous: a first-class international center of learning and research.

Today Göttingen is a charming little place which still corresponds to a romantic concept of a "typical German" university town. The narrow alleys are lined with gabled houses, each with its own artfully carved beams, bull's-eye glass and frivolous alcoves. A rampart surrounds the ancient heart of the city. The classical, white-golden main hall of the Georgia-Augusta University rises in its center. Town and university survived the war unharmed, but only externally. If student sayings like *"Extra Göttingam non est vita"* sound hollow everywhere, nowhere do they sound as presumptuous as here. Before 1933, great jurists, philosophers, biologists and mathematicians had spread the fame of the university throughout the world. Talented scholars and students from all countries came to Göttingen.

"A few months, no, only a few weeks in spring, 1933, sufficed," Jungk writes, "to destroy its reputation." With the dismissal of Jewish and "semitophile" professors, Göttingen sank to the level of a banal provincial university. Fires were lit in front of the Great Hall and books burned. Professors in brown uniforms raised their hand to the Hitler salute. One announced solemnly: "We are proud to wear the honorable appellation, barbarians."[*]

Within two years, fifty professors were expelled from Göttingen, among them the Nobel Prize winners Max Born and James Franck. The faculty of mathematics and natural science was hardest hit during this purge, losing more than half of its staff. Robert Jungk reports an incident that occurred during a visit by Nazi Minister of Culture Rust. At a banquet, Rust sat next to the famous old mathematician David Hilbert. "Is it really true, Herr Professor," Rust asked, "that your institute has suffered so much because of the departure of the Jews and their friends?"

Hilbert answered: "Suffered? No, it hasn't suffered, Herr Minister. It just doesn't exist anymore."

Today the almost two hundred-and-fifty-year-old university

[*] Formal address by the Rector of a German University on May 1, 1933: quoted in Rudolf Degkwitz: *Das alte und das neue Deutschland*, Hamburg, 1946.

has an enrollment of about ten thousand students, more than twice as many as in 1933; almost one-tenth are foreigners, chiefly from Scandinavia and the developing countries of Asia and Africa. The Rector of the university is a Swiss, Professor D. Zimerli. Books that were publicly burned in 1933 have been replaced in the great university library. Some professors who were dismissed came back after 1945, or at least were named honorary citizens of the town. A new generation of professors is beginning to emerge. A generous investment program has made it possible to construct modern facilities, comfortable student homes, institutes and a large athletic field. And yet Göttingen has not succeeded in regaining even a fraction of its former worth. Göttingen has lost its special place on the academic map of Europe. The Georgia-Augusta University is regarded as not much above average in any of its fields.

Göttingen rather dramatically illustrates the difficulties of German postwar intellectual life, so oddly unproductive in comparison with the past. By eliminating entire fields, by relegating some of the best intellects to exile or to the silence of internal emigration or the oblivion of the gas chambers, the Nazis and their "academic" fellow travelers perpetrated immeasurable damage. Some people fear that it may be irreparable at least during this century.

In the previous chapter I mentioned that only five schools were built in all of Berlin during the entire Third Reich. Universities were victimized by this disinterest even more profoundly. A considerable decline of German education would have been unavoidable even if Hitler had won the war. By 1939 there were only half as many students in Germany as in 1933. Here lies one interesting difference between Stalin and Hitler. Both dictators suffused education with politics and smothered it under a paralyzing doctrinairism but, in contrast to the Third Reich, the number of students in the Soviet Union under Stalin grew tremendously. New schools, universities and research institutes were being built all the time.

Today, twenty years after Hitler and despite widespread reconstruction, university education in West Germany still lags behind that of other western European countries. Elsewhere in

Western Europe, a higher education is no longer a middle-class or upper-class privilege. The percentage of "working-class" students at higher institutions in West Germany hovers around 6 percent (compared to England's 25 percent, Sweden's 20 percent, the United States' 30 percent). What this means for the future of learning, research and the accumulation of talent seems clear. A breakdown of general figures further illustrates this situation. Of the 280,000 students currently at West German institutes of higher learning, approximately 170,000 are expected to complete their courses. In England, the figure is 120,000, but a German student studies almost twice as long as an English one. Thus, England produces 120,000 persons with academic degrees at the same time that West Germany produces 80,000

The description "Nation of Thinkers" has probably never been as threadbare as now. Whether it be in Göttingen, Heidelberg or Tübingen or at the relatively young universities of Bonn, Munich, Mainz or West Berlin—everywhere there are bitter complaints about the inadequacy of education and the mediocrity of research. German universities are not drawing foreign students as they once did; he who wants to study mathematics or philosophy, economics, medicine or physics with the great masters of our time no longer goes to Germany, as was the custom forty or fifty years ago, but to other countries in the Old and New World. Today, young German scholars must emigrate to France, England or the United States to reach the sources of learning and significant centers of research.

Munich Nobel Prize winner Werner Heisenberg (he himself studied in Göttingen during the "beautiful years" before 1933) describes the demise of natural science faculties in West Germany: "After World War I, Germany was in an almost hopeless economic condition. But only a few years later, after 1920, it occupied a leading position in scientific research despite its economic misery. After World War II, Germany recovered economically much more rapidly than after the first. By 1950, its economic situation exceeded all expectations. But even now West Germany still plays only a subordinate role in scientific research." Of course, it is true that research now demands entirely different prerequisites than it did forty years ago when a piece of chalk and the back of an envelope were enough to figure out new mathematical formulas. Today, large teams are necessary, huge laboratories, expensive computers. Thus, it may be argued that in the natural sciences money could help German universities to repair the damage wrought by the Nazis. In the humanities, the situation is different. Here, as the past fifteen years have shown, money is not enough. Professor Walter Jens of Tübingen says: "In 1945 the German university stood on a moral, ethical and intellectual rubble heap . . . the destruction was great, and its traces are still visible. . . . Some university people made it too easy for themselves after 1945; we see the result. By acting as if nothing had happened, relatively little happens even now."

German universities have, of course, changed considerably since 1945. Many young teachers have replaced Nazi-infected older professors. Professors who are devoted to democracy and humanism can be found anywhere. During the Weimar era all professors loyal to the Republic, as Jens says, "could have been placed on a single expulsion list." Today, liberal nonconformists like Jens are no exception at West German universities.

Within the new West German state, among its new public institutions, universities occupy a unique spot. Since 1949, West Germany has had a new, better political system. There are new mass media, run by new men. Even the army seems to have been thoroughly reformed; new rules have replaced old Prussian principles of blind obedience. German soldiers—who once were told to "quake in their shoes" at the sight of an officer—are probably less victimized by their superiors today than their French, English or American counterparts. Of all important institutions of public life only the Catholic church and the universities in Germany have survived the great collapse with no apparent reform, almost as though nothing had happened. German universities must share the blame for the disaster. The spirit of their teaching—especially in law and German philology, also in theology and medicine—intentionally or unintentionally served the advent of Nazism. Later its teachers justified a system that culminated in the gas chambers. After 1945 the universities shirked their responsibility; they neglected to examine their own role in the Thousand Years Reich, they did not seek an understanding or explanation of their capitulation to evil.

The lesson which the politicians had learned from the past and to which they gave expression in a new and wise constitution, the universities did not learn. After 1945 they returned to the same point from which, a few years before, an ominous, "idealistically" transfigured way had led to National Socialism. The hierarchal structure of the German university facilitated its total submission to Nazism. It is still a strictly supervised and hierarchically ordered organization. Professors govern like gods; assistants and lecturers who achieve independent status in other countries—in many cases serve as high class errand boys, ghost writers and file-index keepers for the almighty Herr Professor. Teamwork—an imperative in modern science—is made extremely difficult by this system. This is one reason why West Germany, in Heisenberg's words, plays "a subordinate role" in scientific research. It has already led to the emigration of capable young scientists who could find no opportunity for further development. A well-known example is Professor Mosbauer from Munich, who went to the United States and there received the Nobel Prize. He returned to Munich only after receiving assurance that the absolute power of the professors would be abolished and the departmental system introduced at least into his faculty.

The National Science Foundation of the United States estimates that between 1957 and 1961, more than two thousand scientists emigrated to the United States from Germany. In 1963 four hundred German scientists served as professors at American universities.. Germany is not the only country that loses scientists to the United States, but an important reason for its loss is the traditional hierarchical order prevailing in German universities. Its major facet is commonly described as *Professorenherrlichkeit* (Professorial Majesty).

It is proverbial; German novels are full of it. But a foreign visitor is still astonished to witness it firsthand. The groveling and submissivness of students and lecturers before the professor, so conspicuous at German universities, is a rare thing in the Anglo-Saxon countries or in France. It is not just politeness or respect; it is subservience. At lectures and seminars one notices the large number of students faithfully taking notes and the very few asking questions. Most people who have attended both German and foreign universities notice the difference. "Here you don't question a professor," an English exchange student in 1964 concluded an article on German university life, published in a West German student magazine. "Most students think it just is not done."

This habit seems to be already ingrained on the secondary school level. In 1964, Dr. Reinhard Tausch, a German educator, compared the behavior of West German and American children in the classroom; he discovered that American students ask on the average 7.3 questions per hour, West German students a mere 2.2. Tausch complained that German teachers hardly ever say "Thank you," and are autocratic in comparison with American colleagues. "Autocracy in the schools is related to dictatorship in society," Tausch concluded.

A West German student does not easily—in contrast to an American or Englishman—establish a personal relationship with his professor. Of course, most universities today are so overcrowded that it is no longer easy to establish a true community of teachers and students. But during the many months I spent in German university towns I met only one student who was able to say that he had paid a private visit to his professor. A peculiar class-consciousness separates German professors even from their own personal assistants. I must have been present at at least two dozen social gatherings in homes of West German professors, but only once—in Berlin were the "ranks" mixed. A Rector is not addressed as "Herr Rector" or "Herr Professor," but as *"Magnifizenz"* and, moreover, in the third person: "If *Magnifizenz* so desire, I shall leave this book with *Magnifizenz*." A dean is no common mortal either, but a *"Spektabilität"* and is also addressed in the third person. "If *Spektabilität* will allow me to rewrite this sentence in the sense of the suggestions made by *Spektabilität*." Not every student pays such court, yet enough of them do to give the West German university the atmosphere of an Italian operetta.

A visitor to a well-known Hamburg theology professor arrived punctually at five, was left waiting for more than one hour. When he reminds the secretary of his existence, she answers bluntly: "You must get used to that. That's the way great men are."

I would not much want to be the student of this great man, let alone his assistant. Such incidents are no rarity at most West German universities. Under different circumstances you would attribute no significance to them. But not, it seems to me, here.

The Free University of West Berlin was founded in the blockade year 1948 as a symbol of freedom, a protest against the Communist-dominated East Berlin Humboldt-Universität. Its charter speaks proudly of a "free community of students and teachers." But how free are professors and students? Can their political utterances diverge from those of the rector? Professor Kurt Sontheimer, one of the best-known West German political scientists, invited the philosopher Karl Jaspers to give a lecture at the Free University upon the twentieth anniversary of the collapse of the Third Reich. The *Allgemeine Studentenausschuss* (General Student Commission) at the same time planned to hold a panel discussion led by West Germany's leading nonconformist, the Munich journalist Erich Kuby. "It was to be expected," the *Spiegel* reported, "that both lecturers in their view of the past and outlook for the future would not stick to usual theses but would treat May 8, 1945 as a salutary defeat of Nazism rather than as a shameful day of German capitulation."

Professor Herbert Lüers, Rector of the Free University, denied Jaspers—who also favors the recognition of the Oder-Neisse border and cooperation with the DDR—the right to speak at the university. He then persuaded the academic senate to support this decision in secret session. His *Magnifizenz* informed the Student Commission at the same time that Erich Kuby could not speak at the university either, since he had criticized the faculty seven years before. His *Magnifizenz* based his decision on the legally defensible but academically dubious "right of the landlord."

The students demonstrated in protest and even held a partially successful strike. Yet Kuby was forced to give his lecture outside the university in an overcrowded hall. An assistant at the Free University, by the name of Krippendorf, protested against the arbitrary decisions. He published an outraged article in the Berlin daily *Spandauer Volksblatt;* he attacked the Rector personally. German rectors are sensitive creatures. The Rector did not renew Krippendorf's contract which was just expiring. The majority of professors supported the Rector for the sake of "order" and probably because of something called "caste solidarity." The entire incident could lead to only one conclusion: Students don't understand anything about politics. They ought to study and leave politics to the authorities. This is the traditional view in Germany.

The historian Golo Mann reports a conversation he once had with a "very well-known" German professor of philosophy: "I have nothing to do with politics," the professor remarked. "But wouldn't you try to help if the house were to go up in flames?" Mann asked.

"No," the professor answered carefully, "if the house began to burn I would call a fire engine."

To fight the fire, to participate in a political or economic crisis, was a profession that first had to be learned. He, a professor, had not learned it.

Rather, he had learned to philosophize. . . .

"But," Mann concluded sadly, "if a professor should ever get involved in politics, it was all too self-evident that he would champion the interests of the state and support it with historical arguments."

This little anecdote may help to explain the otherwise mysterious failure of many decent and humane professors during the Nazi time; simultaneously it sheds light on a state of mind which—to a lesser extent—still persists today. Universities are supposed to be dedicated to the search for truth. They are supposed to transmit knowledge, to help young people find a moral base. When the academician abdicates politically out of so-called professionalism, when caste-consciousness is stronger than the demand for political and moral rectitude, when it is not *contra bonos mores* that former Nazi professors continue to teach, become deans, even rectors, and solemnly represent the spirit of their university in public,* then

* One of the best-known cases of this kind, that of Professor Hugo Moser of Bonn University, which the *Zeit* vainly tried to make into a test case, has been described in a previous chapter. Another instance occurred when the Bavarian government named as Rector of the New Regensburg University Professor Götz Freiherr von Pölnitz who was well known for his Nazi utterances during the Third Reich. Bavarian Minister of Culture Huber protected his choice for a long time. "In order to safeguard his

something is very wrong with the system. It is frightening to think of former Nazi ideologues posing today as intellectual or even moral authorities.

Arguing that universities were not as strongly influenced by Nazism as foreign observers assumed, a Göttingen professor cites "the fact that universities were able to take up their work again relatively quickly after 1945." It is true that universities were able to resume normal teaching activities relatively quickly. Yet in many cases, this was possible only because they hushed up, over-looked or minimized their part in Nazism. Professorial caste-consciousness and solidarity prevented a purge.

There were all sorts of people at the Nazi universities: some who resisted, some who remained silent, some more or less enthusiastic followers of the regime. Real heroes, like Munich Professor Kurt Huber, who died for his convictions, were as rare as the fellow travelers were many. There were the silent fellow travelers, who watched mutely when their colleagues' books were burned; the silence of the intellectuals can often be more disastrous than the roaring applause of the "uneducated" masses. And there were the men who were the tyrants' conscious helpmates. In innumerable lectures and treatises, they went to great lengths to prove the "legality" of a criminal regime. On the rare occasion that they were later asked to account for themselves, many explained their be-havior as "concessions to the spirit of the time," or, what is worse, belittled it as "not having exceeded the norm." If they praised and scientifically justified the Nazis, they had done it only to "camouflage" their "true revulsion" of the regime.

It would be incorrect to say that these men are still Nazis today. They completely affirm "the norm of today." They are ready with historical arguments to justify present-day democracy just as they

economic existence Pölnitz camouflaged himself," said the Minister in justifying the incriminating writings of his protégé. When the material turned out to be too damning, Pölnitz resigned from his office. As the first Rector of a second new West German university (Bochum) the government of Northrhine-Westphalia appointed the Hamburg Professor Hans Wenke. Wenke, too, had seriously tainted himself with Nazi and racist utterances during the Nazi era. In this case, the state government bowed to public criticism. It was a rare occurrence.

provided "scientific foundations" for dictatorship and racial madness. They constitute the most flagrant example of intellectual opportunism in our time. For, unlike a simple worker, a professor cannot exonerate himself with the excuse, "I did not know Hitler's intentions," or "I supported him because he stopped unemployment and built *Autobahns*."

One of the most striking examples of academic opportunism is the case of Martin Heidegger. As the Rector of Freiburg University in 1933, he told his students: "The rules of your being ought not to be doctrines and rules. The Führer himself constitutes the German reality of the present and the future and its law." After the war Heidegger continued at Freiburg, became professor emeritus only in 1952 at the age of sixty-three. Ludwig Marcuse, a Jewish professor who has returned to West Germany, and a colleague of Heidegger, commented: "To me, an inveterate admirer of Heidegger, it seems he should not be allowed to teach, not even if he guaranteed that he would not disseminate one further drop of Nazi propaganda. He cannot be allowed to teach because he is a notorious unforgettable example of the moral depravity of German intellectuals."

The case of Heidegger is famous but not necessarily exceptional. Just as there are no official numbers on former Nazis in the government or in the police, there is no reliable information about the number of former Nazi activists in the universities. Private estimates can run anywhere between several hundreds and several thousands. To uncover the past of even such public figures as professors is uncommonly difficult. Most bibliographies do not list the Nationalist Socialist works of those in question; many *curriculum vitae* bashfully stop in 1933, to begin again in 1945 (as though they had exercised different professions during the Nazi era). However, Rolf Seeliger, a young Munich journalist, has succeeded in compiling a still incomplete list of fifty well-known Nazi professors still teaching, plus appropriate references to their work. Seeliger's work has been repeatedly interrupted by a series of cease-and-desist actions brought against him by the academic dignitaries he has exposed.

One such complaint came from the present Professor for Penal Law, Trial Law, Philosophy of Law and Civil Law at Marburg University, Professor Dr. jur. Erich Schwinge. Seeliger printed a pamphlet in which he quoted from *Wesensschau und konkretes Ordnungsdenken im Strafrecht* (Phenomenology and Concrete Orderly Thinking in Penal Law), a book published in 1937 and co-authored by Schwinge. The quote was:

> The blood-community of the German people is the basis and simultaneously the highest and ultimate value from which all German judicial thinking must derive. The existence and the well-being of the German people therefore constitute the ultimate criterion for what is justice and injustice. . . . The National Socialist ideology, as expressed in broad outlines in the Party Program and the speeches and writings of the Führer, therefore concretizes this criterion, for justice and injustice.

Professor Schwinge, who calls himself a democrat today, asked the courts to forbid Seeliger's accusing him of being partially responsible for Nazism. The Freiburg County Court thought differently and rejected Schwinge's suit, maintaining that "anyone who had professed his political beliefs so vigorously during the Nazi period, could not expect immunity today."

A few other examples assembled by Rolf Seeliger:

Professor Dr. phil. Wilhelm Helmich

Field: German language and methodology of German language instruction.

Now: Full professor, University of Kiel.

Before: In an article in the *"Rassenpolitische Unterrichtspraxis,"* in 1939, he laid down his views about the "danger of the Jewish population in Germany" and wrote: "During the time of the Jewification of Germany there was the danger that . . . Jewish words would become part of German everyday speech. . . . These words are of a racially separate origin, therefore the danger is that they will not be used with a clear value judgment. It is every teacher's task to fight for an education by means of an unambiguous language together with the ideological fight which has to be fought down to the racial basis. . . ."

Professor Dr. jur. Herbert Krüger

Field: Civil law with special emphasis on international law.

Now: Professor, Law Faculty, Hamburg University. Director of the Seminar for Civil Law and International Law, Director of the Research Program for International Law and Foreign Civil Law, Director of the Institute for Foreign Policy.

Before: In his speech "Trust as the Psychological Basis of the Community of the Folk," held during the solemn immatriculation on June 5, 1940, at Heidelberg University, Krüger announced: ". . . The Führer unites a maximum degree of external freedom with a maximum degree of internal obligation. . . . He is completely free in his decisions; neither the people nor the *Reichstag*, nor the government of the *Reich* have the right to have a voice in the decision of the Führer . . . he is not a private person, but when he makes a decision the embodiment of the German people acts."

". . . our enemies are mistaken if they believe they can defeat us first psychologically and then militarily as during the [last] World War. Not only the military, but also the psychological inferiority rests with the other side today. As sharp as our weapons, as firm is our trust in our Führer. The union of these two will not let victory elude us this time."

Professor Dr. theol. Michael Schmaus
Field: Theology
Now: Professor, Dean of the Theological Faculty, Munich University. Chairman of the Seminar for Dogma and of the Grabman-Institute for Reasearch into the Theology and Philosophy of the Middle Ages. Munich University Rector 1951-52.
Before: In his book *Encounters Between Catholic Christianity and National Socialist Ideology* (1933) he wrote: "National Socialism places the idea of the people grown out of blood and soil, destiny and mission into the center of its ideology. Creating Germans as a people is the essential objective of the National Socialist Movement. . . . Political equality does not exist within this sphere . . . nothing is less Catholic than an extremely democratic evaluation of being . . . National Socialism is not an invented system, not an ingeniously prepared ideology, but a movement that has originated in the very roots of life, something that comes from the original instincts. Therefore it is justified when National Socialism claims: A National Socialist stance cannot be adopted through reading or thinking but only through experience. . . . The deeper all German men and women penetrate to the wells of nationhood and belief, the more confidently we can look into the dawn of the future . . . can we be confident that the construction of the Reich which has been started, will succeed. . . ."

Professor Dr. jur. Friedrich Schaffstein
Field: Penal law, criminal trial law and philosophy of law
Now: University Professor, Law Faculty, Göttingen University.
Before: In "The Science of Political Penal Law," an inaugural address as Professor at Leipzig University (1934):

"... One of the more profound reasons for the superiority of National Socialism and its racial ideal over the political ideology of the Enlightenment and of Marxism is that the former originates in the biologically inherited inequality of mankind whereas the latter originates in its alleged equality ... an outdated older (purely physiological) stage of development of scientific thinking. ..."

Dr. rer. nat. Gottfried Kurth

Field: Anthropology
Now: Teaching fellow, faculty for Mathematics and Natural Sciences Göttingen University.
Before: In his book *Race and Caste in Four Thüringen Villages* (1938) he wrote:
"... The peasantry is still the greatest carrier of Nordic blood in our people. ... The greatest achievements of our people are based on the talents and strength of the Nordic race. The future of our German nationhood depends on securing a broad basis of Nordic blood from which the leadership of the Reich can grow ... The Führer is building the Reich for the coming millennia; it is up to us to make sure that the people will be available for these millennia, who are capable of fulfilling and carrying on the Führer's will. ...

These men were not Nazis in the sense in which members of the Gestapo were; it is an historical irony (or an oddity of the totalitarian state) that the Nazis were at times even suspicious of some of them. Heavily imbued with nineteenth-century romanticism, they easily managed to reconcile their traditional nationalistic attitude with Nazism. Perhaps the opportunity to inherit the positions of expelled Jewish or anti-Nazi professors was also a temptation. The reinstatement of hundreds or thousands of these men as teachers of postwar youth was not imperative, but in the light of the conservative restoration that marked the rebuilding of the German universities after 1945, it seems a logical consequence.

The resurrection of the "dueling" or "fraternal" societies is the counterpart of this restoration among the students. Some student societies—"*Korporationen*," "*Turnerschaften*" or "*Burschenschaften*"—are a peculiar psychopathological phenomenon; they are again an integral part of West German university life. In number, political activity and social influence they surpass all other forms of student organization. The Occupational Powers prohibited the

Korporationen because they had opposed democracy and had engaged in active antisemitism. It is now generally forgotten that long before the Nazis—in the nineteenth century, student societies in Germany had held *autos-de-fe*, prompting Heinrich Heine to prophesy: "That was only a prelude; where books are burned, people are burned in the end." The top societies solemnly decided in 1896 to acept no more "non Aryans" in their ranks; in 1921, they opposed the Weimar democracy; in 1932, they proclaimed Nazism as "an essential part of the national liberation movement."

After the Occupation, several West German rectors tried to prevent a revival of the *Korporationen*. But tradition prevailed. The courts, teeming with former members of *Korporationen*, ruled in their favor.

Today, about 40 percent of all male students belong to various *Korporationen* and *Burschenschaften*. A quarter of these practice the so-called "*Mensur*," that is, dueling. The *Mensur* is a ritual which German students share with certain primitive African or or Australian tribes. The resulting facial scars, called *Khanti* in Guinea, are called *Schmisse* in Germany. In both instances they are proof of masculinity and honor. According to the so-called Philosophy of the *Mensur* there is an "inner pig" living in each man, and only dueling can get it out. The inner pig is identified with cowardice, laziness or even "humanitarian hogwash."

Whether these student societies practice dueling or not, an unpleasant chauvinistic and authoritarian atmosphere imbues them all. In 1954 the present West German Foreign Minister Dr. Gerhard Schröder warned in a speech before students:

> One cannot ignore the fact that certain forms of student behavior in Germany's past expressed opposition to democracy, were signs of an aggressive nationalism and proof of a certain caste spirit. We witnessed that such behavior was practiced by those students who drew sharp lines between themselves and German democracy. . . . There is the danger that some student associations have gathered again around the old traditions and will revive their old content as well as their old form.

Today the *Korporationen* enjoy the blessings of the church, of politicians of all parties, as well as the consent of most rectors; some receive subsidies from public funds.

Two notorious hallmarks of the *Korporation*—the duel as the obligatory form of conciliating quarrels among "men of honor," and antisemitism—have been "officially abolished." The first President of the West German Republic, Theodor Heuss, saw to the adoption of the first of these two concessions in the early fifties. The second concession was more easily realized. The problem of Jewish students at West German Universities for all intents and purposes ended with the explusion and extermination of the Jews.

Some student societies originated in the Middle Ages; others grew out of the liberal independence movements of the first half of the nineteenth century. By the end of the nineteenth century, no liberal ideals had survived. If they have ideals today, they are in most cases Wilhelminian myths, prejudices and notions: a mixture of kitsch and inferiority complexes, feudalism and nationalism, sexual prudishness and lewdness, blind faith in authority, a vague faith in the mission of Christianity and elitarian contempt for the processes of democracy. West German student societies today work in behalf of the German cause in southern Tyrol (Italy); in 1959, individual members were involved in bomb throwings there. Some societies regard the Republic of Austria as an integral part of the Reich, which must be re-established, of course, within its old borders.

The *Korporationen*'s main source of strength is the patronage they can bestow and receive. In government, in finance, and at universities strategically placed "old boys"—their tribal membership visible from their reddish facial scars—can easily accelerate the professional advancement of an ambitious corps brother. The *Korporation* is a "bond for life."

Korporationen are not merely snobbish fraternities or "eating clubs," nor are they honor societies like Phi Beta Kappa whose membership depends on academic accomplishments; they are called "blood brotherhoods." One *Korporation* publication announced in 1962 "a more positive value should be assigned to traditions which have been ennobled with blood than to statutes or pledges written in ink." The *Mensur* serves this ennobling process. It has nothing to do with the usual sport of fencing. Fencing with foils is an elegant sport; speed, agility, ability, practice, and intelligence determine the winner. The *Mensur* has nothing elegant, nothing sporting about it; its aim is mutilation.

The *Mensur* is fought regularly in the elegantly furnished club-house of the venerable Borussia *Korps* in Tübingen ("old boys" help pay the bills for both bar and doctors). Two duelists (*Pauker*) stand facing each other, the upper part of their body, neck, arms and nose protected or wrapped in bandages. Skull, forehead and cheeks remain exposed. The opponents wish each other "*Waffen-schwein*" (luck with their weapons), and then begins an unwieldy flailing about with sabers above their heads until an exposed spot is struck and the opponent has his dueling scar. In the *Mensur*, the duelist does not fight his antagonist, he fights himself. His enemy is his "worse self," his "inner pig." Neither of the duelists comes out victorious—the ideology of the blood does, proof of which are the nauseating, blood-encrusted dueling jackets, sacred relics kept along flag-draped walls.

The *Mensur* is obligatory in dueling *Korporationen*. Each *Korporation* determines the number of obligatory *Mensurs* each member must engage in. The *Korporationen* are ruled by a strict hierarchy: from the "*Erstchargierten*" and "*Zweitchargierten*" to the "*Burschen*" (orderlies) on down to the lowly "*Füchsen*" (foxes), accepted on probation to perform menial services (such as fetching beer for the Burschen, and shining shoes). Professor Theodor Adorno of Frankfurt writes of man's simultaneous longing for submission and absolute rule. The *Korporationen* satisfy this longing, and at the same time rationalize it by emphasizing "national tradition."

What is the meaning of the massive revival of these societies? It means, I think, the withdrawal of a large part of university youth from modern life—an escape from the twentieth century into a romantic dream world; a carnival-like vacation from the present, tolerated by the universities and subsidized by the taxpayers; a massive process of stupefaction.

The upheavals of recent German history have had little effect on the societies. *Korps* students are again easily recognizable in all university towns, by their "colors," their peculiar garb and freshly lacerated faces. Participating in their beer evenings at society houses, one hears demands for the return of "stolen Eastern

Territories" and sees them raise their sabers. Hoarse beery voices roar in chorus:

> Where courage and vigor flame in a German soul there's also
> the shining sword and goblets are clinked.
> We stand united and loyally hold together
> and shout loudly in fiery song:
> whether rock or oak shatter we will not be shaken
> Youth, in the throes of the storm, is torn away
> to go into battle and die for the Fatherland.

A small number of West German students recognize this danger and reject the *Korporationen*. They are a pathetically tiny minority —the majority of students either belong to these associations or remain indifferent to politics. Opponents of the *Korporationen* are often found in the editorial offices of independent student papers.

Two such papers are particularly noteworthy: the Tübingen student paper *Notizen* and the Göttingen *Politikon*. Both started as general student organs; both became independent in order to retain a freedom of opinion. Subscribers and advertisers outside of the universities, appreciating the courage and wit of the young editors, give them the financial support they need. Their content is on a par with their best counterparts in the United States or England. Both papers constantly attack the *Korporationen*, which can be risky, or ridicule them, which is not difficult. They criticize themselves as well, attack students and faculty alike. Both papers protest the presence of former Nazis on the faculty, but they emphasize, too, that not professors but students capitulated first to National Socialism in the twenties. This concern is the basis of their criticism of the *Korporationen* and the right-radical splinter groups.

In Tübingen, in 1965, the young editors succeeded in forcing the university to discuss its own role in the Third Reich in a series of lectures. No other West German university has performed a similar self-critique. "Dignity in rational man is his admission to himself of what has happened and what has been done. The indignity of merely living is to blot out the past, to forget and go on motivated solely by demands of present existence. Indignity is intensified when this blotting-out of the past ends in demands on others." So said the German philosopher Karl Jaspers, who has lived in Basel since 1948.

16

A Soft, Gentle Roar

ⅅⅅHERE PEOPLE have caused horrible suffering or allowed it to occur, and today peacefully drink their coffee as though nothing had happened, spend their holidays at the Mediterranean and read James Bond; where, according to Karl Jaspers, "the lack of dignity in merely living" is "simply blotting out the past"; where life goes on as it must to enforce humiliating compromises that widen the no-man's-land between good and evil—there the temptation is great to hearken to certain voices, and be they ever so soft. The Bible calls them, in a different mood, "soft and gentle." They are heard after great fires, earthquakes or similar natural catastrophes. Ralph Waldo Emerson said they speak for the conscience of their society.

Such voices are rare everywhere; in the Bible they are called miracles. In Germany they have always belonged to writers. Beginning with German baroque poet Friedrich von Logau (1604-1655), who, standing on the ruins of his homeland devastated by the Thirty Years War, came early to a conclusion that is still pertinent, "Iron poduces its own rust, which corrodes it; we Germans have ourselves produced that which devastates us today," to the humanists Goethe and Schiller (celebrated by their countrymen as national heroes even though Schiller regarded patriotism a quality of uncivilized people and Goethe admonished "Germans, vainly you hope to make yourselves into a nation; make yourselves—you can do it—into free men instead"), on to the most recent period, to the brothers Mann, to Bertolt Brecht, Herman Hesse, Herman Broch, Karl Kraus or Carl Zuckmayer. These are few of many fearless thinkers; serious admonishers, soft gentle voices of conscience. Despite differences in style and in artistic vigor, their tradition is unbroken even today.

Marcel Reich-Ranicki, the West German literary critic, begins his essay on literary life in contemporary Germany with the words "Anyone who writes provokes society." It is a conviction many young West German writers share with Reich-Ranicki. Most of them have long ago left the "ivory tower" of pure estheticism into which not a few of their predecessors had locked themselves. Contemporary West German literature is "engaged" as never before in its history. Its favorite form is the "period novel," a hybrid between fiction and reporting.

Thus, here too as everywhere in the world, writers destroy the cliché conceptions of life, in an attempt to discover what people are really like. Their works have one thing in common: an apparent lack of real effectiveness. They are no force. They are, Thomas Mann once said, "consolation." And perhaps a hope for the future, although the past more than once has proved their impotence. Nonetheless we must have faith in their words; life would be senseless otherwise.

The defeat of 1945 was followed by a dumbfounded silence on the part of most writers who survived it, a silence that stood in sharp contrast to the noise of economic recovery. Some German writers must have been silenced with finality by the Nazi experience; others, like the poet Ernst Jünger, are still writing. But

Jünger had not much to say that sounded convincing to the defeated youth of 1945 as it slowly returned from prisoner-of-war camps. In *Man the Measure*, Erich Kahler has written that Jünger was the German intellectual who "bore the greatest responsibility for preparing German youth between 1920 and 1933 for the Hitler state." An excerpt from Ernst Jünger's *Diary* (September 21, 1929), illustrates his version of estheticism:

> But we are drifting toward the elemental forces that became visible to us for the first time in many years in the hellish abyss of war. We will stand nowhere but where the flame has cleared a path for us, but where the flamethrower has cleared away nothingness. Since we are the genuine, true enemies of the bourgeois, we delight in his extermination. We are no bourgeois, we are sons of wars and civil wars, and only when all this, this spectacle of circles emptily circling about, has been wiped away, will we be able to unfold within us what is natural, elemental, truly wild, and the capacity for real creation with blood and semen. Then the possibility for new forms will have been created.*

Jünger's obscurantism saved him from being imprisoned after 1945. Subsequently, the Bonn Government even awarded him a high decoration, a characteristic of the moral schizophrenia of the older generation. It did not alter the fact that younger readers and, mostly, younger writers still reject the rehabilitated poet.

Many people are still surprised that West Germany has "literature" at all today. From the beginning it was obvious that the spiritual consequences of Nazism would be harder to remove than the millions of tons of rubble. There were those who felt that literature would be completely out of the question for the forseeable future. Some expected a desolation and coarsening of literature similar to that which had visited Germany after the religious wars.**

During the middle of the fifties, a Swiss observer (Walter

---

* Within a few years it became clear what "truly wild" and "the capacity for real creation with blood and semen" signified. Soon this sorcerer's apprentice was not to be able to free himself of the spirits he had unleashed. He regretted it only after it was too late.

** "The German lands," the nineteenth century, French historian Jacques Bainville wrote "have been a kind of province since 1650 where the common people still speak a coarse patois, while the people of the world employ our language."

Muschg: *The Destruction of German Literature*) thought he saw the temporary end of German literature. In his opinion it had been destroyed; he was not sure that it could be rebuilt. Most German authors "were dispersed, silenced or killed" during the Hitler era; the disappearance of the Jews "also meant the elimination of much talent and intelligence." Also there seemed to be "no young talent . . . The air is filled with the laments and curses of the emigrated and the murdered, by the silence of the dehumanized. . . . The ignorance of young people presents no way out of this predicament."

Another problem was language. A language that served for twelve years to express the unspeakable, to plan and operate and carefully catalogue an Auschwitz, to pervert age-old concepts, lies into truths, truths into lies—what can still be done with such a contaminated vehicle? What can you write in such a language other than newspaper articles or business letters of the new Ruhr industry? George Steiner, an American essayist and literary critic, Fellow of Churchill College in Cambridge, investigated the evident mediocrity of German postwar literature in 1960 and reached this conclusion:

> The thing that has gone dead is the German language. . . . A language in which one can write a *Horst Wessel Lied* is ready to give Hell a native tongue. How should the word "*spritzen*" recover a sane meaning after having signified to millions the "spurting" of Jewish blood from knife points? It cannot. Languages are living organisms. Infinitely complex, but organisms nevertheless. They have in them a certain life force and certain powers of absorption and growth. But they can decay and they can die.

This, others had feared even before Steiner. The poet Karl Wolfskehl was thinking of Germany when he wrote from his New Zealand exile: "And if you have a thousand words, the word, the word is dead." The Viennese Karl Kraus wrote: "The word passed away when that world awakened."

West German cultural life is neither so empty as these gloomy forecasts, nor as full as the student of past German greatness would hope. Foreigners who visit West Germany after England, France or the United States will find West German cultural life politically interesting, but often artistically one-sided, provincial, uncreative and sometimes terribly boring. Not a few West German poets have a preference for extremely avant-gardistic abstractions. In part this may may be a flight from the contaminated language, in part an understandable reaction to the lower-middle-class prudishness of the Nazi period (which persists to some degree in East Germany). The same reaction is noticeable in the field of experimental music to which great attention is paid in West Germany. But with

$$aa \qquad aa \qquad aa$$
$$bb \qquad bb$$
$$x$$

a German critic complained recently, it is difficult to solve any human or moral problems. Not that this is the sole task of art, but it is certainly one of them.

An unsurpassed number of generously subsidized theaters in Germany confronts an unsurpassed dearth of original plays—123 subsidized German stages receive roughly 280 million marks a year in public funds. East Germany, too,—with approximately one-third the population of West Germany—has eighty-six state-supported theaters. The German public is unusually receptive to good theater; foreign observers time and again are impressed by the seriousness and fervor of the German theater public. For years, the English theater critic Kenneth Tynan has been singing the praises of the German audience. He has called it "an audience of critics." And yet contemporary English, American or French playwrights—from Eliot and O'Neill to Giraudoux, Beckett, Anouilh, Sartre and Ionesco, Tennessee Williams, Arthur Miller or Thornton Wilder—have no parallels in Germany. Foreign authors keep alive the German stage; the only German-writing authors of some standing are the two Swiss dramatists Max Frisch and Friedrich Dürrenmatt, and Peter Weiss, who left Germany to become a Swedish citizen in Stockholm (now also the home of the venerable poetess Nelly Sachs, perhaps the greatest among all living German poets). Peter Weiss and Nelly Sachs are of Jewish descent; both of them were driven out of Germany by the Nazis. Neither wants to return.

Nor does Germany have much to offer today in film making, although before 1933 it was the pioneering center of international movie production. The ruins of 1945 did not produce a Rosselini or De Sica. The subsequent affluence produced no Polanski, Bergman, Antonioni or Resnais.

The loss of the Jewish population can be felt everywhere and is immediately obvious to a visitor coming from France, England or the United States. Germany is not the first country to surrender to provinciality with the expulsion of its Jews. But no country went about it so thoroughly. The few Jews who returned to Germany after the war were mostly old or sickly, pensioners or small businessmen. Creative artists with but rare exceptions did not return. One appreciates Germany's loss by contrasting the flourishing, pulsating cultural life of other countries, particularly that of the United States during the postwar period, where Jewish literati and writers, publishers and directors, critics and editors are inevitably at the center of artistic achievement. "By God," Walter Jens laments in his essay "Contemporary German Literature," "by God, the German poets have never had greater need of the judgment of a metropolitan court than at this moment when they have been robbed of their most faithful friends, counsels and opponents, the Jewish intellectuals." He adds: ". . . a modern literature is unthinkable without Israel's voice."

In 1958 a Polish Jew who had attended school in Berlin before the war alighted from a train at the Frankfurt railroad station, clutching his total possessions—two suitcases. He had fled from Communist Poland where he had worked as a literary historian and critic. His name—Marcel Reich-Ranicki, a man in his early forties, of slight build, with friendly eyes in a round, soft face. It is no accident that this *literateur*, who had been completely unknown in Germany, soon became West Germany's leading and most controversial literary critic. For, he had brought along something other than his two valises, something that has become rare in Germany: a love of literature as though it were the most beautiful of all women, a critical talent, a Jewish moral passion and a sense for language all the more acute because he is a foreigner. Reich-Ranicki also brought with him an unshakable belief in the future of German literature, despite the destruction it had suffered. A biting opponent of Reich-Ranicki once called him the "De Gaulle of literary criticism—noble, tearful, blindly invoking a lost grandeur." Reich-Ranicki had come out of Eastern Europe. It is an interesting fact that Eastern Europe is the only area in the world where the Germans are still taken absolutely seriously; the only area where one either expects or fears great things of them—be it in literature or in aggressive *revanchismus*.

There are other contradictions to the findings of Steiner and Muschg. It is not true that most younger writers try to ignore the past. To the contrary, the Nazi past is their favorite obsession. Germany, a lamentable land without lament, has found an age-old remedy for an old grievance during the last few years. It has delegated its sorrow to its poets.

It happened slowly. At first there were only a few, like Wolfgang Borchert (*Draussen vor der Tür*), who died at an early age. Then came Heinrich Böll, Alfred Andersch and Wolfdietrich Schnurre. The number has increased steadily over the last five or ten years. Very slowly, very hesitantly, they began to grope back into the past and simultaneously critically to appraise the West German present. The new writers in many instances interwove the Nazi theme with social criticism of the contemporary scene. Today they dominate West German literary life; they are the literary "establishment."

Most are in their thirties or forties. Some learned to read during the Hitler regime, made early attempts to write but, says Heinrich Böll, "found the right words" only much later. Others, even younger ones, grew up in the crumbled landscape that was Germany after 1945; fields of rubble were their textbooks. Their names are Günter Grass, Hans Magnus Enzenberger, Wolfgang Koeppen, Siegfried Lenz, Martin Walser, Alexander Kluge, Günter Herburger and Rolf Hochhuth. They have little international recognition. Outside of Germany they are practically unknown, with but few exceptions like Grass, Böll or Hochhuth.

The best among the younger writers carry the past as a stone around the neck that becomes heavier rather than lighter with time. The more the past recedes, the more present in the literary sense, it becomes. Every West German publisher's list, every fourth book review confirms this. The best and best-known West German writers cannot free themselves of the past. Their bookshelves are crammed with the testimony of the Nuremberg or Fankfurt Trials, packed in next to the classics. Günter Grass, the most successful and probably also the most talented, imaginative, and daring of the new men, declared in an interview in New York in 1965 that it was possible to write a book that ignored the past in the United States; however, one could not in Germany. Here you are forced to look back time and again.

Perhaps they have only now found the right words, perhaps a new, untainted generation of readers had to grow up, perhaps criticism inside and outside Germany is more effective than one thinks; the literary confrontation with the Nazi past is today so great that some people speak—gladly or ironically—of a "frontal attack" of the literati against the Third Reich. There is talk of a massive *"return of suppressed matter."* Its exponents are different from one another, with diverse backgrounds, styles and artistic talents. Their public effectiveness varies. They write literary "white papers" of a kind that can only be found in Germany nowadays. Dramas, novels, historical reports, poems, Brecht's words could serve as their motto: "Let others speak of their infamy. I'll speak of mine."

Among them one finds "fantastic realists" like Günter Grass, whose fierce novels abound with figures reminiscent of Hieronymus Bosch; "moralists" such as the pacifist and devout Catholic Heinrich Böll, a successor of Remarque; emigrés from East Germany like Uwe Johnson, who has succeeded in breaking most of the political taboos about the DDR.

For Rolf Hochhuth the stage is a moral institution. He wrote a Christian passion play *The Deputy*, whose main theme is the partial responsibility of the Catholic Church for the extermination of the Jews. Hochhuth was the first young West German author who called out, like Hamlet: "The play's the thing wherein I'll catch the conscience of the king." Other authors followed suit. Peter Weiss wrote a piece called *The Investigation*, a concentrated dramatization of the Frankfurt Auschwitz Trial. He had once considered calling it simply *The Camp*. It opened simultaneously in a half dozen West German theaters. Heinar Kipphardt, author of the recent play about atomic scientist Robert Oppenheimer, has written a drama about Joel Brandt, the man who tried to barter English trucks for Jewish lives with Eichmann. There are the poets Enzenzerger and Ingeborg Bachmann, and cool, sober documentarists, registrars of hell, like Alexander Kluge.

Thomas Mann's novel *The Magic Mountain* is often considered the representative work of the first German Republic which collapsed in 1933. Are there works that are just as representative of the first decades of the second German Republic? It seems to me there are two such books. The first is Günter Grass's *The Tin Drum*, whose hero is a perverted, archaically cruel, drumming child who refuses to grow up. It is the first West German novel since 1945 that can be compared with the best English, American or French novels of the period. Grass' razor-sharp irony, his gargantuan lewdness, introduced a refreshing note into German literature.

The second is Heinrich Böll's *The Clown;* it symbolizes West Germany in the figure of a mute, terrified boy. His clown, descendent of a wealthy Catholic Rhineland family which disowns him, withdraws from life. At the end of the novel we find him begging for alms at the Bonn railroad station. His mother, who only a few days before the entry of the Americans had cried for the "defense of German soil against Jewish Yankees," is now a member of Adenauer's party and dedicates "Anne Frank Houses" all over West Germany.

German literature is not dead. It was not destroyed, despite Hitler, but it was changed. Its heroes are perverted, crippled figures who stammer their protests out of Teutonic nightmares.

Politically most young German writers are left-of-center. Asked about their ideal state, their ideal society, many would answer: a hybrid between Sweden and England, a minimum of "nation," a maximum of social welfare and political freedom. Strikingly different was the Weimar Republic when leading writers, both of the left and the right, actively opposed or ridiculed parliamentary democracy: Weimar times are over. The defeat of 1945, in contrast to that of 1918, has not produced a literature that glorifies war or is imbued with hatred for the victors. West German postwar writers do not idolize the "masculine" adventure of war as Ernst Jünger did after 1918. They regard war rather as the embodiment of boredom.

A significant figure in German letters since 1946 is Hans Werner Richter, pacifist, son of a North German fisherman, former bookseller and, during the thirties, briefly a member of the German Communist Party (which soon disappointed him). Richter's extraordinary accomplishment far exceeds his actual literary production. He is the founder, organizer and master of ceremonies of a singular literary circle which he brought to life in 1947, and therefore calls itself "*Gruppe* 47." During the past eighteen years, the *Gruppe* has had a decisive influence on West German literature; it is a piece of the Paris Left Bank removed to the Rhine, and a constant thorn in the side of the Bonn government. The poet Hans Magnus Enzensberger, who attended his first *Gruppe* meeting in 1956, considers it the traveling "central coffee house of a literature without a capital." It is, in Richter's words, a "circle of friends" without permanent members.

Since 1947, the *Gruppe* has been meeting once or twice a year, each time at a different place—last year even in Princeton, New Jersey. Richter alone determines who is invited. Those invited since 1947 include almost all younger writers who later became famous in West Germany. From Böll, Schnurre, Walser to Enzensberger, Bachmann, Celan, Johnson and Grass. The meetings of the *Gruppe* are not merely social gatherings or "salons." Their focal point are public readings. What is read must be new and unpublished: a part of a play, a half dozen poems, a chapter from a novel. A reading lasts between thirty and forty minutes and can often be a harrowing experience. The "delinquent" (the reader) sits next to the "*Obersten* Richter" (the supreme judge) on the so-called electric chair. The general critique begins as soon as the reading is over. Sometimes a reader is stopped even before he has finished his text.

The audience will criticize his uprightness, the precision and cleanliness in his use of his mother tongue so bady contaminated by the Nazis. Implied will be a moral commitment of great passion. An occupant of the "electric chair" may not defend himself, and under no circumstances may he be a "bad loser" or he will not be invited back. This form of criticism—improvised on the spot—is certainly not ideal. Its disadvantages are obvious and are often questioned. However, the *Gruppe* 47 has had a fortunate influence on the development of young German writers and its fight for a literature of humanism goes on. Today, publishers anxiously await invitations to *Gruppe* meetings.

Hans Werner Richter is a broad-shouldered, short man with dark, gleaming eyes and pitch-black hair beginning to grey at the temples. His vitality is infectious. The unusually long life span of the *Gruppe* 47, its political and literary influence, are proof of his rare pedagogic talent. "The origin of the *Gruppe* 47 is of a political and journalistic nature," Richter wrote in 1962. "It was not created by literary people but by politically committed journalists with literary ambitions. Our intention can only be explained by the collapse of the Third Reich and the atmosphere of the first postwar years." The young people who returned from prisoner-of-war camps, Richter recounts today, sought to prevent a repetition of horror. They wanted to create a literature fully aware of its responsibility to society. They felt they had to make an entirely new beginning; "they recognized as one of their main tasks, an all out attack on the traditional German sense of history. They resisted the theory of collective guilt but regarded German literature before 1933 as partially responsible for what had happened."

Today Hans Werner Richter says it was no accident that their first intention was a cleansing of the language ". . . each word had to be painstakingly tested as to whether it was still sound." The language had not only to be freed of Nazi perversion but also of the dishonest circumlocutions which the literati who had remained in Germany had introduced to circumvent Nazi censorship. The first members of the *Gruppe* 47 began with the ABC's, with the simplest words. They concerned themselves with "the addition of the parts and little parts of the action . . . they wrote the primer of a new prose," Richter says. "First they were mocked, then they received literary prizes." Richter likes to quote a typical poem of that time; a poem that deals with words only; its author is Günther Eich, one of the first members of the *Gruppe* 47.

> This is my cap
> this is my coat
> here my shaving kit
> in the linen bag.

The tin can:
my plate, my cup,
I have scratched my name
into the tin plate

Scratched it with this
valuable nail
which I hide
from eager eyes.

In my knapsack
is a pair of woolen socks
and a few things
I don't tell anyone about.

Thus it serves as a pillow
for my head.
The cardboard here
lies between me and the ground.

Most of all I love
the lead refill:
in daytime it writes verses for me
which I invent at night.

This is my notebook
this my ground sheet
this is my towel
this is my thread.

Where do the German writers live today? During the fifties it
sometimes seemed as though one had to travel through half of
Europe to visit them. "What have I lost here in this country into
which my elders have brought me, through lack of guile?" the poet
Enzensberger asked at one time and emigrated to a distant island
in a Norwegian fjord. Others followed his example. Günter
Grass moved to Paris, Heinrich Böll to Ireland, Ingeborg Bachmann to Rome, Alfred Andersch to the Ticino. But this literary
diaspora has abated in the meantime and many have returned. Grass
is in West Berlin, as is Enzensberger part of the time, Böll is back
in Cologne. But in this country of widely scattered provinces,

without a center and capital, you still must travel in various directions if you want to visit poets. They live dispersed, much more so than in England, France or even the United States. The "central coffee house" of the *Gruppe* 47 meets only once or twice a year.

Alexander Kluge, born in 1932, and one of the younger members of the *Gruppe* 47, lives in Ulm, a small town on the Danube at the border between Bavaria and Baden-Württemberg. There is not much in Ulm to dispel general boredom. After the destruction of the war about the only architectural site worth visiting is its famous Gothic Münster Cathedral. There is also an office building from the Nazi era with a stone eagle suspended above its portal. Where the eagle used to hold a swastika between its claws you now see a smooth square of cement.

After the war American philanthropists provided the money for the construction of the College of Design which sits just outside Ulm. Its first director was Inge Scholl, a sister of Hans and Sophie Scholl. In a sense, the College is a successor to the famous Bauhaus School in Dessau (which today belongs to the DDR but has not been resurrected). Alexander Kluge has been a member of the staff for several years now. He is a slim young man with large, intelligent eyes and fine, sharp features. He is generally considered one of the most intelligent of the young West German writers; I mention him because he is a good example of the youngest generation of writers, the generation which is even more oppressed by the past than their older colleagues.

Kluge was thirteen years old when the war ended. The two books he has published since 1962 are fascinating attempts to approach the German past through literary means. *"Lebensläufe"* (published in the United States under the title *Attendance List for a Funeral*) and *Beschreibung einer Schlacht* launch a major attack on the traditional German historical conscioueness. Kluge wants to "paint new historical pictures instead of the old ones." I asked him what he wants to achieve. "Clarity about myself," he answered.

Kluge questions tradition. He pursues it, somewhat like Hochhuth in the last act of *The Deputy*, to the most brutal end, to the mass grave, to the gates of the gas chambers; few authors have ventured as far. He calls things by their names. Others, like Heinrich Böll or Alfred Andersch, often employ symbolic concepts. They do not call Nazis by name in their novels, but speak of "the others" or of the "buffalo eaters." Even a historian like Golo Mann, in his *German History of the Nineteenth and Twentieth Century*, calls Hitler by his full name only up to the point where he comes into power. From that point on Hilter is only called "H." ("H." wanted. . . . "H." planned . . .").

As we were sitting opposite each other in the functionally furnished office of the College of Design in Ulm, Kluge quoted the Frankfurt sociologist and musicologist Professor Theodor Adorno: "No poetry is possible after Auschwitz." You reach the limits of realism at the camp gate with the inscription "Work Makes Free." "One cannot really describe it," Kluge says. "However, it is possible, even terribly necessary to take stock. Make inventories. I attempt to erect fences. I hope that the reader's imagination can move between these fences."

Kluge's two books are unique. Perhaps they indicate new possibilities for fiction writing. They are sober inventories of a catastrophe, cool, dry and therefore more gripping. A card index of all imaginable inhumanities. Kluge's books consist of excerpts from diaries, telegrams, official reports, sermons of army chaplains, expert opinions of concentration camp doctors, all joined together in a seemingly offhand manner. Much of the writing intentionally retains the official style we know both from the trials of former Nazi murderers, or for that matter, from the correspondence of today's rulers. Fantasy and reality, invented and documentary matter have come together here in a unique mixture. Parody, properly handled, it has been said, can be the highest form of criticism.

"Our world consists of the rules of language," Kluge says by way of explaining his technique. "Pure language, the pure concepts, do not exist because we do not have a pure world. There are only jargons, especially in Germany. Each profession has its own language. The SS had one. The camp doctors. The judges still have it, as do policemen or teachers. When I describe people from the Nazi era in *Attendance List for a Funeral*, people who lived then and who are often still alive today, I try to refer to them in their own terms."

In *Attendance List for a Funeral*, a group of short stories which are "partially invented, partially not," Kluge recounts "a melancholy history." The word "history" has a double meaning in this instance. For Kluge "history" does not begin in 1933 or 1918, as it does for so many others; it begins earlier: in the moral schizophrenia of the educated German "who nursed his intellect without using it." It is rooted in the traditional "conspiracy within good society not to raise questions about the rightness of a particular course of action." Kluge's *Attendance List for a Funeral* contains a "scientific report" about an unsuccessful medical experiment on two concentration camp inmates. SS doctors seek to induce erotic tension in the test subjects in order to determine whether X rays produce a permanent or only passing eclipse of sexual attraction between male and female. The test subjects are unaware that they are being treated with X rays. It appears that "no tension whatsoever" is generated by the two when they are placed naked in a room, even though their love for each other has been established. Question: Why did the experiment not succeed? "Has everything been tried?" writes Kluge's fictitious reporter. "I cannot vouch for the fact that everything was tried . . . after all we couldn't go in there ourselves and try our luck, because that would have been a racial crime . . . but had we become excited? Well, in any case, more than those two in the room. On the other hand, we wouldn't have been allowed to. Therefore I don't believe that we were excited." Is that to say, the reporter asks finally, that at a certain point of misfortune, love can no longer be generated?

Everywhere there are questions. Whether we are dealing with "Lieutenant Boulanger" or "Chief of Detectives Scheliha," both are prototypes of a "past" whose records Kluge pours through as though he were possessed. Lieutenant Boulanger executes "Jewish commissars" at the Eastern front "for the purpose of securing important cranial material," which will be used at a university for research on "the inferior Jewish race." His instructions say: ". . . After the death of the Jew has been induced (in the prescribed manner), whereby the head may not be injured, the head is severed from the trunk and then sent to its destination embedded in a preservative fluid and in a tin container which has been expressly manufactured for this purpose and can be tightly locked."

Kluge's little biographies not only develop characters but their careers as well. For Boulanger, his ghastly mission meant the "abbreviation of the path to advancement"; the prospect of an academic career had been held out to him.

In the short story "Chief of Detectives Scheliha," a Prussian bureaucrat wanders with two assistants, one secretary and two policemen through the Eastern front no-man's-land to clear up a murder case at a time when the Reich is about to collapse. There must be order! Scheliha is captured by the Russians. Returned to Germany, he has, by 1961, advanced to Chief of Police and delivers a lecture at the Rotary Club on the subject of "justice and criminality," in which he recounts his own vain and problematical pursuit of the murderer at the end of the war. Kluge transforms the lecture and subsequent discussion into a devastating parody of German legal thinking.

Kluge's second book, *Beschreibung einer Schlacht*, describes the "organizational structure of a calamity," "the well-known calamity of St., whose origins either lie 30 days or 300 years in the past." He means the battle of Stalingrad. In Kluge's book, Stalingrad is not a defeat caused by "technical mistakes" made thirty days before. Rather it is a defeat which has evolved out of all of German history, out of the hypocrisy of the "clerics" and "educated" as well as the politics of Iron Chancellor Bismarck.

Alexander Kluge has many occupations. Actually he is a lawyer; in Ulm he teaches movie-making. He has made several interesting documentary films, one of which *Brutality in Stone*, deals with the architecture of the Nazi era. The idea for the film came to him in Nuremberg when he saw the monstrous toilets on the former Party grounds. "It occurred to me to make a film which would blur the distinctions between Auschwitz and the Ulm Revenue Office here that most people walk past these days, unaware of its antecedents." Another Kluge film traces the career of a West German policeman; it is supposed to be a true story. The good man faithfully fulfilled his duty during the Weimar Republic, most likely thrashing Nazi demonstrators when duty required it. Later he served the Nazis. Currently, now in the service of the West German police, he continues to protect the public interest. At the end of his long career—and of the film—he threatens to bash in the head of everyone, but everyone, who is not a democrat.

Along a narrow, winding village street, near Cologne—the village has since been incorporated into the Rhenish metropolis—a small villa stands in the shadow of old trees. Its façade is unadorned brick, a few stone steps lead up to the curtained glass door; the ground-floor windows are barred. A teen-age girl opens the door and leads visitors to a small summerhouse behind the main building. Here lives and works—when he is not in Ireland ("there I rest up from Germany")—the West German writer Heinrich Böll. He is one of the "oldest" of the writers of the postwar period, author of such war stories as *The Train Was Punctual* (1949), *Kommst du nach Spa* (1950) and *Where Were You, Adam?* (1951).

His stories, in their sharp rejection of war—the embodiment of the most horrible ennui for Böll—as well as in their characterization, are occasionally reminiscent of Erich Maria Remarque's famous antiwar novel *All Quiet on the Western Front*. It is odd that (in the past as in the present), the Germans should be the ones who write the most extraordinary antiwar books. Böll has also written a series of novels about the postwar period such as *"Und sagte kein einziges Wort* (1953), *Billiards at Half Past Nine* (1959), and his latest work *The Clown* (1963). In these books, the angry moralist criticizes society, politics and religion. But the past is almost always present, almost physically perceptible. The heroes of Böll's novels are variations of Cain, haunted men, women and children branded for life. They are, as Böll claims he himself is, both victim and culprit.

Heinrich Böll was born in 1917 in Cologne. He is an athletically built man with a broad, high, deeply furrowed forehead and thin hair combed back. The large, wide-open eyes below the thick brows, his gentle, often slightly open, somewhat childlike mouth lend his face a permanently questioning look. In this torn-up land where people are almost as much on the move as in the United States, Böll is the only well-known writer who still lives in the city where he was born, a fact that endows his books with a local authenticity rarely found in other West German postwar novels.

Böll loves his city; he loves it more for its beautiful Romanesque churches than for its famous cathedral. And though Böll likes to claim that Cologne "is not really Germany," or "here one never took Prussia and worldly power really seriously . . . and even threw flower pots at Hitler and publicly derided Göring"—he makes no attempt to transfigure his hometown in his books. In his work Cologne appears first as a rather hypocritical, Catholic prewar city, then as a rubble heap and finally as a resurrected postwar miracle in the dubious, cold and harsh light of the neon lamps. Cologne, Böll writes in a short autobiographical note, is also that city which "sheltered the oldest Jewish community in Europe and delivered it up to the Nazis; sense of citizenship and humor (horrifying in their official garb) were of no avail against misfortune."

Böll is one of the few well-known writers of the postwar period who experienced National Socialism in full consciousness. He was sixteen years old when Hitler came to power. He says he knew at once "what it meant." But not because he could see through it, he says, "It was none of my own doing," his father, a carpenter, had explained it to him. In 1939 Böll became a soldier; he spent a long time in France, then in Russia, but does not like to talk about it. He was an American POW at the end of the war. The earliest memories of his youth, he writes, were unemployment, disturbances, strikes, Red flags. "A few years later the unemployed had been accommodated, they became policemen, soldiers, hangmen, workers in the armament factories—the rest moved into the concentration camps; the statistics worked out, the Reichsmark was abundant; the bills were paid later, by us who had in the meantime unexpectedly become men who tried to decipher the misfortune and did not find the formula: the sum of suffering was too great to attribute it to the few who were unequivocally guilty; a part remained and has not been accounted for until today." Böll feels pursued by this part. When he published a travelogue about Ireland several years ago, certain critics expressed relief that he had finally thrown off the burden of the past. His subsequent books showed how wrong these assumption had been.

In his small summerhouse, Böll sits behind a large, roughly hewn wooden table, surrounded by bookshelves, travel souvenirs, a few reproductions on the walls. "Yes, I cannot free myself of the past. . . . It speaks to me out of the present. . . . It is a letter addressed to us and which most of us have left lying unopened." He finds it difficult to answer direct questions about West Germany, for how can one make clear statements "about such an imprecise land?" But to a visitor from England who asked him several years ago, "Are there still Nazis in this country?" Böll answered, "Of course, did you expect that a simple date, May 8, 1945, could transform a people?" Now he is sitting at his table and says softly: "I find this country sinister . . . and we writers, who write the way we write, are camouflagers in a certain sense. . . . We are read, we are successful authors. But the same old things keep happening."

Like so many writers of his generation, Böll is shocked by the "perversity of German rearmament . . . that was not necessary, not here . . . I wouldn't have given these people weapons again." Why? Because one "shouldn't lead them into temptation." "You cannot form a new army and simultaneously bring people to trial because they obeyed orders." Böll does not exonerate the individual of guilt; yet his main accusation is directed against "conditions." They are always more powerful in his books than the single, helpless average person.

Böll shares this attitude with other writers of his generation; it seems to have profound religious roots in his case. But Alexander Kluge, who is many years younger, confronts Böll with Montaigne's well-known saying: "The fact that society lies, murders, is not a necessary consequence of having a state but of our not being able to control it." Böll's heroes have never controlled it, Kluge complains. However, Böll's great accomplishment consists of having at least shown the consequences of this situation.

Günter Grass, born in 1927 and *enfant terrible* of the young West German literature, belongs to a different generation than Böll; the two men's attitudes toward the world also differ markedly. Born in the former Free City of Danzig, the "refugee" from the lost Eastern territories often attacks the political activities of the refugee organizations; and they in turn attack him for being "unpatriotic." In his books Grass paints an outstanding, plastic, living picture of his hometown, which now belongs to Poland. Hans Magnus Enzensberger has remarked: "The fact that this town enters into German literature only now that it is irrevocably lost to Germany constitutes more than an irony of history. A conquest like this presupposes the loss."

Grass has a dark mustache à la Stalin and his boyishly parted hair falls onto a large, muscular face. His brown eyes are strikingly clear. He lives in West Berlin. Grass receives visitors either on a small veranda that leads out into the garden or at the top floor, which serves as his studio—for he is also a sculptor and graphic artist.

I asked him about his childhood. He was in the *Hitlerjugend*, then with Air Defense. Shortly before the end of the war, as a seventeen-year-old, he was inducted into the army and wounded. "My father was a typical opportunist who joined the party in 1936. He had nationalistic, Germanic feelings. He also wanted to wear a uniform."

Both of Grass' main works, *The Tin Drum* and *Dog Years*, depict the Nazi era and its consequences through the eyes of the petit-bourgeois. Of all the books we now have about the Nazi period none is more disgustingly convincing than *The Tin Drum*. None points out more clearly how the huge dung heap had been piled from many little scraps; and how everything then became a veritable hell-on-earth. Grass himself does not use the word "Inferno." This is typical of him. For he is afraid of the big words and mainly wants to "rid the past of its demons and its mythology." Only in this way, he believes, can it be made at all tangible. Only in this way, he believes, can it be used "as a lesson also for our time." He feels that "many years were wasted in making Hitler a demon . . . that clarified the fronts, but also made a verdict impossible. Hitler was no demon. We are doing him a favor if we call him a demon and thus make him inaccessible to comprehension. He was a small hideous piece of dung."

More than a half million copies of *The Tin Drum* have been sold in West Germany. "Anyone who has observed the world caught like a beast in this book," Enzensberger writes hopefully, "will recognize its anarchical face at his own front door."

With *Dog Years* Grass seems to want to say to those who still have not seen the light: the Nazi years were not great years. They were dog years. The novel describes the peculiar friendship between the ambivalent Nazi Walter Marten and the half-Jewish scarecrow manufacturer, Eduard Amsel. After the war Marten tries to suppress his memories of the Nazi era. However, he does not succeed in eluding Amsel's irony. The book contains a devastating satire on the prodigies of the West German economic miracle, the millionaires and press lords.

Grass is the first young West German who has succeeded in drawing convincing, authentic pictures of Jews. All others who have attempted this so far have succumbed either to their own self-consciousness or to some need to pay literary reparations. In most West German postwar books, Jews are sentimentalized, idealized figures who have been "alienated" as dark beauties, sensitive spirits or pensive philosophers. Grass' main Jewish figure in *The Tin Drum* is a poor fool by the name of Feingold, who goes half mad with suffering. "More Jews like Feingold were murdered than sensitive spirits like Anne Frank," Grass said when I brought up the subject. Grass once discussed this problem with the novelist Alfred Andersch, who never called the Nazis by their name but always talks about the "others." "I told Andersch, that is not the way to do it. One has to call the things by their name." Andersch answered: "I suffered a great deal under the Nazis. I can't take the word into my mouth." Grass replied: "When you describe an SS man you must crawl inside him . . . otherwise the reader won't know what he is dealing with."

Before leaving Grass, I brought up a question I had always wanted to ask him. In reading *Tin Drum*, you get the impression that everyone without exception was guilty; no one in this book is innocent.

"Yes," Grass replied, "this impression is correct." But he hesitates to use the words "collective guilt." Not because there is none, but because its use makes it too easy for too many people. "They say *mea culpa*. The rest of the world is satisfied. And that is the end of matter."

17

Dr. Jekyll and Mr. Hyde, or The Many Faces of a City

Τ HERE ONCE was a town called Frankfurt that lay in the heart of Europe, where the beautiful Main, after meandering through snug forests, abundant vineyards, past gothic churches and crenelated castles, writhes like a huge question mark toward the West and flows into the majestic Rhine. Frankfurt-am-Main has always been the intersection of many intellectual and commercial routes.

It is an old town with a long, checkered history. Charlemagne, the first great "European," once owned a villa here, a stone's throw from the place where exactly a thousand years later a European banking house with the name A. M. Rothschild & Sons was founded.

The city has always been an important trading center point for cloth, wine, grain, books and kings. In earlier times, the German princes assembled in the old Frankfurt City Hall, the *Römer*, to elect an Emperor after long negotiations and much horse trading. Here Johann Wolfgang Goethe was born in 1749. Ninety-nine years later, eager Goethe readers, politicians, humanists, professors and other esthetes from all the German states assembled here in the *Paulskirche* to plan a liberal democratic constitution. Probably not since the Constitutional Convention of Philadelphia had there been a parliamentary gathering of so many educated, idealistic men. The members of this national convention wanted to lay the cornerstone for a united, free and peaceful Germany. But nothing came of it, though it must be noted that already in the *Paulskirche* voices claimed there was absolutely nothing that forty million united Germans could not accomplish.

Many respectable citizens of Frankfurt, honorable businessmen, workers, dentists, firemen, voted voluntarily for Adolf Hitler in 1933. Others saw through his many promises and voted against him. But that was all they did. They lived on as best they could as honest taxpayers, conscientious watchmakers and dexterous technicians. Soon most of them were shouting "Heil." Books were burned in Frankfurt in 1934 and synagogues in 1938.

During the last years of the war, the city was blanketed with bombs and huge stretches of it devastated. In 1945, it became the headquarters of the American Occupation Forces. For years high barbed-wire fences cordoned off the districts from which the victors governed the defeated land. In 1948 the city missed becoming the capital of the new West German Republic by a hairsbreadth. Frankfurt instead developed into the transportation metropolis and financial capital of the new state. The barbed-wire fences were dismantled and the last ruins torn down. Modern, cold and impersonal huge new warehouses, office buildings and honeycomb-like apartment houses sprang up in what used to be the old part of the city.

Goethe's native town, the town in which Schopenhauer sought refuge from a Berlin ruled by the Hegelians, is today the seat of the new public relations industry. High above the noisy streets sit the modern taste-makers, writing verses about automobiles and detergents. Many people regard Frankfurt as the truest reflection of the West German postwar society—but also its most devastating one: much hurrying and little *"Gemütlichkeit,"* many sober conversations about the discount rate and stock market quotations, little romanticism.

The history of Frankfurt reaches forward into the future as much as back into the past. In the very same *Paulskirche* in which the humanists of 1848 conferred in vain, President John F. Kennedy stood on June 25, 1963. Kennedy said: "I would not diminish the miracle of West Germany's economic achievement. But the true German miracle has been your rejection of the past for the future."

The past, however, finds its way into the present. Even those who seek to relegate the more recent past to an imaginary Stone Age are bitten in their heels as by a fossil suddenly come alive. Eighteen months after Kennedy's speech, twenty-two staunch West German citizens were standing on trial in Frankfurt. They were accused of murder or aiding and abetting the murder of an indeterminable multitude of people, committed with premeditation, nineteen, twenty or twenty-one years ago at Auschwitz.

The Frankfurt Auschwitz Trial soon became almost as famous as that of Nuremberg. Not because it was the "largest" for many years, or because here, in contrast to Nuremberg, the Germans were sitting in judgment on each other. But rather because these mass murderers seemed like the average clientele of almost any West German barber shop. They were, spectators remarked, "people like you and me." This had not been commonly realized when the so-called monsters of Nuremberg were condemned. In Frankfurt Mr. Hyde sat in the dock as Dr. Jekyll. Mr. Hyde was a mass murderer. Dr. Jekyll is an honorable West German citizen, and in this capacity has no lack of supporters. "What do they want from poor Dr. Jekyll," supporters would say. "While he was Mr. Hyde he only followed orders. It was war; duty is duty and schnapps is schnapps."

Others—they were in the minority—took a closer look at this average human being. They compared him with contemporaries bearing striking resemblance to the accused, some old, some even brought to trial, or too young to have become guilty of anything. If it is as easy as it seems to change from Hyde to Jekyll, might it not be just as easy to do the opposite? Is it just as easy to change a mass murderer into an affable druggist as it is to transform the friendly pilot of a passenger jet that flies the route between Palma de Majorca and Frankfurt to a mass murderer? Duty is still duty and schnapps is schnapps. Our age has means of extermination at its disposal that make the Auschwitz gas chambers look like paleolithic weapons. Today, Dr. Jekyll sits in the prisoner's dock, and there are judges, witnesses and lawyers to conduct the proceedings against him. The "final solution" of tomorrow, the poet Hans Magnus Enzensberger has written, will leave no witnesses.

There was once a businessman by the name of Robert Mulka, who founded an import-export agency in Hamburg in 1946. He bred goldfish as a hobby. Doctors who had examined him considered him completely normal. Like most Germans after 1946, Mulka was industrious and honest and, like so many, he became wealthy. His slim, slightly bent figure, his finely cut, sensitive face framed by silvery hair, lends him the mien of a dignified Hanseatic merchant. On business trips he stayed only in the best hotels. He was seen frequently at the bar of the elegant Frankfurter Hof while he was waiting for his verdict at the Frankfurt Trial. For, he seemed so respectable and honest that he was allowed to move about freely. This man, his demeanor and figure reminiscent of a character from *Buddenbrooks*, was the Senior Camp Adjutant of Auschwitz. His hands were stained as much with blood as with ink. As Senior Adjutant he was responsible that all orders of the Camp Commandant would be duly executed. He made sure that the wheels of the extermination machine would never stop, be it for lack of fuel or human material to be processed. He ordered the Zyklon B needed for the gas chambers; he was responsible for the "care" of the arriving transports. The Frankfurt court found the Hamburg merchant Mulka guilty of "aiding and abetting murder in at least three thousand cases" and condemned him to fourteen years imprisonment.

There once was a cashier by the name of Karl Höcker, who was thirty-four years old when the war ended. Since that time he has lived in a small villa in Engerhausen, in the district of Lübbecke where he was chief cashier of the district savings bank. A respected citizen, of medium height and thin dark hair, he was entrusted with sizable amounts of money. His hobby was gardening.

Like Mulka, he too had been a camp adjutant in Auschwitz. The press interviewed Höcker's neighbors. Many expressed sympathy for this "unjustly persecuted" man, who was generally liked. Only the manager of the savings bank seemed to have been inconvenienced; he suspended the defendant until further notice. Höcker was found guilty of "collectively assisting the collective murder in at least three thousand cases" and was sentenced to seven years in prison. His sentence was relatively light since it could not be proved that he had been "zealous" in the performance of his "duties."

There once was a dentist by the name of Dr. med. dent. Willi Frank. He lived in Stuttgart-Bad Cannstatt, where he had a flourishing practice. He was always nice to children; children liked going to him with a toothache. In January, 1964, circumstances forced a change in Dr. Frank's practice. He affixed a new sign at his door informing his patients that he would be available " 'until further notice' only on Tuesdays and Wednesdays from nine to twelve-thirty and from four to six-thirty." Mondays, Thursdays and Fridays the dentist would be out of town; he was sitting in the prisoner's dock in Frankfurt. In 1944 he had made "selections" at the railroad platform in Auschwitz. He had also been responsible —as chief of the SS Dental Station—for melting down the gold teeth extracted from the mouths of corpses. For aiding and abetting in the murder "in at least six thousand cases" he was given a seven-year prison sentence.

There was once a certified engineer by the name of Klaus Kylewski. He belonged to the SS staff in Auschwitz from September 1940 to August 1944—his duties there were interrupted a few times "for the purpose of continuing his university studies." In Auschwitz, he too was on duty at the platform. He told those prisoners fit for work to march to the right, others he told to go left to die. After the war he completed his studies at Humboldt University in East Berlin and then was employed as a teacher at a trade school in Düsseldorf. For "aiding and abetting in the murder of at least fifteen hundred human beings" he was sentenced to five years in prison. The court gave the following reason for its relatively mild verdict: "He did it without evident zeal and without personal interest." At one time, crimes of passion were regarded as extenuating circumstances. Today, in the atomic age—depersonalized murder, the absence of feeling and thought is the extenuating circumstance.

Once upon a time a druggist from Göppingen . . . a male nurse from Berlin . . . a teacher at an agricultural school near Cologne . . . they, too, were on trial in Frankfurt. They were all "little people," who had been required for the great murder and of whom Hannah Arendt has said: "They were prepared to do anything, absolutely anything for a raise, for another star on their epaulets."

The Frankfurt Trial was not a single instance, trials of this kind have multiplied since 1958. Their number has been increasing because a small but vociferous minority in West Germany demands them; and because of the pressure exerted by public opinion abroad. Within Germany, polls time and again give the same result: most Germans do not want these trials. In 1965, 63 percent of the men and 76 percent of the women asked were of this opinion.

Nonetheless, and for whatever reason, the trials are continuing and should keep the West German courts busy until the middle of the seventies. Before 1960, grotesque incidents, such as revelations and unsolicited confessions or accidentally opened documents triggered many of the trials. Since 1958, a central office in Ludwigsburg near Stuttgart has been systematically tracking down war criminals.* The office investigates not single cases but whole complexes of mass murder, inasmuch as this is still possible. Approximately ten thousand investigations are being conducted at present. By 1970 two thousand more will be added. The statute of limitations now scheduled to go into effect in 1970 will not cut these proceedings short. Once started they can be pursued until there is a verdict. Thus these trials will remain an integral part of West German public life for some time to come.

The spectator galleries are often overcrowded, and there are many young people in attendance. What do these trials accomplish? German television regularly presents detailed reports about the trial proceedings, as do the better dailies and magazines. Is anybody listening?

This question is more important than that of the degree of punish-

* Ironically, even the head of this central office, Dr. Schüle, was exposed in 1965 as a former Nazi. Schüle at first denied the charge, later he admitted to it.

ment. The sentences are often astonishingly mild. By 1967, most of those convicted at Frankfurt were free again, for medical and other reasons. But humanity will neither be impoverished nor enriched if a man with a thousand lives on his conscience is sent to prison for five or seven years or for the rest of his life. Humanity gains when the spectators succeed in translating what they see and hear into an ethical attitude. Humanity gains when the experience of these trials becomes a factor in the conduct of the individual's everyday life.

What then do these trials achieve? Certainly they give satisfaction to the rest of the world because they "prove" that the Germans are making an effort to "overcome" their past. They also satisfy a sense of justice in Germany, a strongly developed sense even under the Nazis. The answer of a prominent West German, Fritz Bauer, Attorney General of Hessen, who is better informed on this subject than most others, is pessimistic. It is said that the Frankfurt Trials might not have taken place without Bauer's assistance and urging.

"The educational effect of these trials—if they have one at all—is minimal," says Herr Bauer. "Some positive effects would be a willingness to practice self-criticism, tolerance, humanitarianism, *Zivilcourage*, to make personal sacrifices when sacrifice can prevent evil or to revolt against unjust orders of authorities." Has anything basically changed? Herr Bauer does not believe so. If newspaper reports about the trials are read at all, they are probably read like the reports about any other murder or morals trial. Bauer speaks of the immense difficulties he had with legal authorities all over West Germany. It had been necessary to set up carefully selected groups of investigators whose sole task was the search for Nazi criminals and to process available material. Previously, researchers "were often thwarted by too many cases of collusion, of deliberate sabotage." There were hundreds of such cases, most of which never became known to the public. Since 1962 or 1963 the situation has somewhat improved; many young people have joined his staff and they facilitate Bauer's task.

A journalist covering the Auschwitz Trial put an unexpected question to a young policeman: "If your superior ordered you to shoot at these people here, what would you do?" The policeman was guarding one of the defendants; in the course of many weeks he certainly had become acquainted with the consequences of an unjust disciplinary system. Nevertheless, his answer was: "An order is an order. When you get the order to shoot then you just have to shoot." Bauer himself cites this story from hearsay, but considers it completely credible. "These trials have not created a new moral code; they have accomplished just as little as has the DDR where an economic revolution has not solved the human problem."

Bauer is an unusual man. On the side he writes treatises on *Zivilcourage*, that is, the general lack of it. In 1965 he edited an anthology *Resistance Against the Power of the State*, which contains documents from Egypt of 2000 B.C. to Hochhuth and Jean Paul Sartre. "I'm often asked why I go on despite the inefficacy of these trials. I am asked why I don't go to Palma de Majorca where I like it better than here. Well, the answer is simple." It is in the final scene of Saul Levitt's play *The Andersonville Trial*, after the verdict has been pronounced. Bauer quotes it in his anthology:

After the death sentence:
Defense Attorney Baker to the Attorney General: Perhaps. It was a worthwhile effort though it hasn't anything to do with the real world. Men will go on as they are, most of them, subject to fears—and so, subject to powers and authorities. And how are we to change *that* slavery? When it's of man's very nature?
Attorney General Chipman: Is it?
Baker: Isn't it?
Chipman: I don't know. We try.

A Note about the Author

Amos Elon is an Israeli journalist; his book is not written from any one point of view, but is a work of objective reporting. Educated in Israel and England, Mr. Elon has represented the distinguished Israeli daily, *Ha'aretz*, in Washington, New York, Paris, Bonn, and Eastern Europe during the last ten years. He is forty years old and presently lives in Tel Aviv with his American wife.